The Full Power Bike Ride

BY CODY MOIR

DEDICATION

I would like to dedicate this book to all the people in the world that provided me with unconditional love and support during this massive two-wheeled journey. I am infinitely grateful to the kind-hearted people who hosted me, fed me, or simply smiled at me as I cycled down the street. The kindness of strangers was overwhelming, and to them I want to dedicate this book.

I would also like to dedicate it to my parents, who supported me in many ways throughout my trip, and without them – I wouldn't have been able to do it in the first place. Thank you! I hope you all enjoy.

FOREWORD
(BY HARRISON FANNON)

I met Cody on the substitutes bench at a game of college football, and it soon became apparent that I had met someone special. Here was a peculiar curly-haired fellow with a warm indigo aura finely tuned to his vibrational surroundings. Our conversation was interrupted by Cody getting called onto the pitch, and as I sat there on the bench, watching his auburn afro bouncing about midfield, I felt strangely touched by a spiritual encounter that would affect me henceforth.

Fast forward two years and the sun strikes down on the top of Cheddar Gorge, Somerset. The views stretch out across the Avon plains to the West, goats bathe languidly in the heat, and large blue butterflies float above the marjoram and thyme. Cody and I gaze quietly on the hazy vistas around us. They are the promise of future travel and adventure, of a life to jump into, a life to grab by the hand and run around with. Cody embodies this approach better than anyone, to see life through the eyes of a child, yet in a twenty-two-year old's body.

A child's view is one of wonder and sensation, a view one tends to lose in the ordered frameworks of adult life. Playfulness fades, routine sets in, and slowly but surely, we get fitted in to the mould that society has prescribed for us. But for Cody, a resolute attachment to the playfulness of youth is a weapon of resistance to this order. There is no better resistance than movement, no more so movement with a totally arbitrary goal in mind.

When he first told me of his plan to cycle to New Zealand, I thought only Cody has a level of insanity capable of pulling off such a plan. Most would get talked out of such a proposition, choosing to settle on one of many reasonable excuses to rethink and backtrack. But the difficulty and absurdity only served to fertilise the seed laid in Cody's heart that one fateful evening. When the voice of reason asks "Why?", Cody asks "Why not?", like the mischievous serpent that taunts Eve with the apple, the infinite possibilities of adventure excite those filled with the courage to enter the realms of "impossibility".

Cody's journey is an Odyssey into the unknown, into the unknown fathoms of one's mind, and the unknown roads that lead East. I hope the reader can vicariously travel along the tread of Cody's voyage as I did along his way. Such thoughts brought a smile to my face during the mundanity of daily routine, as I imagined this alien figure painstakingly traversing the barren steppes of Central Asia.

Simply by the presence of Cody's boundless energy, my life has been infinitely improved for the better. He is an inspirational example of what one can achieve by defying the expectations placed on us by society, creating new realms of possibility by daring to dream and having the courage to follow these dreams to their actualisation.

Follow his journey and let it awaken the movement in your soul.

Table of Contents

PART ONE – A TWO-WHEELED ODYSSEY THROUGH EUROPE

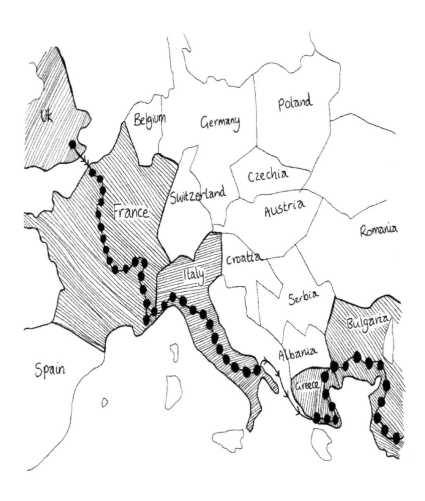

Chapter One

The Birth of a Full Power Idea

I had always wanted to go to New Zealand. Honestly, ever since I was about ten years old. Yet, unlike a lot of people, this had nothing to do with the Lord of the Rings. Whilst with my very first girlfriend, at the mere age of ten (I know that's a bit young for a girlfriend, but for lack of a better word - it will do) I saw a picture of her father who had moved to New Zealand, and he stood there with epic mammoth mountain ranges behind him, in a state of calm bliss. It just struck me straight away in my youthful little cranium, that this land was certainly a magical one. When I asked them some questions about this land, I learnt that it was the literal antipode of England and that if I dug a hole straight through the centre of the earth - that is where I would come out. Absolutely fascinating to my younger self, a land which is so far away that you couldn't physically get any further. This tickled an imaginative part of me that has felt the same urge ever since, to go explore this unknown place of mystical anythingness.

I knew that after I finished university, I would definitely go there, have a gap year to explore and then return back home. This was still my belief even when I had finished university, until I had one particularly important conversation with a friend, Alex, at a party. A big group of us were having a gathering in the forest to celebrate our graduation from university, and had brought our turntables and sound-system into the woods in order to have a jolly good time. Little did I know that it would be one of the most important days of my life thus far.

During an intense chat about life after our studies, Alex convinced me there and then on the spot, that to fly straight from England to New Zealand was not a viable option - for it was boring, bad for the environment and that's exactly what everybody does, ultimately lacking any flare of uniqueness. I had a sudden epiphany that flying certainly wasn't the right way to arrive at the antipode, and I instantly started to think of alternative ways to get there. I considered the possibility of hitchhiking, but then quickly dismissed it due to the disadvantage of waiting around a lot, but I then thought about trains and buses, to which I also rejected in my head for the lack of routes. I felt a bit stuck and almost sad that my plans had changed, even starting to consider the possibility of not going to New Zealand at all - until it hit me.

"I could cycle?" I said out loud, questioningly, with slight hesitation. The thought simply verbalised itself from my brain and out of my mouth without my personal choice in the matter. It felt like I took a long time to reach this conclusion, whereas in reality all of those thought processes must have been over in milliseconds.

"One hundred percent you should!" cried another friend whilst laughing, nudging me in an enthusiastic way.

We were standing in a small circle of about five of us, all close friends, equally as close in proximity. As soon as I mentioned the idea of me cycling from one side of the world to the literal opposite point, their eyes lit up with a sense of wonder and humour. They all exploded with excitement and liveliness telling me that cycling is certainly the best option. Right as the word "cycle" left my mouth, it instantly felt right intuitively and a spark within me was lit, and this little flame began to burn brighter and brighter as time went on. I took a couple moments to consider the logistics of my claim, and thought about cycling long-distance with baggage all day, and then simply repeating that process over and over until I reached the antipode. It seemed logically possible in my mind, albeit difficult. But what hit me the most was the degree of excitement that it evoked both within me and my friends. As soon as I had confirmed the plausibility in my head, I verbalised it once more.

"I will! I'm going to cycle from England to New Zealand!" I bellowed, in a firm and assured manner. Once again it evoked another wave of excitement and amusement within my friends and I had a big beaming smile plastered across my face, knowing full well that I had just birthed an excellent, yet crazy idea. Awesome! I proceeded to speak to every member of the party telling them about my grand new plan of cycling to New Zealand, and every single person reacted with equal enthusiasm to my own, simply confirming how much of a glorious idea it really was.

Unlike most people who create ridiculously obnoxious plans and claims at a party, I decided to stick to mine and actually do it. The next morning when I woke up, I was able to recall the creation of my travel plans, and it delighted me just as much as it did the night prior. I guess, if it had been an awful idea then it would have filled me with gloom or regret in the following morning, but instead - it did the opposite. As soon as I could, I got to work with the preparation of the trip. First and foremost I googled "Cycling from England to New Zealand" just to make sure it was possible, and behold, there was indeed a couple who had already done it. They were middle-aged and did the whole thing on a tandem bicycle, which really reassured me about the plausibility. This was basically the green light for me to start the serious planning, and for the next seven months I spent every evening on the computer researching things that I needed. I had to look into the best possible bike for the trip, all of the baggage required and all the things to put into that baggage. I came across so many articles about long distance cycling and learnt a lot about the whole field. Slowly but surely, I got together all the gear that I would need for every single season and every type of country.

Another essential part of the planning process was the route. I knew that some countries in the world are a little bit too dangerous to cycle through due to them being at war and suchlike, so I had to research the details of which countries I could actually pass through once I'd left Europe. Once again, I read article after article trying to ensure that I didn't make any poor choices and end up losing my life or just generally have an awful time.

Furthermore, once I'd figured this out, I then had to think about funds. I knew it was going to cost me some considerable amount of money, although I did read a lot that once you start cycling, it is one of the cheapest forms of travel possible. Regardless, I tried to make as much money as I could before I left, working with my dad full time as a labourer for his building business. I worked in the day, got back in the evening and did some more research about the trip. I was just positively obsessed with my oncoming project, and it didn't stop exciting me from the birth of the idea onwards.

Chapter Two

The Departure

The morning that I set off on the humongous journey, I first ensured that I put some time aside to write down a few challenges for myself. Obviously cycling to New Zealand was to be quite the challenge in and of itself, yet I also wanted some micro-challenges within the macro. I will list them for you here:

1. Get to New Zealand merely by bike and boat.
2. Don't take any cars or lifts along the way.
3. Remain vegetarian the entire way.
4. And don't spend any money on accommodation in Europe (live predominantly in the tent).

So, these were my informal rules that I laid out for myself that morning, and they would come into play, for better or for worse, during the trip.

On January the first, New Year's Day 2018, I got on my brand-new bike, "Rasta Bike" with my new best friend, Peace Bear on the handlebar - and simply started cycling towards the antipode. The reason my bike was called Rasta Bike is simply because he was a Rastafarian. Basically, I had all my hair cut off towards the end of university for charity, back when I had long curly hair and loads of dreadlocks. Some of the dreads went away to the lucky people who auctioned money to cut them off, but the rest I kept. In the will of not wanting to waste, I decided that they would make a great addition to my otherwise bald bicycle. I couldn't help but compare it to an adult version of the pink and white tassels on the side of most girly children's bikes, and the thought made me chuckle, rather immaturely. So, then my brand-new Surly Ogre bicycle had his new dreadlock tassels - thereby making him "Rasta Bike".

Oh yeah, you may also be wondering about what the hell "Peace Bear" is. Well, as I said, he was my best friend. I found him in my hometown of Aldershot, on a stall that was raising money for donkeys...He had multi colours all over his body, and a big striking peace sign on his chest. It was almost as if he looked at me directly in the soul and declared that he wanted to join me on this epic voyage. I paid the asking price for this little fellow, and then the rest was history. He was a little piece of home - a constant reminder of where I was leaving, and where I would return. Let alone, he was also my Full Power Disk Jockey, playing all the old-school-bangers during the long daily ride.

New Year's Day simply seemed like the perfect time to leave on such a huge journey. New year, new me, New Zealand...it just makes sense doesn't it? In some ways I can be slightly obsessively orderly and leaving on the first calendar day of the year is just quite neat and tidy. It was quite an emotional morning to say the least: saying goodbye indefinitely to my loved ones. I really didn't know how long I was going to be away for but considering that I was planning to work along the way to keep me going, I knew it was going to be quite a while. They knew it was going to be a while too, until they saw me next. My mother was crying, my sister was crying, and if my dog was a human he would've probably been crying too (my dad doesn't cry because he's a builder. But if he wasn't a builder, he would likely have shed a tear or two also). Anyway, it was certainly emotional. I knew that I'd planned my route carefully to avoid anywhere stupidly dangerous, but I was also well aware of all the dangers involved with cycling all day every day on roads with many motor vehicles on them. I wasn't particularly fearful, because as far as 21 year old boys go, I was pretty fearless, but I was also well aware that my family were well aware too of all the life threatening risks I was about to plunge myself into. This made the goodbye drastically more challenging than saying goodbye for a normal holiday, because we all knew that this wasn't going to be a normal holiday by any means - we all knew it was going to be a Full Power Bike Ride.

I straddled the saddle of my Rastafarian stallion and pushed the very first few pedal strokes of millions to come. I slightly wobbled side-to-side for a while, adjusting to the strange feeling of having thirty kilograms of baggage attached to a bike. I straightened out and gradually built momentum, but before turning the corner I turned to give one final wave to my family. After I turned onto the main road they were out of sight, and now there was nothing but me, Rasta bike, Peace Bear, and the incredibly arbitrary, crazy mission of cycling to New Zealand.

My first leg of the entire trip was on home turf - the Motherland. And I didn't actually say goodbye to my entire family in Aldershot when I left that morning, because I had another sister living in Brighton who I was planning to stay with, before taking the boat over to the Continent the following morning. So off I went.

I shan't write an account of every tiny detail that occurred along the way, because otherwise that would be awfully tedious for you. But I will, however, account for the interesting details (or what I'd deem to be interesting, anyhow). So, I got onto the main road and followed my maps on my phone, leading me towards the coast of Brighton. Within the following ten kilometres I already had heaps of drama occur. I had my very first fall off the bike, whilst in the forest. One factor was that the forest floor was quite muddy, but the other factor was that I was trying to video myself whilst cycling and I clearly didn't have enough coordination to pull off this degree of multitasking, and subsequently fell off my bike into the mud. It was very amusing, and I laughed at myself a lot, continuing to laugh even more when I realised that I'd accidentally caught it all on camera. Ten minutes later, a big tree had fallen on the path blocking my route entirely. So, for the first time during the trip (first of many), I had to attempt to drag the entire fifty kilograms of bike and baggage over the big tree trunk, struggling massively in the process. Luckily, I didn't fall again, because otherwise I would have left the forest looking like a proper mental mud monster.

Eventually I made it out of the woods, back on to a normal road, relieved to be cycling on a sealed surface. But after a mere five minutes of this, my back-rack broke. I almost cried. I thought that the entire thing broke under too much weight and started considering having to turn around and go all the way back home, which would have been rather embarrassing considering I didn't get very far at all. But luckily, upon closer inspection, it was only the bolts, which had come loose. I got out my multi-tool and simply screwed them all back in, this time much tighter than they were before. Everything was unharmed, and I was free to continue. It was a pretty challenging first day of cycling, showing me that this trip wasn't going to be easy, at all. I thought that I was going to arrive in Brighton before dark, but the reality was very different and I ended up arriving at about 10pm. Thank goodness, I arrived to my ever so lovely little sister who had already prepared dinner for me, and a comfy sofa to lay my weary head.

The next morning, I woke up early before sunrise in order to catch the boat. I had one more emotional goodbye to say to my sister, and she waved me off from her doorstep. It was pitch black which was a peculiar cycling situation, but it ended up being a beautiful morning for my cycle to the boat port, with the baby pink sunrise on the French horizon, luring me onto the Continent. I got onto the ferry, tied up my bike and took a seat - ready to wave goodbye to my homeland, and to wave hello to the innumerable life-changing adventures waiting for me along the ever-changing horizon.

Chapter Three

Contentment on the Continent

My first day in France turned out to be equally as challenging as my first day in England for this trip. But this time, it wasn't the actual cycling that was difficult, instead it was the night of sleep that proved troublesome. The night before, I had the comfort of my sister's home, but this night I knew nobody in the area and hence why I brought my tent, for nights like these. But unfortunately, just by chance, there was an extremely powerful thunderstorm. I set up my tent next to the cycle path that I had been on the whole day, pretty much from when I arrived at the French port until dark. It was only once I was settled in the tent did the storm hit. It was torrential and tormenting, but just continued to get worse and worse with increasing violence. Luckily I had bought a good tent, and it was proving its worth by keeping out all the rain. But one thing it wouldn't be able to withstand would be a thunderbolt.

They were sounding ever so dangerously close, genuinely making me consider that one may actually hit my tent. I even resorted to looking online as to what someone should do when camping in a severe thunderstorm, and all of the solutions would have required me leaving my tent - and I really wasn't prepared to do this, ending up like a drowned rat. I decided to just stay put and accept my doom if one did hit me. It was empowering to surrender like that, but I still couldn't sleep properly in the circumstances.

The following morning the thunder had subsided, but it was still brutally windy - truly desperate conditions for packing down my tent. The rainfly was being pulled around left, right and centre by the ferocious gales, and if anyone had seen, it would have looked as if I was attempting to fly a big kite. I wasn't. Everyone did warn me that it was crazy to leave during the middle of winter, but I didn't listen and just knew it was right to leave on New Year's Day, regardless of winter weather. People say that the most challenging experiences in life are the ones that build character, and this I deem to be very true. If every day was easy and every moment was cruisy, you really wouldn't learn all too much. But when you have endless hurdles to jump over, you learn both about the hurdle and equally about yourself - which can sometimes be invaluable learning. I'd already learnt a huge amount during a mere two days of cycle touring, so I could only imagine how much I was to continually learn from that point onwards.

I eventually made it to the home of my French cousin, who was happy to host me for a couple of nights. Essentially, my Grandad is French and was a sibling of 13 children, hence why I have about 40 French cousins in the North of France. One of these cousins said she was happy to have me at her family home. I'd barely started my trip and I felt like I already needed this refuge. During one mealtime with my extended French family, her husband, Antoine, said something rather profound that was to stay with me for a while:

"I hope you find what it is you're looking for," said Antoine. I thought about this for a little while before I could respond.

"Thank you, Antoine, but first I must understand what it is I'm looking for, in order to find it."

I've thought about that little conversation quite a few times since, because I'm not sure if there was one thing in particular that I was trying to find on this bike ride, maybe a multitude of things, or maybe I was seeking nothing in particular. There were lots of reasons why I was embarking on the trip in the first place - I wasn't just cycling from England to New Zealand on a *complete* whim.

Well, I wanted to become a man. A well rounded, worldly individual who is firmly grounded in his manhood. As it stood, I still felt like a boy at 21. We lack a rite of passage in Western culture to mark that transition from a boy to a man. So, in a sense, this was my own rite of passage that I assigned myself, and boy oh boy it was not an easy rite of passage. But if I had wanted it to be easy, I wouldn't have done it in the first place.

It was at points when I was plummeting down the mountainside at lightning speed, light rain gently pattering my face with the end of a rainbow just hovering over the sea, that I realised why I started the ridiculous expedition in the first place. Experience! Experience was the main thing I wanted to gain from the whole trip. I wanted the good, the bad and the ugly experience of life: from being far too cold, to being far too hot, crazy rain, crazy shine, feeling overwhelmingly happy to feeling overwhelmingly sad. In reality, I mostly experienced things in between these two extremes, but I didn't wish to shy away from any experience, because I wanted to experience the full spectrum of human existence and truly know what it means to be alive.

After spending a couple of lovely days with my French family, I continued to my next checkpoint - Paris. I'd been to Paris before and will probably return, but nonetheless every time you visit it doesn't become any less stunning. However, first I had to get there. In the car it is a mere one-hour drive, but as my trip progressed, I worked out that roughly one hour of driving equated to one full day of cycling - if, and only if, everything goes to plan. In the North of France, very little went to plan, thanks to an amazing yet awful invention called "Google Maps".

Due to its sporadic spastic malfunctions, it brought me so much grief and hardship during those first few weeks navigating the northern fields of France. Google Maps had a special bike icon, which enabled it to find useful bike paths and shortcuts that you wouldn't be able to take in a car. I know that all sounds fabulous on the surface, but it was all too good to be true. Essentially, it would take me down some tiny side-roads which then turned into gravel, eventually turning into a mud path instead. Then, as soon as you get suspicious that it's taking you the wrong way – behold, the path just disappears into nothing but a farmer's field, in all its muddy and filthy glory. Literally, this happened time and time again during my traversing of Northern France, because it showed the path on the map but in reality, no path existed. It tricked me numerous times, and because I had spent the last hour on a slowly dwindling "track" I simply could not justify turning back around and losing two hours of progress, so I generally just bit my tongue and continued through the muddy field. Once again, I could just hear all of my friend's voices reverberating around my head telling me that it was a silly idea to leave in winter. Once again, I ignored these voices and just trudged along, pedal-by-pedal and puddle-by-puddle.

We give England a difficult time for being awfully rainy but believe me - the North of France in winter is just as bad, if not worse. The rain just simply did not stop, regardless of whether it was in the form of slight pitter-patter, or in the form of relentless torrential downpour, it didn't matter, it was still bloody wet, every day. I soon got used to this, and got stronger in the process, understanding rain as an objective thing, which isn't necessarily "bad" unless you say so. Being in the elements all day every day without choice, really does wonders in the form of teaching radical acceptance and non-resistance. You can't resist it, because ultimately you have no choice. I signed up for it, after all. I mean, I only had to take a leaf out of Peace Bear's book to see how content on the Continent you could be, if you simply relax and let go. He was super chilled, both mentally and literally, but he didn't care about being wet - because he's a legend. Rasta Bike was also rather relaxed about the whole rain scenario. Neither complained once, so I decided to do the same - to allow the rain.

Soon, I learnt not to trust Google Maps and instead stuck to the main roads and carefully shared them with cars (which after a while you realise that they are not in fact cars, but instead awfully terrible things called "Motor Monsters"). This was all hunky dory for a little while during the honeymoon period. It was quicker,

16

more efficient and simply meant that I could stay away from cycling through muddy fields. But alas, the joy came to quite a sharp end, when my phone ran out of battery. It was all well and good following road signs to Paris, but some of them are obviously motorways and some not - but how does one navigate this dilemma in a foreign country? Not very well, is the answer.

It was pitch black and I wasn't all that far away from the city, so I resorted to asking a local for help. His broken English essentially told me to go "that way" and then "this way", showing me with his flippant French hands. I took his advice, and it ended miserably. Well, basically I ended up cycling on the A1 motorway into Paris, one of the busiest in Europe. It was epic, with about five lanes on one side and five lanes on the other. I was doing well considering, and just stayed in the huge hard shoulder. It really was a massive shoulder, and I felt relatively safe considering the circumstances. I just kept my head down and focused on speed and distance, wanting to arrive in Paris unharmed. People were beeping at me on average once every two minutes, probably utterly baffled as to why there was a cyclist crazy enough to be on the A1.

I ignored them, until a particular noise was too difficult to ignore - police sirens. The police van was going the other way to me, but I knew full well that it was for me. The noise went, but soon returned ten minutes later, when this time, it was coming from behind me. It pulled up on the side of the shoulder and a large, bald French policeman jumped out:

Which nationality?" he shouted, in a tone of disappointment.

"English," I replied, much more disappointed than him, to be adding an even worse reputation onto that of British tourists (because we certainly don't need any more of that).

He told me to get into the van, and I was about to tell him how I was cycling to New Zealand and couldn't get in the van, but luckily before I said those words I decided that it would be better not to get arrested, and simply jumped in the car with Rasta Bike and Peace Bear. I felt extremely annoyed with myself, and equally annoyed with the local guy who had purposefully sent me onto the highway. But I soon came to terms with the ordeal, not considering it as cheating as such, because I had not chosen this fate, and I had added into the small print of my challenge before I left, that if the scenario included flashing lights of any form, it is justifiable to get into a car. I think that's the lesser of two evils, over getting arrested. His sharp glare and ferocious frown didn't look overly friendly in any way, shape or form. And regardless, it was a mere 10km before they dropped me in the outskirts of Paris. That's what made it more frustrating that I had gotten so close before they picked me up.

On a brighter note, they decided not to fine me or bring me into the cop shop, so they just let me go with a slap on the wrist. That was good, but it taught me a valuable lesson to keep enough charge on my phone. The ongoing battle between choosing the small roads or big roads had only just started and remained a constant challenge for the rest of the trip, but that's to be expected, no?

The evening became even more challenging when I managed to get lost in the middle of Paris, still without any charge on my phone, now getting later and later. My hosts lived in the opposite end of the city and I was anxious to get there in time before they went to bed. I was starting to think that I wasn't particularly good at this whole cycle touring thing, but then again - I hadn't had all too much practice.

I did eventually make it to their place, with the help of some renewed battery and some genuinely helpful Parisians (unlike the previous guy who sent me onto the motorway). I even made it in time for the family dinner which was super scrumptious. I spent a couple well-needed days of rest to recover from the whole ordeal, eternally grateful for the hospitality. But once I had rested, I was ready and excited to get back on the road, for the trip was still fresh and promising with a poignant scent of adventure.

Most of the middle of France simply consisted of more muddy fields, which I was progressively getting better at avoiding. There wasn't all too much else to see, and at times it did get a little bit tedious, but it was broken up by some quite quaint little towns, and eventually the further south I got the more scenic it became.

As I approached the Alps, it became very hilly very quickly. The region is called the Rhone-Alpes, and it is basically all a large mountain range. Until that point, it had been quite flat, but now I was in for a shock. The mountainous peaks in the distance were snow-laden, beautiful yet intimidating. During my first proper climb, where I'd eventually made it up and over the summit - I had my first experience of dangerously cold feet, when plummeting down a rainy descent with minus temperatures which froze my feet to their very core. They honestly felt so very fragile at that moment, that if I slapped my feet hard enough, they surely would have fallen straight off my ankles and shattered into a million icy pieces of foot. But I quickly stopped, made a fire and warmed them up again. In general, it just made for much more challenging cycling, constantly climbing up and going down - where the descents were equally as dangerous as the ascents, when the roads were icy.

Despite this, I decided on taking a huge detour to cycle up one of the mountains in the Alps, to visit my friend who lived near a ski resort. I already told him I was coming, but when I looked at the map in more detail it looked like it was going to be too much hard work merely for a wee visit. I told him I was thinking of changing my mind, and *he told me* plain and simple:

"Well, you signed up for it." These words struck me, and at any point after that during my trip when I started to give up or complain, I would tell myself exactly that - you signed up for it, Cody. I decided to stick with my plan and cycle up-hill for the entire day until I got to 1000m above sea level, where he lived. It was the hardest part of the trip by that point, and the snow and ice didn't make it any easier. I finally arrived at his wooden alpine cabin, exhausted, but the wood fire and good food made it all worthwhile. We spent the following day skiing together and then I made my way back down the mountain towards the French Riviera.

There were quite a few more literal ups and downs, to say the least, before arriving on the South Coast of France. One day I woke up at the Gorge du Verdon, by a gorgeous lake, and I said to myself that it would make sense to both start my day and end it in two equally beautiful places - so I decided to arrive in St. Tropez that night, rather than in two days' time. I started the momentum, which was to continue for the remainder of the day. I thought I was to arrive around 10pm, but just like all my other previous calculations, I was quite far off. I instead arrived at 3am in the morning, which took a huge amount of motivation to continue heading towards an arbitrary micro-goal, within an even more arbitrary macro cycle trip to New Zealand. I felt sick in the evening, genuinely having to suppress vomit from leaving my tired mouth, but I managed it, and carried on cycling through the darkened mountains regardless. I did introspect at one point and think "what the hell am I doing right now?" but I stayed committed to my weird and wonderful goal. Eventually, I arrived at the view of multi-million-pound yachts, unthinkably expensive mansions, and a beach with absolutely no body on it. I decided this would be a perfect place for me to place my portable hotel (my tent) and truth behold, I had a wonderful night's sleep uninterrupted, without a single soul, even in the morning. Usually, in the summer this beach would have been absolutely packed, but in the middle of the freezing winter, I had it all to myself, and I felt like a rockstar. It was a good decision to set that target the day before, to arrive in St. Tropez, because once again I was able to wake up to a stunning view, this time of the turquoise and teal Mediterranean Sea, glistening in the winter's sun. The water was littered with the long white masts of glorious yachts, all in slumber during their hibernation period. I left my tent up all day and no one seemed to have a problem with it, which showed just how much January really was the "off-season".

That morning, I was having my morning meditation in the sun, getting my day off to a good start, and a random lady came and sat very close to me. She distracted me, not just because that's naturally what happens when someone sits next to you so close, but also because she was quite beautiful. She was of Moroccan heritage, with a thick French accent flowing from her mouth. She had luscious curly locks, and her face was most certainly sun kissed. She apologised for disrupting me, and out of nowhere gave me a private tour of St. Tropez. It turned out that she lived there, with her husband, and they sold super-yachts to the super-rich. Rather fancy, I do say. She showed me the thin cobbled streets, lined with old pastel coloured buildings and even the rich old men in the town square, playing French petanque - a game where you throw the larger silver balls as close as possible to the small white ball. It was an enjoyable day, but it went wayward when she said that she'd only just had a massive argument with her husband and was trapped in what she called "a prison with golden bars." She went on to tell me her entire life story, and how she had everything she could possibly want with all the riches imaginable, yet she still felt trapped and thereby hated her partner. She had clearly been drinking alcohol that morning to somehow try to dampen the pain inside, but it hadn't worked. She took a fancy to me, clearly displaying her affection towards my kindness and started trying it on. Of course, I wouldn't do such a thing, especially not when she told me that I should run away if we bumped into her husband.

That was officially my cue to leave St. Tropez promptly. I didn't want to be brought whirling into that tornado of an experience. In fact, I'd merely wanted to finish my meditation in the sun. But I'm happy I did have that weird and wonderful experience, because after all, a wide-ranging, diverse experience is what this trip was ultimately about. But nonetheless, I packed up my tent that was still on my wintery private beach and I hit the road, to escape what could have been a rather awkward love triangle.

I carried on down the French Riviera, heading towards the border of Italy. I passed through some notably famous towns, such as Cannes and Nice. Cannes was equally as nice as Nice, being home to the world-renowned Cannes Film Festival. The city of

Nice was full of obscure architecture and had the remnants of a previously very wealthy coastal city, where 18th century English aristocrats would've strolled down the promenade with their wives on their arms. The actual cycling each day on the Riviera was glorious with the coast hugging my side. It made quite a pleasant difference to the muddy fields I'd become accustomed to.

Then, after being in the same one country for over a month, I passed into two different countries in the space of only one day. Firstly, I crossed the border into the microstate of Monaco, the second smallest country in the world. I only had a short look around, but I was surprised to find out that it had its own monarchy, and the best lamp posts I've ever witnessed in all my days. I also visited probably the nicest public toilets I've ever been in. The whole country had a peculiar vibe to it, and it was clear that the entire place was a tax-haven, because everything stank of dirty money, let alone the casino. With a tiny population of 35,000 people (same as Aldershot), there are a total of 125 different nationalities living within its borders, so it's certainly multicultural. And I wonder why? Maybe something to do with hoarding cash. Who knows?

I then went back into France, and a few hours later, at sundown, I passed through my final French city, Menton, into the third country of the trip - Italia.

Chapter Four

Pillars, Plazas and Pizzas

I talia, Italy, Italia - the home of many people's romantic dreams: with the rolling hills of Tuscany, an ever-flowing reservoir of red wine to indulge in, and swimming pools full to the brim with pasta. Okay, well, I doubt anyone truly fantasises about the latter, but you get the idea. I had been to Italy before, so I knew not to get hopelessly engulfed in these romantic notions, but I was excited nonetheless to be in a new country, and to explore Italia in a novel and nourishing way - by bicycle.

I'd viewed this country previously from the comfort of a train, where you can sit back, relax and take it all in - going from touristic location to touristic location. However, seeing it by bike is very different. For example, the concept of distance is dramatically unique, simply due to the fact that you have to work for it. Every inch of distance that you cover, is created from your own physical exertion. Especially in terms of topography, you can't help but notice every slight lump and bump of Mother Earth's body, mostly because you feel a certain level of pain in order to get over her bumps. But despite this, there is something so everlastingly pleasurable about traversing those kilometres by yourself. A bicycle moves at such a great pace. Not so quick that you can't process the beautiful home on the Italian Riviera, but not so slow that you get bored of it and see the cracks. A pace where you can still smell the flowers on the wayside. Yet, it's a speed that is still only relatively recently available to us as humans (relative to our thousands of years of existence) so it still brings us this giddy, childish feeling whenever you pick up some speed. It's the best way to see a country, hands down, if you want a genuine cultural experience.

This verdict hasn't even yet taken into consideration the difference in personal experience with locals. By train, you can go from hostel to hostel, only meeting locals who are paid to be nice to you. But by bike, you can meet the most random of locals in the most random of situations, and see their true kindness shining through. Merely three days into my Italian chapter of the trip, and I'd already been fed free pizza from a lovely restaurant owner in San Remo and hosted by an Egyptian chef who refused to let me camp outside in the cold. The kindness was overwhelming in such a short period of time. I was blessed.

By the time I reached Italy, I had already cycled two million metres, which is an obnoxious way of saying I'd cycled two thousand kilometres (but you do have to admit though - it does sound better when you write it as in the former). Within my first week of Italian cycling, I had seen a lot of pretty beaches, eaten a literal tonne of pasta and been barked at an awful lot by farmers' dogs. "Bork bork" they said, "bork bork" they repeated the second time just in case I didn't hear them. Sometimes I got so annoyed with them and just shouted back to them what they shouted to me, because that was as far as my Doggo language stretched at the time. I didn't hear them say anything else, so of course I couldn't expand my Doggo vocabulary. Yet, it seems that all Doggo languages that stem from Latin (well, both French and Italian) use this "bork" term to say hello. I was interested to see if the Greek doggos had a different word for greeting me.

The Italian Riviera wasn't dramatically distinct from the French one - in that both were beautiful and expensive. Once I had come off the coast into the mainland of Italy, I had one main incentive for pushing forward - visiting my good friend Alex in the capital city, Rome. It's good to have an additional reward for the otherwise arduous mission of cycling all day every day. And this was certainly a good reward awaiting me – a true friend.

Meanwhile, on the way down to Rome I spent a few days in Genova, with my amazing host Pietro, where we went to a silent disco, and an authentic Italian football game. After this I volunteered for a week with a local family, helping them to build large inflatable boats, and we collectively knocked down a wall, which was quite a bit of fun. If you've never knocked down a wall before, you should try it one day. Towards Rome, I rolled over the lush green undulating hills of Tuscany. It was an absolute pleasure, speeding past long lines of evergreen cypress trees, which winded up towards lonesome yet gorgeous Tuscan farmhouses. The Tuscan towns were a sight to behold too. One night I literally camped *inside* the walls of an ancient fortified city. I can't say I've ever done that before. I, of course, took a stereotypical selfie with the leaning tower of Pisa, and marvelled at the renaissance remnants of the marvellous Florence. As one does, I wrote a wee poem about the famous bridge of Firenze - here it is:

The Old Bridge

Look at how the reflection dances
Rippling
Continuous, yet entirely novel every millisecond
No flicker of illuminated droplet is ever an exact replica
of the one before it
It may appear in the same place
But the light is new,
and the water too.

Sun slowly ceasing to have any influence over the sky
Darkness regaining its reign.
Rain
Hovering above
in fluffy-white-space-candy-floss.

I'm stood
Essentially hovering over a river.
The only thing stopping me from falling
is the sheer fantastico magnificence of
human engineering,
and the capabilities of the human mind
manifest in stone.

A bridge,
Just a bridge.
A bridge does what a bridge does.
I've seen them before,
I'll see them again,
But not for one minute does it take away
from the craziness
that I'm essentially flying right now.

Could a bunch of badgers build this?
Pigeons...wouldn't need to build a bridge in the first place,
So I shan't bring them into the equation...
But still,
What is it that makes us ever so different to the rest
Of the natural world?
Did this knowledge come from space?
From the Sun Gods?
Who bloody knows...
Either way, Firenze has me in awe,
Of the capabilities
Of
Human Kind

I had a little bathing break in a thermal spring further south, but ultimately kept on pushing pedals towards Roma. I planned to meet Alex a day later, next to the central obelisk in the Vatican

City (the smallest country in the world) at sunset, but out of nowhere central Italy was hit by a freak snowstorm. This was certainly freak weather for this part of Italy in late February, but the whole of Europe, pretty much, was hit by snow. As you can imagine, that's not great for a cyclist carrying 30 kg of stuff - but I'm a warrior at heart, so I single-handedly cleared all of the roads on my route, (all littered with about 20 inches of snow) with nothing but my own teeth. That's right, you read it correctly the first time, I used my two front teeth to eat all the snow, just so that I could cycle to the Vatican. Okay, yeah, that's total rubbish as you probably already worked out, but anyway, the snow didn't stop me from getting to Alex for the subsequent Vatican sunset.

I made it in time. He was waiting for me, sitting on the central obelisk, in an equipoised and meditative posture (as always). I made a full power entrance into the micro-state, by playing Tame Impala, who have a psychedelic rocky style, and happen to be one of his favourite bands. His smile showed me that it was a successfully fashioned entrance. We embraced, and had a reunion party with Peace Bear, and the rest of the animated inanimate crew (Blue Tac the blue cat, R2D2, Rubber Fish and Wooden Fish - essentially all of my other mascots that accompanied me on the ride). We had a jolly good boogie, before heading towards our host, Claudia, who I knew from my host in Florence, who I knew from some girls I met in Genova (and so on and so forth). We were welcomed by Claudia and her housemates with a beautiful meal and equally lovely company.

Alex was a big part of the reason as to why I decided to cycle to the antipode in the first place. He was the person who single-handedly changed my perception of taking aeroplanes for travel and reminded me how pollutant they are for the environment. When deciding where he will visit me, we knew that it had to be Rome. For some reason it felt like the perfect place. He hitchhiked from Bath (which is a Roman town, believe it or not) and managed to get to Rome for zero pounds and zero pennies which was his main goal.

We had a great few days exploring the capital of Italy and the old "capital of the world", as the Romans once self-proclaimed. But from the very beginning of our exploring, it seemed that the authorities were straight on our backs. For example, on our first day, at the start of our walk into the centre, Alex started to climb a tree. This is what Alex does. It's part of his authentic character. A child at heart, full of freedom, if he wants to do something, he will do it - without the overpowering pressure of social norms having any control over him. Once, he even held an up-the-tree protest at our university when the security told him it was "unsafe" to climb a tree on campus, and to get down immediately. He found this suggestion preposterous, for humans have been climbing trees for millennia - and therefore displayed his adversity to the command to get down, by staying up there for the rest of the day.

Likewise, that morning in Rome, his monkey movements were met with opposition once more. As soon as his hands touched the branch, a loud "*beep*" came from a police car nearby, with such a rapid reaction, to the point where they must have been watching our every move prior to the branch grabbing. I mean, does that mean we looked suspect in some way? It seems alarming that we could have looked like anything but conventional Romans going about our normal Thursdays. I fail to believe that our stretching on the wall, or perpetual chanting of "*The Grand Old Duke of York*" could have aroused any suspicion of mischievousness from either of us. But alas, the Roman police were on our backs from the start of the day, and their commands are slightly more serious than those from our university security, so I said sternly "Alex, get down" and luckily, he did.

But the authorities had no plans to stop surveying our sightseeing after that incident. For the rest of the day they were watching us as closely as 1984's Big Brother himself - and that's very closely. Next up, they had a problem with us sitting on some grass to have lunch. Can't sit on grass in Rome apparently. Fair enough. So, we sat on the wall instead. Can't do that either. Okay...therefore we were only left with the option to stand and eat our lunch. I'm not quite sure what their problem was with us, but I must admit that Alex did look slightly alien - being a little bit smaller than a giant, and wearing his red Christmas jumper with a bright green dinosaur on the front covered in tinsel, with the words "tree-rex" printed along the bottom. I found it to be a rather hilarious jumper, but maybe for the Romans the joke was lost in translation. Ultimately, we saw everything there was to see in the glorious imperial place-of-old, and continued southward, down the boot of Italy - with me cycling, and Alex hitchhiking.

As if we hadn't already had enough opposition over the previous few days, on my way cycling from Rome to meet Alex at our next town, Latina, Google Maps took me on a peculiar route. It was a very small road, and I was always sceptical when I saw those on the map, especially at night, but it looked like a shortcut and I thought that I'd go for it anyway. I cycled hesitantly down the path and it was strangely close to a house, and eventually ended up being a dead-end with only cow sheds surrounding me. "Okay, turn around then, that was a waste of three minutes of my precious time," I thought to myself. But whilst I was cycling back onto the main road, with my flashlight unavoidably shining at the same house I had just had to closely pass, an old Italian lady came running out of the house with a broom in her hands shouting at me super-duper angrily. I stopped. Okay, clearly not a great situation to be in, much confusion, but a broom isn't going to kill me. But...*what the frippery flippets!* Her equally flustered husband on the other hand, was carrying something that definitely *could* kill me! He was literally holding a loaded rifle at the head of a poor innocent cycle tourist - me! They were both now shouting in Italian, and it's not so much of a sexy language in this context. I just shouted back saying:

"Excusa! Excusa! I am lost!" I tried to look as much like a lost tourist as I possibly could, to avoid getting shot. Eventually when their adrenaline levels came back down, and when they had seen that I wasn't trying to steal their cows, they lowered their weapons and cleaning tools, and looked severely embarrassed (and rightly so). I said that I needed directions to Latina and the old man proceeded to give them to me, gun still in hand. I mean, who would have thought it - that the stereotype of farmers with guns is actually true? They were proper Italian Hillbillies. Who would genuinely try to steal a sheep from him? Or even steal his lettuce? Even then, is that actually a crime punishable by death? Maybe in that part of Italy. But all I can say is I was a very happy bunny leaving that farm alive, and it was unbelievably good to meet Alex in Latina, in one full, non-decapitated piece. We cooked a yummy yet simple meal on our camping stove, slept in our tents in a park and woke up rejuvenated.

We took the coastal route down to Napoli, with an onslaught of rain making it slightly more dramatic. But luckily during the rainiest of days, a lovely restaurant owner allowed us to sleep in the outside heated area of his restaurant. We dried our clothes (although I accidentally dried my gloves too thoroughly and they melted on the heater) and warmed up for our final leg towards the city famous for its mopeds and mafia.

We eventually arrived and spent a couple days engulfed in the whirlwind of Napoli and were able to experience the "best pizza in the world" at Michele's Pizzeria (and I think it probably lived up to its title). We browsed the old cobbled streets, and all day narrowly avoided getting hit by reckless teenagers on their little Vespa mopeds. We didn't have to dodge away from any mafia, but who knows - we may have been walking the same streets as infamous organised gangs. But probably not.

After we escaped the craziness of Napoli, we travelled marginally south to climb an active volcano, Mount Vesuvio, while thunder threatened to strike us down. We can't say for sure, but whilst climbing up to the summit in the thunderstorm, we both thought that we saw two wolves staring at us from deep within the woods. They weren't cats, and they were too big to be wild dogs. It was an epic atmosphere, and the thunder was somewhat alarming. Yet, this is one of the most surveyed volcanoes in the world, so we knew we would be fine, but it was quite a scary atmosphere nonetheless. We were soaking wet and hiked for six hours relentlessly uphill in order to get to the crater. So, with this in mind, we were certainly quite annoyed when we got to the top and were told that the volcano was closed early, due to bad weather. How can you close a volcano? No way, we weren't having any of it, so we snuck in under the fence. That's right - we broke into a volcano. Then, at the very top, near the crater we were faced with even more authoritarianism, to which we once more prevailed, and managed to talk them around - finally getting to see the infamous crater. Thank goodness. We had a bit of a celebratory ceremony with a big pinecone that we found in Rome, and collectively threw it deep into the boiling crater. It marked a feeling of achievement and novelty - not many people can say that they threw a Roman pinecone into the bubbling mouth of Vesuvio.

The following day we went to Pompeii, the very place that Vesuvio famously destroyed. It wiped out nearly all its beautiful buildings and killed nearly all its beautiful inhabitants, yet some ruins still remain - hence the UNESCO World Heritage Site. Even though I cycled and Alex hitchhiked, he was still later than me to arrive. He fancied a relaxed morning walking barefoot and smelling the newly sprung spring flowers. Fair enough, not a problem. But it *was* a problem when I arrived there and they said, "we're shutting early today at 4.30pm." What the hell, it was 2.30pm already and we only had two hours left before closure. Where was Alex? His phone was off (of course) so I bought us both tickets, gave Alex's ticket to the security guard and told him, "to please give it to the tall bloke with the red dinosaur Christmas jumper," and off I went in alone to explore the ruins. I had already planned concretely to hit the road the following day, so it was my last possible opportunity to explore this great wonder of the world. He finally arrived, and I randomly stumbled upon him in the main square. We ran around (literally) taking in as much history as possible in a short space of time. We ran past ancient coliseums, archaic residential homes and so many other beautiful assortments of ruins.

We had one final night camping in Pompeii, went to a Catholic church service in the morning (which was very intriguing) and then finally said goodbye to each other, until next time. It was such a fun journey with a very close friend, and an important person for the fruition of the trip. It was a shame to leave him, as he hitchhiked back to the UK, but it was a glorious feeling to get back on the bike and carry on cycling towards New Zealand.

My next mission was to cross the entire centre of Italy from the west coast all the way to the east coast. It was fine, albeit really quite hilly in places. The rural countryside was a nice rest from the hustle and bustle of places like Napoli. After cycling the whole width of Italia, I arrived at the "heel of the boot", Puglia - the southern region of Italy, with primordial olive trees everywhere I turned, and amazing fairy stone houses defining the landscape. Back home, before my trip, I never really used to drink coffee, and I would generally avoid bread. But in Italy I was essentially living solely off coffee and bread. There's just so much of it there! It's a slight exaggeration of course, as I was eating ample amounts of peanut butter as well, but still – I consumed enough wheat products in Italy to last me a lifetime. Pasta for lunch? Yeah go on then. Biscuits with the morning coffee? Okay, fine. And what for dinner...well, pizza would be nice. But despite the overdosing of wheat, it is still undeniable that the Italians know how to make really good food. Either this stereotype is very true, or I was just super hungry the entire time due to all the cycling. Probably both.

They take the pasta making seriously, with hundreds of varieties, but so do the tourists apparently. I met two Swiss guys in the South of Italy who were also bicycle touring. I was spending some time in a charming town called Matera with an Italian guy who had previously waved at me from his car and pulled over on the side of the road. He exclaimed that he had the same bike as me and that he also loved bicycle touring. We decided to meet the next day for a coffee. While I was with him, we met two other cycle tourists in the exact same situation on the side of the road. All of a sudden, four total strangers were now connected through one common factor - bicycles. The Italian guy, Genaro, unfortunately had to go back to work, but me and the Swiss guys continued our journey together for a couple days. One thing they were adamant about in particular was finding the old ladies in the historic centre of Bari, who make pasta with their hands. After an hour or so of searching fiercely for these old pasta-women, we finally found them. It shocked me that during the pasta making process, the Swiss lads were making notes about the whole thing, literally with a pen and paper - learning the ropes from the very best in the pasta game. So there you have it - both Italians and tourists alike take the art of pasta very seriously. But for me, even after five weeks in Italy, I concluded that pasta is pasta - and if I wish to mix the curly ones with spaghetti or slightly over boil it, then so be it! I shan't hand over my autonomy to the Pasta Police. It's quick and cheap, and that's why pasta is ultimately a king of foods, so let's cut out the blibber blabber.

After one more little cycling leg of Italia, I was then ready to hop over the sea via a boat from Brindisi to Patras, Greece.

Chapter Five

The Birthplace of Western Civilisation

Oh Greece, what an amazing place to cycle through! With constant sea and mountains gently surrounding me the entire time, relatively flat cycle routes, a good level of English and an absolute abundance of history, what more could one want?

Yet, saying that, when I first arrived at the port in Patras, Western Greece, there were scenes of chaos. It was during a time of particular pressure for refugees to escape their war-stricken countries. The whole port was surrounded by barbed wire, like most, but here there were hundreds of young men trying to jump over the fences, simply being met by police sirens and thereby scenes of them fleeing back to their camps. This was quite an unnerving start to a country I knew quite little about. I cautiously cycled out of the port and past the groups of asylum-seeking men. There was no direct hostility or violence towards me, but you could tell by the way they were looking that they envied anyone who wasn't in their current position - and rightly so. War is an evil thing and will unfortunately continue for as long as countries like ours make money from selling weapons.

I really didn't have a clue about my plan or my route other than visiting Athens. But luckily my good friend Stefanos was able to flesh out my itinerary and link me up with lots of his friends all over the country- and once you have one connection, it's crazy how that suddenly transforms into two, three, and four connections very rapidly. I knew little about Greek culture, and not a thing about the language but I was intrigued by the history of this country, and everything that the Ancient Greeks gave to Europe. In fact, this was one of the main reasons that I planned my route as such. Because I had already seen Eastern Europe before on the trains, and I figured that if I spent longer in Italy and Greece, I could properly pick up some interesting historical information. They call it the "birthplace of Western Civilisation" and you can see why, considering the sheer number of influential philosophers, scientists and artists that have come out of this country during the last 3,000 years. Athens, for one, was full to the brim with ancient ruins. Particularly mind-boggling was the huge Acropolis complex, which is still standing today despite numerous explosions taking chunks out of its very body.

Another Greek friend from University, Maria, was also a massive help by having her family host me in Athens. It was an incredible city with such a gloriously symbiotic mix of old and new. Her parents were ridiculously kind, feeding me so much food and even plentiful amounts of their own home grown olives. In the deepest sincerity, I say these words – they were the most glorious olives that have ever passed my tongue.

The myth goes, that Athens was originally named after the Goddess Athena, after she won a competition against Poseidon. In order to end the dispute over land, Zeus demanded that both Gods offer a gift to the people of the city, and whichever was the best gift, they would name the city after that God. Poseidon gave his gift first and struck the earth, producing spring water, but the people weren't pleased to find out that the water tasted of salt like the sea. Athena decided to gift a seed, which grew to become a bountiful olive tree, which would provide abundant residual food and firewood. The people unanimously decided to name their city after her - Athena, thereby we have modern "Athens". News of this story made Maria's family olives taste all the more scrumptious. It was fascinating to learn about these

Greek myths which are so timelessly rich in imagery and allegory. As stories of an eternal past, they enrich life in the present. Here are some poetic thoughts I wrote whilst overlooking the famous Acropolis:

His-story

History oh history
So many old old things
Artefacts and treasures
Littering the cityscape -
as if dropped there by thoughtless teenagers

I also see a sea of modernism rising stories high
So very starkly contrasted to these gems of the old.
Columns oh columns
of the Athens from the ancient world -
still stood strong and unshakeable
Despite thousands of years
and millions of hours
Ceasing to erode their standing

They stand
As a symbol of the symbiosis of science
The coming together of different fields
meeting each other head on.
But what are these historic monuments,
but another opportunity for a selfie?
Why is history so boring at school?
Well...it happened back then,
it's not relevant now to the world of Google and Apple,
no?

But surely we must look back in reflection of what once was

To inform
The present
To learn from the ancients and to use this knowledge,
to save the possibility of the human race
destroying everything in its sights

Yesterday, the last male northern white rhino passed away.
Essentially another species wiped out
by the unforgiving bulldozer of economy
with no regard for ecology.
Profit over planet.
So to be sat
In the very birthplace of western "civilisation"
The irony screams in paramount proportions
And reminds us that
what we are doing now to the planet
Is anything
But
Civilised.

So history oh history
Let us learn from you
Well and truly
To bring equilibrium to this blue-green-sphere
that we are so very lucky to inhabit.
If we are civilised,
then please let us act like it.

If we are "evolved" beings
Let us evolve once more
Into peace.

Along with the historical side of the city, Athens has a strong anarchical undercurrent with many young people vocally displeased with the political situation. The economic crisis that they've been facing during recent years, has highlighted the inherent corruption within the financial system and has led to huge levels of disenchantment within young people. This can be seen through the huge amount of graffiti around their cities, and anti-government sentiment everywhere. This doesn't threaten me at all, as I share some of these sentiments with them, so in a way it was welcoming to see so much distaste for the economic system. There wasn't any outright violence, just a perceptible undercurrent of counterculture which was somewhat refreshing. Yet this subculture was rubbing shoulder to shoulder with another, that is much more nationalistic and orthodox. Especially in relation to their Turkish neighbours, there was still quite a bit of macho beating of the chest from both nations, and a sense of jingoistic pride in their home nation. This isn't necessarily good or bad - for they are more like disagreeable brothers, with more similarities than contrasts between them.

The actual cycling between cities in Greece was a delight beyond delights, constantly next to the dark blue sea. I'm not sure why, but the colour of the Greek sea had a different quality to it. It seemed to look deeper and more vibrant, and sight of it never failed to make me smile when I looked over the road, into the oceanic abyss. One thing that shocked me about Greece was the large number of tortoises that were strolling along the road. I'm not sure why, but I never imagined Greece to have loads of stray tortoises cruising around. I would do my best to make sure that they didn't get squished by oncoming cars. But unlike the benign nature of the tortoise, there was an unlikely animal threat, believe it or not, in the form of dogs. Quite different to the Latin Doggos which were annoying but harmless, the Greek dogs were both annoying and potentially harmful. It didn't help that a friend of mine from Bath, in her early 60's actually got eaten alive by stray dogs during a holiday in Greece. It was a savage death which surprised everyone back home, but with over one million stray dogs in Greece at the moment, a lonely human may pose a target for a pack of starving dogs driven to afflicting vicious attacks in their desperation. It was another product of the Greek economic crisis, where dog owners could no longer afford their canines, and sent them out into the streets to fend for themselves. I had this untimely death of my friend firmly in my mind when passing packs of stray dogs, and unfortunately for me, it seemed they loved chasing bicycles.

I'm not sure what it is, but they think that the bicycle is a running animal and they simply love to chase it. But with the context of my friend's death, this was far from fun on several occasions. When first cycling into Athens, my maps took me on a strange shortcut through an industrial estate. I know what you're thinking, those bloody maps once again! I was cycling along happy as Larry, when out of nowhere from behind a corner, came sprinting a pack of ten ferocious dogs. One of them was relentlessly persistent, snapping at my heels. I was cycling literally as fast as I could, yet the dogs were running just as quickly. The sandy shaggy ring leader was frothing at the mouth and I genuinely think that if he had bitten me I would have had to be rushed to hospital to get an instant rabies jab, because that would have been a genuine threat to my life. I was shouting at the top of my voice to try to scare them off and even tried to lash out my right leg as a deterrent, but luckily the car behind me was beeping its horn and even tried to swerve into the pack of dogs to stop them from getting to me. They eventually scurried off and I sprinted away on my bike. I thanked the car behind and tried to calm myself down. I mean, they probably wouldn't have killed me, but it still sent my heart racing as fast as a Formula-One car, and my adrenaline was through the roof. There were only a few other minor incidents like that, but this was definitely the most concerning.

Whilst on the road in Greece, I spent most of the time sleeping wherever I could find a place to chuck my tent. But I also managed to find some cool communities to stay with. One of them was near Larissa in central Greece where a family lived in beautiful earthen homes, made from a combination of clay and straw (otherwise known as "cob"). My own home for a couple nights was an underground hobbit hut, a perfect size for me, and with grass covering the roof, which created a little secret door to enter. I really did feel like a little hobbit. They were also experimenting with natural farming techniques on the land, with methods such as seed bombing. It was truly inspirational to see people living in an alternative way, sowing the seeds for a different future - where we can live as communities in unison rather than in isolated cities full of strangers, all trampling on each other for relentless financial gain. Another cool place that I stayed for a couple of nights was a wonderful unknown spot just past Thessaloniki. It was a community of travellers from all over the globe, staying in an old abandoned hotel complex next to a hot water spring. By all means, it wasn't a five star hotel and some people would have turned their nose up at it, but for me – quite accustomed to my sweaty tent, it was amazing to have creative company and have a morning bath which was naturally heated by Mother Earth herself.

Overall, Greece was an awesome country to cycle through with lots of cultural idiosyncrasies, an abundance of history bubbling out from every corner, and natural wonders everywhere you looked. Potentially, if these creative centres of communion, and the countercultural shoals of youths are nurtured in a nourishing way - we could see yet another birth of "Western Civilisation", yet one more holistic and healing. Who knows, Greece may yet have a significant role to play in the evolution of our culture. Although I had loved my time there, I was at the point where I was sincerely ready to leave the continent that I called home, and to venture into the unknown.

PART TWO – A TWO-WHEELED ODYSSEY THROUGH ASIA MINOR

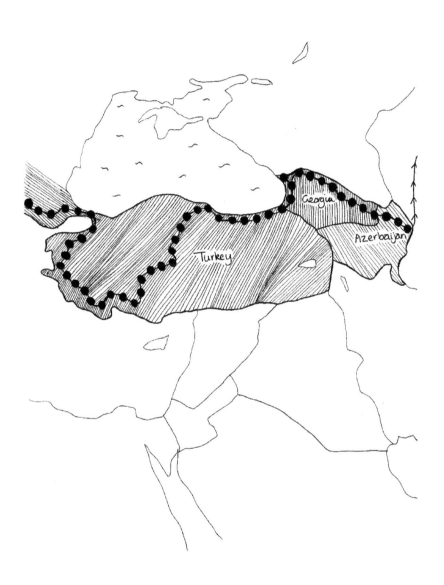

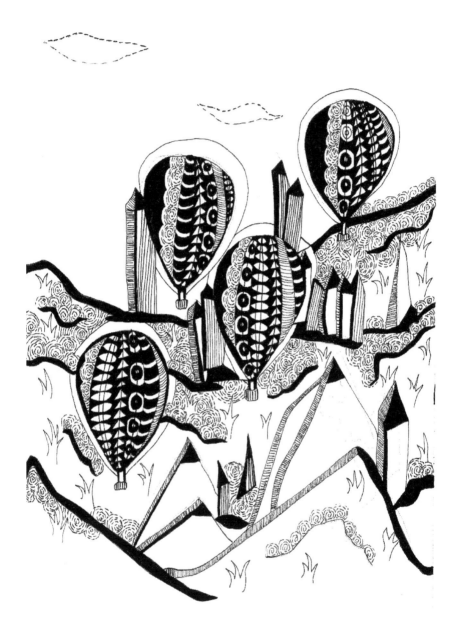

Chapter Six

Orientalism

The waves were gently slapping the rocks below, with the sun having already gone down, a pinkish sky accompanied the distant murmur of a brass band. Istanbul - the meeting place of both Europe and Asia, the only city in the world that literally crosses two continents. And the mix is clear, with the two rubbing shoulders, side by side, as if dancing some form of cultural waltz.

It took me three months and three weeks to cycle the entirety of the European continent and to finally arrive in Asia. But the very last stretch of that huge journey was one of the most dangerous roads (if not *the* most) that I have ever been on in my entire life. I know that you will probably read about the dangers of Motor Monsters many times in this book, but believe me when I tell you that this main road from the border of Greece into Istanbul was severely deadly in every conceivable sense. On this 6-lane monster motorway, I had an utterly absurd level of adrenaline shooting through my body for the entire day. I was completely on edge, almost starting to come to terms with the possibility that this could be my last day on Planet Earth.

Essentially, it was the only road coming from the Greek border and there were no other options. But I didn't think that I would need another option, because no one warned me about this road. Maybe I should have assumed it would be busy, considering that Istanbul is the fifteenth largest city in the world, but still - there was no preparing for the danger of this road. The problem wasn't the amount of traffic on it, I'd already been on plenty of busy roads that weren't all too dangerous, but the issue here was the truck drivers. These truckies must be driving this road all day every day back and forth across the border, because they all had a huge sense of complacency, allowing themselves to switch off completely, to go into autopilot, and barely even take their eyes off their mobile phones to look at the road ahead. Literally, they were all just looking down at their phones instead of looking at the road. It was a dead-straight road, so they obviously felt that there was little need to look at where they were going, but little did they know that there was a poor feeble cyclist merely a few inches from their gigantic wheels, who could get crushed against the concrete reservations in the blink of an eye due to their incompetence. This lack of awareness from the drivers was further accentuated by the fact that there was barely any hard shoulder at all. Let's compare it to the A1 motorway I accidentally went on in Paris – a huge dangerous road, but the massively wide hard shoulder made it comparatively safe. But this road on the other hand, with the lack of a hard shoulder meant that you were so much closer to the violent wheels of these disgusting Truck Dragons. The drivers, on autopilot, would accidentally swerve slightly from left to right, albeit merely inches, but almost running me over in the process, nearly scraping my left ear. I had to confront death and look the Grim Reaper dead in the eyes that day. I had to become more comfortable with the prospect of my own end, because it could have easily occurred at any moment.

Luckily, only God knows how, I managed to remain in one piece and I eventually arrived in Istanbul. I'd put it down to a small sprinkle of luck, but mostly thanks to my unwavering relentless focus on keeping going in a straight line. I was the most focused that I have ever been before. As some form of reward, Istanbul was a magical city, full of ancient mosques, little corridors of bazaar markets selling Persian carpets, tropical dried fruits from all over the Eastern World, and all the spices imaginable. Istanbul was always an important point in my planned route, as a checkpoint where I would ensure I had everything sorted with my bike and all the stuff I needed to successfully traverse a surely difficult environment in Central Asia and beyond. I had so much to think about, such as things to help me guard against the harsh summer sun that I would be slowly cycling into day by day.

But of equal importance was my psychological preparation. Of course, it is merely a different continental landmass, but this unavoidably brings many new challenges that aren't present in Europe. There are extreme weather conditions, insects that can kill you in an instant, and of course some Asian cities where you must watch your belongings with the eye of an eagle. So yes, there were reasons for me to use that interim of geographical transition to prepare wisely. And furthermore, my Australian elevator friends (who I met in an elevator, in case you didn't guess) helped me to imagine the innumerable ways that I could die on my trip beyond Europe. They also helped to remind me that the Australasian continent beyond Asia would be equally as life threatening, if not more.

Yet at the same time, there was this deep and loud longing for these far away exotic countries that would bring the unknown and the novel in a myriad of ways. A strong orientalism, a fascination with some of the cultures that awaited me in this new landmass - China, Korea, Japan - the very idea of visiting these places had excited me from a very young age, and soon I was to be traversing them by bicycle. This notion of "The Orient" was traditionally seen as the opposite to the Western World, novel and fascinating, yet also seen as less civilised too. With or without knowing, that concept has infiltrated our contemporary common conceptions of these faraway places. This remains the case, despite modern globalisation creating a much more homogenised world, where most major cities are simply major cities, regardless of east, west, north or south. Maybe some people today still see Asia as being a savage place, where they don't even eat baked beans and very rarely play cricket, but for me, throughout my youth I had always seen Asia as an unbounded land of anythingness. It was this positive sense of Orientalism which was one of the big catalysts for me to actually begin the crazy voyage in the first place, and to fully allow the caterpillar of my idea to transform into the butterfly of actuality.

For me (I can't say the same for you) these potentialities of oriental wonder and beauty, by far outweigh the dangers that they stand beside, on these distant lands. And anyway, what young man doesn't wish to experience the constant dangers of adventure? Well, probably loads, but regardless, I was one young man thirsty for excitement, and this is what I pursued.

Ahead of me lay not one homogenous Asian culture, with one Asian cuisine, and one Asian style of architecture, but instead a sheer multitude of diversity within all the above. So many differences of peoples and places, throughout "Asia Minor", "Central Asia" and "Far Asia", all distinct and varied in a multitude of ways.

I took the ferryboat over to the Asian side of Istanbul. It was a precious moment for me, with live traditional music playing on the boat. I wanted to cycle over the bridge, despite knowing that it was forbidden. But, luckily before doing so, I decided to ask a local traffic policeman to see if it was at all possible, and he said that if I attempted it, he would cut off my willy. It was a joke...I think. So, I decided to get the ferry boat, as any sane man would (just in case this was genuinely the formal Turkish penalty for cycling across the main bridge).

Now that I was technically in Asia, well rested and mentally open for what was to come, I was ready to continue the adventure and start cycling once more. My next checkpoint was down in the south of Turkey, where I was planning on volunteering at two music festivals, so that I could have some well-needed socialising and boogying. Most cyclists would simply stick to the Black Sea and go in a straight line from east to west across northern Turkey, but instead I chose to take a huge detour all in the name of fun and music! En route from north to south, I slept in some interesting places - one night in a police station, believe it or not.

Yeah, you did read that correctly - I slept in a police station. Luckily it wasn't for having committed a crime, because if I had, I probably wouldn't have been treated with the excellent hospitality that I received. I was given my very own wooden out-house, with enough room for Rasta Bike, Peace Bear (although he needed very little space) and me staying all together in one delightful sleepover. There was a really lovely selection of benches for me to choose, on one of which I laid down my sleeping mat, pillow and sleeping bag, and boom - I slept like a baby (well, a baby that was fully conscious that it was sleeping in a police station, on a bench which only supported half of the sleeping mat. And one that gets woken up at 5am by the loud singing of a mosque).

You may be wondering why, so do allow me to explain. The man from the cake shop had taken me to the police station, and with good intentions too - to help see if sleeping in the town park would be an issue or not. I've slept in parks before, but this dude seemed to be a full-on law-abiding citizen, thus marching me to the police just to be on the safe side.

Yes, they said it was fine, but it would likely be noisy, with a risk of drunken youths disturbing my sleep. Thus, they offered for me to sleep on one of the benches within the police yard. I thought that this was a slightly odd offer, yet when I thought about whether to accept it or not, I was struck by a strong sense of novelty and a new experience at hand. For I have never ever slept in a Turkish police station and probably never will again. And after all, new experiences were what I wanted from the trip. The senior officer even offered to arrest me for the night and let me go in the morning, but I couldn't tell from his tone whether he was joking or not, so I kind of grunted a semi-laugh and looked away. He didn't pull out his hand cuffs, so all was okay.

It was a rather peculiar way to end a rather challenging day, to say the least. Earlier, in avoiding a premature death via Truck Dragon, I gave myself too much room to the right and I accidentally hit the barrier of the hard shoulder, due to my attention slipping for a split second. Upon falling, my left arm instinctively shot out straight to support the blow, but a loud *click* sound came from my elbow and "*ouchies*" was my natural response. To make matters better, my front wheel was as wobbly as wibble wobble jelly on a plate. Great. After applying some ice and ice creams on my elbow, I just about soldiered on to the nearest village four kilometres away, where the only mechanic for miles managed to at least help the wheel straighten up a tad. I was a bit shaken up by the whole ordeal, but on I went regardless. After all, I still had the Southern Hemisphere to cycle to.

In direct response to the awfully busy main road, I took to the other option - the unpredictable, sometimes terribly surfaced smaller road. It seemed like it could be a life-saving plan. But, of course, as with any challenging day, all the challenges get thrown at you at once, somewhat like having an entire PE class throwing basketballs at you simultaneously at once. So I had the other opposite end of the spectrum. My cycling app took me through the tiniest farming villages, and eventually ended up taking me into a barren, desolate, Mars-like landscape. This turned out to be a humongous construction site, where all the workers stared at me as if I was an alien. It was a bumpier terrain than anything I'd ever experienced before. Of course, this was absolutely fabulous for my still slightly wonky wheel, and still slightly dodgy elbow - good stuff.

So yes, the prospect of sleeping in a police station would at least prevent all my stuff from getting stolen in the night - saving me from a totally devastating day all together. They gave me a traditional Turkish chai tea, and even brought me some bread in the morning - all amongst good chats. A pleasant police experience for sure. Definitely better than the Roman police! The following morning, I went to the hospital to get more ice for my swollen elbow, and I was the talking point for all the bored patients in the waiting room. Fair enough, I don't mind being the point of conversation or laughter - for I have always secretly loved the limelight, ever since acting in school plays. I've always been a drama queen, to the core.

Afterwards, I went to the park that I was originally going to sleep in the night prior. My meditation was interrupted once again, but this time not by a pretty French lady but instead by some religious guys that asked me interview questions for some famous humanitarian dude to answer on TV. They told me to think of a question to ask, so I asked how to stop war, and if one possible way to reduce violence is to stop the UK from selling large amounts of weapons to countries which use them to kill? Of course, it was a loaded question.

And shortly after my interview, I was taken from the park amidst my morning gratitude affirmations in order to speak with some Turkish man's ten-year-old daughter. She was taking English lessons at the time, and I guess my conversation with her was to supplement her learning. So all within an incredibly short period of time, all in the same village, I was a guest at the police station, an interviewee, and an English teacher. At least it wasn't a boring time there. But Turkey was full of surprises, and the police station wasn't the only weird place that I rested my head.

One night, I slept in a truck - a big orange truck, parked in a petrol station. It didn't faze me, and it certainly didn't feel odd to accept the offer. In fact, it came with great pleasure to know that my poor broken back would rest on some form of bed for nine hours, rather than having to endure another night of broken sleep in my tent.

Sleep is so important, as everyone knows - because when you have a bad night's sleep you generally act like a sour faced sulky brat the next day. It's especially important when cycling 100km a day, as you need every ounce of energy to keep pushing pedals the following day, on repeat. However, I set myself a challenge before I even left home - which was to not pay for a single night of sleep throughout Europe, and I had managed to complete this challenge!

And I managed to keep it going into Turkey, beyond Europe. So, for five and a half months, I had not paid one penny for sleep. I camped an awful lot, slept in the homes of many friends (mostly friends of friends of friends) and the rest of the time I laid my head in some very unexpected, random places. When permitted, I slept in restaurants after closing hours, in many parks, on people's crop fields (avoiding the crops themselves, of course - I'm not immoral) and on the odd bench here and there (like a proper homeless cyclist). Benches were the worst-case scenario, but the best-case scenarios were staying at hostels and hotels some nights free of charge, because I knew a worker or owner. I experienced all forms of sleeping spots, but only if it was free. All in all, I'm so grateful for having slept in a myriad of different places and positions during those months, rather than my one bed in England over and over, for I wouldn't have learnt a fraction of what I did by sleeping in a multitude of weird and wonderful locations. That night, in my private orange truck, I was so peaceful and tranquil, and had a fully nourishing sleep. Come the morning, I felt like a fully charged mobile phone ready to make phone calls all day.

The sheer unwavering hospitality of the Turkish locals was one of the multitude of reasons that I loved cycling through Turkey, and why I will always regard it deep in my heart as a truly special place. People were simply so very kind when they would see me struggling along on my bike at night, and they would relentlessly offer whatever they could to provide me with comfort. I wouldn't even have to ask for help, because people would already offer for me to stay in their spare room or to eat with their family. Innumerable times, local families in the villages would give their absolute utmost to make me feel welcome and comfortable. Even though some of these people didn't have all too much wealth financially themselves, they had an abundance of emotional wealth and love, and this was so inspiring to see how these virtues manifest in the absence of monetary abundance. Despite not having much themselves, they would give me so much food until I was literally full to the brim, without expecting anything in return. For me, this is the definition of unconditional love. And they were giving it, to a total and utter cyclist stranger.

Before I left for the trip, I was warned numerous times about the inherent evil in humans and how they will always try to benefit from you, at your expense. But the people of Turkey displayed only the opposite, merely giving and never expecting repayment, not even for a split second. They well and truly smashed the stereotype of dangerous strangers into oblivion, and for their hospitality I will be eternally grateful and indebted forevermore.

Whilst all of this was happening, I was still cycling day by day, turning wheels towards the festivals on the south coast. En route I traversed the Mediterranean eastern coastline of Turkey. It felt very different from the rest of mainland Turkey for it used to be a part of Ancient Greece and many Greek ruins remain there today. The cities, like Izmir, are very cosmopolitan and multicultural, and the sea feels like many other Mediterranean coasts in Europe. I was excited to finally arrive at the festivals, because although I'd had lots of social exchanges with locals, I hadn't had all too much fun with youngsters. I stayed constantly motivated by the impending fun that lay ahead, and kept focused on getting closer and closer, enjoying the scenery as I went.

After a few weeks of pedalling, I made it to Fethiye by my deadline - which was the beginning of the first festival. I essentially volunteered, helping the organisers to set up the event in return for my ticket. We organised a lot of the decorations and stages, doing some artwork and making everything ready for the first day of the event. It went rather swimmingly and I made a lot of lovely friends in the process. The festival itself was full of fun and laughter, and after loads and loads of dancing, it was time to head to the next one. It was a similar situation for the second festival, and I aided the preparation process in any way that I could. After two straight weeks of socialising with people my own age and listening to awesome music, I felt like I had sufficiently received a substantial dosage of fun. I met so many people, and some of them will certainly be friends for life. Even Peace Bear had a blooming great time! He danced away to the booming music, and even met a lady-bear-friend (if you know what I mean) and he was very hesitant to leave her, so I kind of had to pull him away. Rasta Bike predominantly just chilled by the reggae stages, but I think he thoroughly enjoyed it too – allowing his dreadlocks to swing in the ocean wind, and to unwind with good tunes.

The first part of the detour was well worth it and quite easy, knowing that there would be a reward in the form of shared dance-floor joviality and collective celebration of life. But the second part of the detour was much harder, having already had the parties, it was now time to get back on track and en route once more towards New Zealand. This meant going all the way back up from the south coast to the north coast once more- and this wasn't just down the road, as such, but instead an entire 1,000km of cycling. What made it even more challenging was the mountain range that I had to pass up and over, straight away from sea level. Sea level wherever you go is usually around zero metres above sea level...which makes sense, but I had to climb up to 2000m all in the space of a couple days. This, combined with the fact that it was a scorching 35 degrees, made for a particularly challenging couple of days which really pushed me to my psychological limit. For the first time truly in the entire trip thus far, I actually considered how idiotic of an idea it was - cycling to the antipode. I was honestly in utter agony and so fed up of climbing this hill in that heat, that I even considered going home, getting a regular office-job and a house and suchlike. But these defeatist thoughts didn't stay around in my weary cranium for long, and instead I brought forth more of my warrior spirit within and kept climbing upwards. Eventually, with lots more pain and agonising thrusts of my legs, I made it up and over the challenging yet beautiful mountains, towards the centre of Turkey.

Central Turkey was a kind of flat plateau, which finally offered some well-needed respite from the laborious task of cycling upwards, then downwards, then upwards once more. Not only this, central Turkey offered the delights of two particular gems. The first gem was the city of Konya, which was home to the poet

Rumi. Some of you may have read some of Rumi's most famous quotes on Instagram and suchlike, but he was a teacher of mystical Islam during the 13th century. He originally came to Turkey by walking with his father all the way from Afghanistan, and you can imagine - back in the day, that would have taken a seriously long time. In most of his poems he spoke about the essence of love and talked about it as if it was the divine itself. His most famous quote is "you are not just a drop in the ocean, but you are the ocean in a drop". For me, this is an incredibly profound statement, showing that each human is a microcosm of the universe, a physical manifestation of the divine itself. The whole city had a feeling of electric spirit which permeated the streets, and some of the historical buildings were a sight to behold, with towering minarets marking the skyline, constantly pointing upwards. Whilst in Konya, I went to one of the oldest Turkish baths in the whole country and had a jolly good sweat session, which was well appreciated. I've been to quite a few hot baths in my time, but the Turkish baths are ones to remember and some of the hottest I've ever been in.

The other main gem slap bang in the middle of Anatolia (the historical term for the Turkish peninsula) was the geological wonderland of Cappadocia. You may well have seen the famous quintessential image in kebab shops after a night out - hundreds of hot air balloons, soaring high above a landscape of otherworldly rock formations, in phallic-like shapes which the locals call "fairy chimneys". It is truly a beautiful place, with hundreds of little hidden caves. In fact, there are entire "underground cities" which the locals have used for almost a thousand years, to hide from numerous different invaders over time.

I even became a true caveman for a couple nights myself, and genuinely slept in a cave. Basically, when I arrived at the place of my host, he said that he'd had some issues and had no space for me to sleep but said that there was a very nice cave nearby where I could reside. To most normal people this may well sound like an absurd suggestion, but to me - that sounded like a bloody great idea! I just had to lay down my sleeping mat and get into my sleeping bag, and baddabing baddaboom I had a home for the night. It was a win win, because I didn't have to deal with the ordeal of setting up my tent and taking it back down in the morning - because after all, the cave was my tent. It provided all the necessary shelter that I required. It was an interesting experience, and under candlelight it was actually a very beautiful place to sleep, waking up in the morning to the sunlit fairy chimneys right outside my front door. It was quite a large space with a big opening at the front, as if it was a wide empty window. Inside, there was an open planned space with a couple separate "rooms" as such. In all the walls were little indentations almost like boxes, which were supposedly for keeping messenger pigeons back in the day. Some tourists paid ridiculously huge amounts to stay in so-called "cave hotels" which were awfully luxurious and fancy, but I on the other hand experienced the real deal for no more than zero pounds and zero pence. Central Anatolia certainly is a remarkable place, with these two beautiful gems and the flat riding, it made for a lovely respite.

However, the rest didn't last for long, because I had some mountains left to conquer, before getting back onto the Black Sea. Once I'd made it up and over, back to the north coast of Turkey, I now only had to follow one road in a straight line towards the border of Georgia. This region on the Black Sea is famous for the cultivation of hazelnuts where they grow in abundance, and most of my cycling was fuelled by the deliciously scrum-diddly-umptious hazelnut-butter spread, which I simply ate straight from the jar in ample quantities. Some may be appalled by such behaviour, but personally, I believe this to be the full-power food of kings.

After three months cycling through Turkey, I was once more ready to experience a new culture and country. I had actually learnt a decent amount of the Turkish language, learnt a fair bit about their history and spoken to so many of its wonderful locals. As I've said before in this passage, Turkey will always have a home in my heart as a land filled with loving locals, gorgeous coastlines, interesting geological features and very tasty tea! But I'd reached another border, and now it was time to leave.

Chapter Seven

Saintly Georgia Days

Usually when I tell people that I cycled through Georgia after Turkey, they get somewhat confused as to why I'd cycle through an American state so far away from Turkey. But, behold, I mean the *country* of Georgia instead. It's a small nation in the Caucasus region of Eurasia. But I truly don't blame people for not knowing much about this country, because before I crossed the border, I knew very little about it myself - in fact nothing in the slightest.

It was always a double-edged sword during this cycle trip when crossing borders from one country into another. On the one hand I was always excited to experience all the novelty and newness that lay ahead of me, but on the other hand I was equally nervous in knowing that I was entirely unfamiliar with the language, customs, culture and food of this unknown land ahead. During this transition from Turkey to Georgia I really did feel this equal split in my emotions – of both excitement and angst. But one thing that kept me pushing on was the fact that I was going to be seeing another one of my closest friends from back home, across the other side of the border - my good pal Harrison! Although the unknown was waiting for me, the very familiar and friendly face of my good mate was always going to balance that out, and he certainly did.

But nonetheless, I crossed the border the evening before he was meant to land. The transition was smooth, and the border guards didn't give me many difficulties and off I went. The first novel thing that struck me was the elaborate design of their alphabet and all the letters - with so much curvature and flow to the individual letters, it looks so easy on the eye. As a basic example, here is "hello" in Georgian: გამარჯობა. I mean, how epic is that! Personally, if pixies had an alphabet, this is the type of script I would imagine they'd use. It's crazy how even a mere bottle of water can look so magical, purely due to the writing on the front of it. I think the reason that I took such an interest in this is because it was the first alphabet other than Greek, that was different to our Latin alphabet.

Anyway, a bit of background about Georgia itself: well, it's a post-Soviet country, meaning that it used to be under the dictates of the Soviet-Union which was essentially a huge conglomerate of independent communist states, ultimately under the iron thumb of the centralised power of Moscow, Russia.

Georgia was the first of many post-Soviet countries that I was about to cycle through - out of six in total. They speak their own language - Georgian, but most people can speak Russian as well, which wasn't very helpful because I couldn't speak either, and I still can't. But luckily, most young Georgians can speak basic English. The period that I was there was during the Fifa World Cup, and although I'm not a football hooligan, I am, after all - English, which means we all genetically breathe, sleep and eat football, without a choice in the matter. So I was quite anxious to arrive in time to the nearest border town, in order to find somewhere to watch the quarter-final match of England Vs Sweden. I stopped off at a little cafe quite close to the border and when I asked if they had a TV they said "yes" (but I think this was just to keep me as a customer). Eventually they came out carrying a little square TV which couldn't have been any more pixelated if we tried, but I was still very grateful to be watching the game regardless. England won and I was feeling jubilant, so I ordered some food. As I looked around, I noticed that there were no other men in the entire outside seating area, and there were only women, dressed in rather provocative clothing. As more time went on, more women came in on their own, scantily clad. It eventually sunk in that this was not only a cafe but must have been some kind of brothel. I felt slightly uneasy being in that environment and knowing that everyone was considering whether I was a potential customer or not, so I left and camped on the beach behind the cafe.

The next morning, I awoke and cycled to the airport where I was to pick up Harrison and his bicycle. Our plan was to cycle together from Batumi on the Black Sea coast all the way to the capital, Tbilisi. It was my birthday in a week's time, and we were hoping to reach the capital together in order to celebrate. I met him that morning outside the arrivals, with his bike in a box and all his baggage beside him - we embraced after half a year apart and began putting his bike back together into one piece, with smiles firmly formed. Harrison is a dapper young chap, who at the time, was still finishing his Archaeology and Anthropology degree at Oxford University. He's a bright lad, but more importantly he's a bloody good laugh and I was looking forward to the adventures at hand.

It's quite a strange experience reuniting with someone after that long. The very nature of cycle touring means that you spend a lot of time alone, getting used to your own company, and this is one of the reasons it appealed to me in the first place. One noticeable difference in my being, was that my own ability to speak English had declined dramatically. It was quite evident for Harrison, having come straight from a heightened academic environment, where advanced vocabulary is thrown around like lexical frisbees. He went from conversations filled to the brim with low-frequency lexis, to a conversation with me, where I spoke like a Turkish corn farmer. Apparently, it was quite comical to hear me say things like "we eat food? Okay we do," rather than "would you like to eat lunch now or later? I'm particularly hungry." This was simply a result of spending so much time alone, and only speaking English with people who knew a miniscule fraction of the language. For sure it was difficult at times, merely having myself for company in alien and unknown lands. But what's even harder than that, is making fleeting yet powerful connections with random strangers, who after a few days become rather close friends. This is certainly a weird feeling, to be constantly meeting wonderful people, enjoying one another's company, but leaving them one or two days after having created such a great bond. For example, during the two festivals in the south of Turkey, I met so many great people and we shared so much together, yet upon leaving, I didn't know if I would ever see them again, which was both beautiful and painful at the same time.

And to accompany this hardship, other than Alex in Rome, I hadn't seen any of my close friends for six months. I know that I signed up for it, but it's a difficult thing to bear considering that I was used to frequent encounters back home with my closest people. You can video-call your friends nowadays, which of course is great, but it's strange that you're seemingly so close on the screens yet so very far away physically. With some of my friends who I class as my extended family, not being able to share laughter, dance, and everything else with them for half a year was quite the challenge. Thereby, with all this in mind, you can imagine that it was a great feeling seeing Harrison and reuniting with a big solid hug.

We spent our first evening in Batumi celebrating the fact that we were back together, excited for the coming adventure ahead. We strolled around taking it all in and had a bit of a boogie in several different places. I found it to be a fascinating city, however Harrison saw it more like the Las Vegas of the Black Sea - with casinos and Eurasian playboys a plenty. It has a long pebbled beach which spans the length of the city, and for the second night in a row it would be the place I'd place my tent and lay my head to rest, this time with company. Harrison brought his own one-man tent and we set up camp underneath a long pier that stretched out to sea. We locked our bikes for safety, and had a jolly good sleep (well, eventually, after the drunken youths stopped making silly repetitive noises behind our tents).

The following morning, we hit the road, with not much time to waste - if we wanted to arrive in Tbilisi in time for my birthday celebrations! We rode slowly but surely, because slow and steady wins the race, as they say. Harrison is a fit young lad so we had no dramas with the fitness side of cycling, in fact, when we both ran the Oxford half marathon a year prior, he beat my time quite considerably - so his keeping up with me was not a concern at all. Instead it was the opposite, as I was quite a bit heavier with my four-season baggage and being slightly battered and bruised from the ride from England to Georgia. Yet he gave me some sympathy and we found a good rhythm to suit us both. He decided to join me in my challenge of not paying for accommodation, so naturally we ended up sleeping in some obscure places. For example, after our first day of cycling we weren't left with many options as to where we could put our tents. After a solid day's graft of pedalling, we were well and truly knackered, and our map wasn't showing all too much green space for us to choose from. In the end, we decided on the village park. I reckon it would have been fine if Harrison hadn't made a rookie error, which he wasn't even aware that he'd made - until he started sleeping. Essentially, we set up camp as normal, said goodnight, and started the slumber process, but at around 1am I could hear Harrison's voice:

"Cody...Cody! Are you awake?" he asked.

"Erm, I wasn't, but yeah I am now. What's up?" I replied in my zombified, dreamlike daze.

"Well, there's loads of ants in my tent and I can't really sleep so I tried sleeping out here on the grass. I'm pretty awake now so...what do you think about starting cycling, like...now?"

I was slightly taken aback by this proposition, considering I was still in a midnight delirium. I quite quickly objected to starting cycling at 1am, but offered for him to sleep in my tent, considering that it was a two-man tent after all. He reluctantly jumped into my stinky tent which had an awful lot of use already, but ultimately, he was able to sleep ant-free. Well, he learned the hard way that one must keep their tent entirely zipped up whilst setting it up. It's things like this that you only learn through trial and error and after being on the road for a while, and my oh my weren't there a huge amount of these little lessons to be had.

I admit that our sleeping arrangements weren't perfect for this holiday, but neither were our eating arrangements either. This isn't exactly because the Georgian cuisine was rubbish, by no means, it was simply a combination of us being awkward customers (vegans) and not having the common language to distinguish what we could and couldn't eat. We largely survived off these potato pastry things that were rather oily but gave us the necessary calories to keep going. Sometimes if there literally weren't any veggie options at all, we would have four or five of these potato pastry things for our whole lunch. We lived and we learned, and eventually stocked up a bit more when we passed shops and managed to vary our diet somewhat.

We had some good charade sign-language conversations with locals along the way and received a lot of kindness. England played their semi-final World Cup game against Croatia while we were together, and unfortunately we lost - so it was lucky that we had each other for moral support (I'm mostly joking here, we both understand that there's more to life than football), but still, it was sad that "football wasn't coming home".

Georgia as a whole is really quite mountainous, in fact, most of the country is made up of mountains. Luckily for us, our route was following a valley which created a flatter part of the land. For sure, it was still hilly in places, and we did have one particular mountain to get up and over together. We had to keep each other motivated, and I guess part of that motivation came from not wanting to look like a puny little weakling, and thus we eventually made it up the mountain. We were greeted at the summit by a long, dark tunnel much to our amusement - tunnels are always fun and definitely safe (ironic statement, in case you lost me there). Yet we survived and had all the downhill to look forward to.

Before we knew it, we were only one day's cycling away from Tbilisi! By that point we were fully motivated because we knew we had a lovely hostel lined up for us - which a wondrous birthday present from my thoughtful Russian friend. The prospect of a proper bed, a warm shower and lots of good music in Tbilisi ensured that our final day of cycling was merely a breeze, and I think we had a bit of a tail-wind as well, so it was literally a breeze too! With that extra little push from the elements, we managed to do two days' worth of cycling in the space of one day and zoomed into the capital city with joy and triumph painted across our faces. We'd made it to our joint goal! It wasn't quite New Zealand yet, so I hadn't made it to my ultimate goal, but still, it was our mutual goal for this chapter and thus an amazing feeling cruising downhill through the Tbilisi suburbs heading towards the heart of the city. We crossed the land bridge, with the sunset lit citadel on the horizon and we knew we were home.

Evening came and we were immersed in the city lights, illuminating space from every angle and corner. To be fair, we'd been in rural Georgia for a good while by that point, and to be in such a large city was a bit of a shock at first, with all the additional traffic and noise. But this is exactly what we were looking forward to - hustle and bustle, people and plans and essentially a jolly good boogie. Considering we arrived a day early, we couldn't stay at my birthday-present-hostel quite yet, so we spent a night in The Rainbow House. Don't worry if you've never heard of this house, I do forgive you, but allow me to explain. Basically, a Rainbow Gathering is a meeting of sorts, where a bunch of international youngsters join in company, in the middle of raw nature in order to share stories, music and food. I went to one for a couple of days in the south of Turkey after the festivals, during my socialising break from cycling. It was an excellent experience and I saw so many smiles from the jubilant countercultural youths. I was tipped off at the end about a "Rainbow House" in Tbilisi where the doors are forever open to the Rainbow Family and baddabing baddaboom, we found out that they were indeed. Harrison and I were welcomed into the house with warmth and hugs, from otherwise total strangers. They were lovely people and we played guitar and sang songs, before falling into slumber - pleased that we'd made it to our goal.

The following day was Saturday, and it wasn't so much Saturday day that we were excited for, but more for Saturday night. It's funny that this is somewhat of a universal concept, that in any city - Saturday night is *the* party time. It's the end of the working week and the start of freedom, and in Tbilisi this is certainly true. Somehow Harrison had heard of a particular club in Tbilisi called Bassiani, and he was rather keen to check it out. We followed his intuition and it was where we chose to spend our night. And behold, it was absolutely bloody epic in every way! The main dance floor was underneath the biggest football stadium in Georgia, in what used to be a huge swimming pool area, now converted into an underground dungeonesque temple of tunes. From the moment we entered the room, a well renowned Berlin-based DJ, DVS-1, blasted us in the face with relentless thumping techno until the moment we left. It felt as if the music had the momentum of a steam engine gradually picking up more and more pace until it reached its ultimate speed, and continued to plummet into the abyss without even thinking of slowing down until it arrived into the station far yonder. We moved our bodies to the music non-stop for the entire night until it was closing time. It was a magical celebration of the feat of cycling we'd just accomplished from Batumi to the dance floor, and of life in general.

We made friends with two Mancunian twins and a Scottish lass who were hilarious company - which made for an eclectic mix of representatives from the British Isles. It turned out that they were also staying at our birthday present hostel and we went to check in as a team. It was called Fabrika and was a huge space that is now a trendy, fashionable hostel, but used to be a massive abandoned factory from the Soviet era, hence the name "Fabrika" (which means "factory" in Ruski). We revelled in the luxuries of a modern hostel and were glad to be sleeping somewhere which wasn't our stinky tents. There was a courtyard outside with trendy coffee shops and vinyl stores, with every single wall of the hostel covered with good quality street-art. Tbilisi was certainly a fashionable city and full of genuinely cool locals. This capital city went from being somewhere we barely knew existed, to being one of the hippest and coolest cities we'd ever been to. The Georgian youth are going through a huge transitional period, where they are coming out of the "red hangover" of Soviet communism and are finally able to explore their autonomy and creative selves. This means that there is an exciting air permeating the city where young people everywhere are exploring their minds and their creative potential, all culminating in boundless amounts of street-art, awesome electronic dance music and creative clothing everywhere you look. We loved it! Well and truly, Tbilisi was an amazing city and one that we certainly could see ourselves returning to someday.

Harrison and I had a few more days enjoying our time together, and even went to a mini festival for my birthday. We danced once more and rejoiced in the gift of life, grateful to still be alive in one piece, breathing breath. I turned 22 at midnight and I genuinely felt a whole year older, considering the sheer amount of condensed experience that I'd just been through, cycling from London to Tbilisi. I was overjoyed that Harrison could be there to share those magical moments with me.

A couple days later he unfortunately had to fly back to the UK. It would have been great if he could keep on cycling with me, but after all, he had to go back to Oxford to finish his degree (which he did, and passed with a First-Class Honours, and flying colours and extra sprinkles on top). We boxed his bike up and parted ways, knowing we'd see each other again, still in one piece, still celebrating the gift of living - just in some other place at some other time. I can speak for us both when I say we thoroughly enjoyed this chapter together, from the more arduous moments of shared mountain cycling, to the gleeful moments of shared techno dancing. Ultimately it is shared experiences that builds friendships and solidifies a brotherly bond, and we well and truly had a lot of that during those ten days. Off he went, and off I went too - heading towards the border of Azerbaijan to experience yet another unknown land.

Chapter Eight

Azeri Sanitary Sanatorium

It was only a short ride from Tbilisi to the Azeri border - a mere half-day of cycling and I was eager to complete it in next to no time. I crossed the border painlessly and had to dodge around all the black-market monetary exchangers on the Azeri side of the border. Azerbaijan is also a post-Soviet country, so in some ways it shares some commonalities with Georgia, but it is also quite different in many ways. They too can speak Russian as their second language, but their primary language is of Turkic origin, which was actually quite handy considering I'd already learnt a decent amount of Turkish and could now apply it once more, but my Russian was still non-existent at this point.

My first impressions were that it was quite a strange place, obviously in the literal sense because it was another unknown country to me, but it did feel a bit weird, energetically. All the old people have these bizarre golden teeth, that I can only assume have replaced rotten teeth (the language barrier prevented me from verifying this, although I tried). It was mostly in the rural areas where this phenomenon existed, but in the first few days of being there - literally every single person I met had at least one shiny gold tooth in their mouth. Like a combination between 50 Cent the American rapper and an old lady from the desert.

There is a peculiar clash of two separate cultures in these central Asian countries. Essentially, they are Muslims and practise the main principles of Islam, with beautiful mosques prominent in the landscape. Yet, due to them having been a part of the Soviet Union, they have a massive drinking culture - and a particular affiliation with vodka. This would usually be a rare sight in many Muslim countries, but here this is perfectly normal for these two cultural aspects to link arms. I think that this is a natural by-product of colonialism, and specifically that of the Soviet type. The forced crumbling of Islamic traditions in Central Asia has led to a desperate relationship with alcohol, yet probably not at all worse than the average Briton's relationship with the holy booze. However, I simply thought it notable that aspects of religiosity and alcoholism go hand-in-hand here, quite different to the Turks where they drink ample amounts of tea, and a drop of alcohol would very rarely pass their tongues.

The first few days were very action packed, and rather challenging to say the least. It was now getting towards August, the height of summer, and it was bloody boiling. Staying in the shade would have been ideal, but the landscape was already starting to turn more and more desert-like, so unfortunately there was very little shade available. It was my intention to get the boat from the East coast over the Caspian Sea to Kazakhstan, so I wanted to cycle across Azerbaijan as quickly as possible to give myself ample time to catch the boat. I had heard it was notorious for being an unreliable service, and that this route was pretty boring at times, so my plan was to just zip across the country quickly, but that was before I got sick - sick as a dog.

It all happened like a whirlwind, and before I knew it, I found myself lying in a bed, in an old people's home. It was a very bizarre scenario for sure. I was essentially in a sanatorium in central Azerbaijan where people live out their final days. An odd place for a 22-year-old, because I wasn't old, and I also wasn't dying (although it almost felt like it, when I was spewing in the early hours of the morning). I felt completely disoriented by the whole situation, and these types of wacky situations had become so normalised by that point that I just let it all unravel in its natural form.

I had been hosted by some very kind people I met at a restaurant and they invited me to their brother's hotel. It was all very nice, until I woke up sweating buckets and violently vomiting. I suppose I was incredibly lucky to have had my own room with an en-suite in this situation, compared to if I had been in my tent - that would have been a bit traumatizing. Thank God. I spent the whole next day recovering and reloading on fluids, before being deported from the hotel for being a bit of an unsightly wreck. They sent me back to the restaurant, where Rasta Bike and Peace Bear were safely staying, and I slept on some sort of foam thing (which didn't quite classify as a bed) where the restaurant staff slept.

The next morning, I didn't feel too sick anymore, so I got back on the road. It was tough, inevitably, in nearing 40° heat. Strong headwinds really didn't help what should have been a comfortable downhill ride from Ganja (yes, there is a city called Ganja which me and Harrison also found rather hilarious when we were looking at a map of Azerbaijan).

It was getting towards dusk later that day and I got called over by a couple local Azerbaijanis, and this wasn't a rare occurrence. Literally all day long it happened, considering that they are so pleased to see a foreign face, they beckon you over for tea. Although it would be nice to meet them all and have a glass of çay (traditional Turkish tea) each time, you have to reject most of the offers and continue pedalling, for if one stopped every time, one really wouldn't get very far at all because you'd simply spend all day drinking tea. But it was getting close to the end of the day, I was knackered, and had just had a powernap off the hard shoulder of the motorway for goodness sake. It was clear I wasn't going to make it to the intended town, and the two geezers waving me over shouting "Çay! Çay!" looked okay.

It turned out they weren't. I mean, they weren't evil, cold-blooded killers or anything, but just very insincere, scheming individuals. One was a security guard, but we all know that means nothing, even though they themselves think that they're police. The çay did arrive after I stopped, however, and they even said they had a bed for me, with no money wanted in return. It was very kind of them. Once again, it didn't quite classify as a bed in my opinion, but it would certainly do, and I was very grateful for the offer. It was in a kind of workshop space, not much more than a shack, which was surely used for work, and rarely used for sleep. But I thought I may as well stay put, just for one night.

But then it all started to get a bit weird when they started making crude homosexual gestures at each other, pointing blame at each other and then at me (a good tip for a way to make a new guest feel uncomfortable). Security Guard Bloke then offered to swap telephones with me which would have been the worst deal of the century, for me anyway, before showing me on his phone a video of him having sex with one of his girlfriends. Great. Thanks for that, Security Guard Bloke. By now, his mate was down to his wife-beater vest, teeth clearly decaying, surely soon to be replaced by the national gold teeth. They then had an arm-wrestling match - a true spectacle of hyper-masculinity for their growingly uncomfortable guest.

We went to get food and even though I'd told them in their own language that I was vegetarian, they ordered a dish with meat and then tried to get me to buy different things for them throughout the whole meal. What a pleasant evening this had been! If they seemed like nice guys at this point, I would have been happy to buy them something, but I was already getting bad vibes from them and this only increased with intensity throughout the night.

The highlight of the evening was video calling my brother Leyth in the petrol station next door, where I happily forgot how much of a shite situation I was in and lost myself in great chats. But when I returned to their workshop space, they started trying to charge me money for the "bed" and saying that I could sleep from 1am until 5am and would then have to leave. They had a strange, sneaky look across their faces and the vibe felt sour. I went to grab Rasta Bike and get myself out of there, despite Vest Guy trying to grab my arm. I threw his feeble arm off mine and ducked out. Down the road I checked my stuff and they had clearly been rummaging through my things. It turned out they stole my pepper spray, and my hand sanitizer. Nothing else.

Fair enough, weirdos. Well that's what I thought at least, however, a couple weeks down the line I saw that they must have been the reason as to why my GoPro disappeared. Whilst I was having that phone call with Leyth, they had clearly been having a jolly good time picking which item they wanted the most. This didn't add to my mood, considering I had my speaker stolen a couple nights prior - but I guess it was partly my own fault for being too flippant and trusting. I'd clearly grown somewhat complacent regarding safety, considering every other rural place I'd been in each prior country had been safe and friendly as ever. Whereas, for the first time properly during the whole trip, it felt quite the opposite in this tiny little town, and in Azerbaijan at-large.

By the point that I fled from their weird workshop, it was about midnight and I was just desperate to find the nearest place to sleep. I did that, within ten minutes. I paid ten pounds there and then (having thereby finished my challenge of not paying for accommodation) but didn't realise what type of place it was. It was only the next morning that I understood it was an old people's hospital. For goodness sake. Once again, I woke up in the middle of the night vomiting with a temperature as hot as hell itself. I wasn't quite sure what it was that was making me this awfully sick, but I was certain it had to be the food. Yet again, this wasn't one of my concerns in the prior five countries, as everything (within reason) was safe to eat and drink. But here, it was clearly a different story. I had the impression I was moving into a wholly different terrain, one which I was not accustomed to. I knew from now on I had to adapt in order to survive.

I spent the whole day resting in the sanatorium and received some funny looks - rightly so. Once more - thank goodness, I wasn't in my tent that night because the entire situation would have been ten times worse, at least. I felt so very lucky and grateful, despite it being a rather unlucky scenario. It felt like it was a day of forced rest from my body, and to resist it would have been insane. For sure, it wasn't the place where I would most want to be resting in the world, but then again, I doubt many people feel that way.

Most of us are in situations which aren't perfect - and the nature of this trip brought forth these moments in buckets. But, ultimately, I had many more majestic, magical moments of bliss, than I did solemn, downtrodden ones. And it made it easier to manage the latter.

Eventually, I felt well enough to move on towards the port where I was to get the boat. I had to say goodbye to my new friends I'd made at the old people's home and started cycling once more. It doesn't please me to say it, but if it wasn't for the final part of my Azerbaijani chapter, it would have been a sour place in my memory: with the boiling inhospitable heat, the incessant sickness and the items stolen. Luckily, the capital city of Baku and the new autonomous region of Portistan saved it as a memorable and not all too horrible country in my recollection.

Chapter Nine

Portistan

G etting onto the boat to Kazakhstan to get over the largest lake in the world, the Caspian Sea, was a particularly lengthy affair, albeit quite an entertaining one too. I had read previously that it was sometimes a long wait to get onto this boat, and even a wait of up to three days at times. Therefore, I had prepared myself, somewhat, for a few days of patience. The reason that I, and most people for that matter, took the boat in the first place was due to diplomatic reasons. When travelling overland west to east via Central Asia, you would otherwise have to cross Russia or Iran. Unfortunately for British travellers and Americans alike, it is increasingly challenging to secure a Russian or Iranian visa, and even if you do, it can be quite a difficult route, whichever country you choose. Thus, due to this, most travellers prefer to just skip this problem entirely and take a boat straight over to Kazakhstan.

There *is* an option, albeit not a favourable one, to take the boat instead to Turkmenistan. But considering that Turkmenistan is an unwavering dictatorship in every manner of the word, it is not the kindest place for cycling. It has a 2/100 rating on the "Freedom in the World Survey 2019" and there are all sorts of crazy videos online displaying the sheer relentless facade of the Turkmeni dictator. They barely give you ten days to cycle through the entirety of their desert nation (which is about 120km every day without a single day of rest) and that's even if they accept your visa application, which is more about luck than anything else. Going through Kazakhstan instead was a much brighter option.

I arrived at the Azeri port of Alat on my own, in the evening, with a boat already full and ready to leave. No problem, I wanted to see the capital city, Baku, for a few days anyway while I waited for the boat. It's a strange experience to traverse an entire country from border to border, when leaving the capital until the end. For a capital city encompasses so much of what a country is. When you think of England for example, your mind rushes into images of red buses and Big Ben, both of which you would never see in the quiet green countryside of Somerset, which is equally as quintessentially English as central London. But by this point I had a warped image of Azerbaijan due to falling ill a couple of times, the overly hot cycling conditions, and getting a couple things stolen by gold toothed weirdos. So, visiting Baku felt like a way of saving myself from feeling completely and utterly sour about Azerbaijan.

There is a lot of oil-money in Azerbaijan, alongside income from huge natural gas reserves. So, like some Arabic cities, you can see this oil-money manifest in the form of golden BMW's, Gucci handbags on many arms, and gigantic modern skyscrapers - all shouting the same message of wealth. This feels morally curious, considering that the rural regions see very little benefit from the economic surplus provided by their native land's natural resources. Actual poverty, rubbing shoulders with supreme wealth is something that has always made me feel uneasy, even in my own land, but isn't this the natural outcome of the game that we call "capitalism"? But, is the Soviet model of State communism, of which they had enforced on their soil for many years, any better? Because, as Animal Farm rightly portrays in its allegory of Soviet-style communism - we are all equal, but some of us are always more equal than the rest.

Excuse me for the slight philosophical detour, but overall, Baku left me with a positive feeling. I stayed with an English friend, Lucy, who I met in Fabrika hostel in Tbilisi. She was finishing her masters in Azerbaijan as an urban planner and lived with her

Azeri boyfriend in Baku. We had some stimulating discussions about the intrinsic insanity of capitalism's model of infinite growth, about the ridiculousness of still using fossil fuels, and the relationship between feminism and veganism. The substance of great chats! And she showed me an interesting, underground cafe with loads of trendy young people in. I found this to be an interesting similarity between Baku and Tbilisi. Both cities of post-Soviet countries where they have only relatively recently gained national independence. This leaves room for the youth to construct new identities in a country that hasn't been "a country" for all too long. And this cultural exploration could also be seen in this cafe in Baku, on a much smaller scale than in Georgia, where you can see these young people flirting with different fashions and cultures, as we all do, to find a sense of self. It left me with an impression that these youths were finding their individuality and creating a new sense of being after the conservative days of the Soviet Union.

I had a good rest, enjoyed the city, and got the info from the port that the boat was arriving later in the day, about 9pm. Off I went, ready to move on, rested. I arrived back at the port and reconnected with some of the people I had previously met there when I first arrived- the Italian girls doing the Mongol Raleigh (where multiple teams drive from Europe to Mongolia for charity), and the Canadian boy with his Indian dad who had hitchhiked from Portugal, to name but a few. It turned out the boat in fact hadn't arrived, but they said it would probably be there by the morning. Okay, so I had to unexpectedly camp in the car park, but no biggie. A few people had to do this for a couple nights prior as well. Oh well, we will all jump on the boat in the morning, and if it arrives early, they will wake us up. That's fine, or so I thought. Neither happened.

The next day it still wasn't there. We asked at the cashier desk and he said maybe it will come later that evening, but probably not because of strong wind. Okay, wow, things were really starting to feel ambiguous now. And when it still wasn't there that evening, I started sincerely doubting if the boat would ever come at all. But luckily that day I met so many amazing people who were also waiting, and it was nice to know that we were all in the same boat (or trying to be, at least, over the Caspian Sea). I had made friends with an Englishman Sam, travelling by motorcycle, and a lovely Israeli guy hitchhiking around the world. Even two other cyclists on very long trips also! One American, and one Swiss. There must have been about 20 of us in total, all different nationalities and traversing kilometres in numerous different ways. The diversity was apparent, and it made for a relatively buzzing atmosphere in an otherwise incredibly boring port. Spirits in camp were high. But that was after having only spent one night in a car park, however after three nights, the group morale was slightly different.

Everyone went a little bit mad. We were told every few hours that the boat would arrive, to only be faced with the reality of no boat. Bad wind still, apparently. Those of us with indefinite travel plans and infinite freedom, were more relaxed on average, compared to those with strict deadlines and limited travel time - where one week in a port really was a big chunk of their holiday. The Italian girls for example, still had to drive thousands of kilometres to Mongolia, and had a strict deadline with flights already booked home for work reasons. They were going crazy, and were oh so angry at the cashier dude, even though he had nothing to do with the decision making of boat safety - he just took the ticket money. They even called the Italian embassy, because, to be fair, the toilets did explode and there was shit everywhere. A couple others who had been living in Portistan for over a week (which is now a self-declared autonomous region of Azerbaijan, which we decided to turn into a nation because we had all been living there for so long), were also losing their marbles a bit. After a lot of democracy, and bureaucracy - we decided to make "Boom, Boom, Boom" by The Vengaboys our national anthem, and we started planning the blueprints of our national flag (but didn't quite get around to finishing it).

In general, most of us had such long travel plans that a week of rest in the port wasn't all too miserable of a prospect. Some of us even enjoyed it, quite a lot in fact. We played a bit of cricket with a rounders bat, which was quite funny, having three English guys trying to explain the rules of cricket to loads of Europeans. We sang songs about spending the rest of our lives in Portistan, with one lyric stating "the Caspian sea is a sea that we're never ever going to see" and we even created an entire song called "The Caspian Blues" where we vented our frustrations with our new stationary port existence, in a soulful and heartfelt manner. As a last resort, we came up with numerous different alternative plans to get to Kazakhstan (in fact plan B, C, D and E) because plan A was seeming less and less probable by the minute. Some of the plans were to pirate a Turkmenistan boat, and even one plan went as far as to suggest that we drain the water of the Caspian Sea and simply cycle across instead.

One highlight of our time at Portistan was our little excursion to the nearby mud volcanoes. We all took a therapeutic natural mud bath which was quite hilarious, because the mud was so thick that when we came out our whole bodies were covered. Sam literally looked like Shrek when he pulled his head out of the mud volcano. We then decided to slide down one side of the hill by creating a little mud slide which was good fun but actually hurt quite a bit with all the stones scraping our backs on the way down. But it was definitely worth it. After our mud frolicking, we camped all together. Some people slept out in the open underneath the stars, but just before going to sleep we saw a pair of luminous yellow scorpions, which was my cue to put up my tent.

Overall, it was a nice sense of community and even at times felt a bit like a festival when we were playing music and playing games. I was simply so happy to have company after a lonely and sickening time since leaving my prior company in Tbilisi. After a week of patiently waiting, the boat finally arrived. Although it didn't appease the anger of the Italian girls, I think that it was genuinely for the best that it took so long to arrive. We found out in the end that it was a very poorly designed Russian boat which was designed too top-heavy, and previously these exact boats had capsized in bad weather and people had died.

When the prospect of boarding the vessel became a reality and not just a fantasy, it felt strange to get on the boat and to split the Portistan populace. What made it harder was that we had to get on two separate boats, and it was kind of sad after having bonded over such a rubbish scenario. Yet, for sure, we were all over the moon that we could finally go through with what we were all there for - crossing the water. Until you spend numerous days in a port, you can't realise how amazing it is to leave. And this is the hidden blessing of these experiences, because it makes you grateful for the outcome. If I just turned up and within ten minutes got on a boat, yes, I would have executed my original intentions, but I would have had merely a fraction of the experience I gained from my time in Portistan.

PART THREE - A TWO-WHEELED ODYSSEY THROUGH CENTRAL ASIA

The Full Power Bike Ride

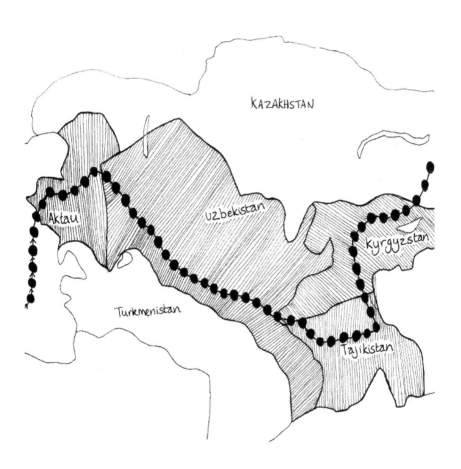

Chapter Ten

Samsung Eagle

It took 24 hours to travel over the largest lake in the world by boat, and when we woke up in our cabins we had arrived in Kazakhstan. We docked in the Kazakh port city of Aktau. "We" rather than just "I", because I certainly was not alone in this stretch of my voyage, I was part of an international community of Portistani travellers, all longing for the allure of Central Asia, the Silk Road and the Pamir Highway. All the Portistani cyclists had made a pact before we got onto the boats that we would link up on the other side and cycle the Kazakh desert all together, in a Full Power peloton. This was essentially the birth of the famous Camel Crew.

The Camel Crew was made up of an international gang of Full Power cyclists. We had: Gunnar, a wrestler from the USA, Fred, (Frederic) a techno lover from Switzerland, Fredward (which wasn't his real name but we couldn't have two Freds now, could we), an engineer from England, with last but not least - Zach and Alize a skater couple, also from The States. We were subjected to an incredibly thorough customs check whilst we were still on the boat, where everyone's luggage was checked extremely scrutinously - to the point where they even flicked through every page of our books to see if anything was hidden in them. They were all very tall men, wearing the Russian style fur hats that curl upwards at the ears, probably made from genuine bear fur or suchlike. This was the most lengthy border control that

I'd been through during my entire trip and it was quite tiresome, bringing through every bicycle pannier through the X-rays about two times each back and forth, with glaring eyes watching your every move. It seemed that they didn't trust us fishy Europeans at all, and maybe rightly so, because we did look like a bunch of bedraggled homeless youths after living in a car park of a port for ten days.

Aktau itself was a captivating city, as it was essentially the major beach town of the entirety of Kazakhstan - of which is a humongous country (the ninth largest in the world by landmass). It's a strange phenomenon, because although they have a beach, they don't quite have a sea and in fact it is a landlocked country, meaning that it borders other nations at every point - the literal opposite of an island. Yet, as I've mentioned before, they do have a large lake (the largest) and hence they have made a beach to imitate a seaside. Thereby, our first images of Kazakhstan were of local youngsters bathing in their seaside town, in bikinis and swim shorts, playing volleyball - living a rather western lifestyle in many ways. This was shockingly contrasted to the scenes of Borat, the film which put Kazakhstan on the map - making out that it was a degenerate Third World country. Another key aspect that differed dramatically from Borat's portrayal of Kazakh people, was that they looked nothing like the Eurasian depictions from the film. Instead they looked somewhat East Asian, almost Chinese in some ways - which is largely due to Genghis Khan and his sons having invaded all the way through this region during the "golden age" of the Mongol Empire, where they even got as far as today's Eastern Europe. As you can imagine, they spread their seed, so to speak, everywhere they went. So, our first glimpse of Kazakhstan was of Asian-looking locals on the beach living a very modern life not too different from our own - smashing our previous misconceptions into smithereens. The concept of Central Asian ethnicity was beyond what we could previously fathom, and considering that these lands are placed geographically slap-bang in the middle of the most important trade route in history - it is easy to see how it is an ethnically diverse part of the world. It was now our opportunity and responsibility to learn about the real cultures of Central Asia and not just fictional ones.

Although the Camel Crew arrived separately to Aktau on two different boats, we reunited the next day and started cycling all together as one entity. It was exciting in every way, to be cycling in a big group of international cyclists, heading towards the utterly unknown - sharing both the wonder and hardship all together. Once we had left Aktau, the landscape barely changed in any way until we were thousands of kilometres further east. Honestly, for a ridiculously large distance, we were surrounded only by incredibly vast plains of nothingness. Of course, there were the odd group of camels here and there, which inspired our group name. We called ourselves the Camel Crew due to the inspiring camels on the other side of the Caspian Sea. We loved them so very much, and we wanted to be camels ourselves, so hence our group name came about. We had never seen camels in the wild before, and they are certainly wacky animals with their huge long necks and their peculiar bumpy humps. They were especially curious when we saw gangs of them in the distance, galloping across the road like a group of long-necked-bumpy-backed horses. Wildlife is a wonderful thing, to say the least - and camels are a great example of this. But unlike the bumpy backs of camels, the actual landscape was plain and dead flat for as far as the eye could see, in every direction, 360 degrees. It is what they used to call the "Russian Steppe" back when it was swallowed up by the USSR.

For the keen geographers amongst you, a steppe is slightly different to a desert, but they share many commonalities. The steppe that we were cycling through was essentially expansive brownish plains of grassland without any trees for as far as one could see. It didn't match the typical image of endless sand dunes by any means, but it was still technically a desert according to the dictionary definition: "any large, extremely dry area of land with sparse vegetation", which is word for word, exactly what we were cycling through for an extremely long period of time.

One of the many issues with this type of landscape is the wind. Ultimately there is nothing at all to prevent the accumulative momentum of wind gales, so it just constantly builds force and power. We learnt this the hard way when we were perpetually pummelled in the face by painstakingly challenging headwinds. We tried to bundle up into a little tight peloton, as if we were in the Tour de France, but unfortunately it didn't really help very much, and we still plodded along at an extremely slow pace. Over the first couple of days cycling from Aktau, we basically got nowhere, and although that's a slight exaggeration - we certainly didn't get very far. This was mostly due to the wind, but also due to there now being six of us, rather than cycling alone. This meant that there were now six people to eat, stretch, rest, go to the toilet, have mechanical issues or injuries - meaning that we were inevitably slower than when we had only ourselves to worry about. But ultimately, it was quite a nice pace and we were all enjoying the benefits of group cycle touring. It reminded me that I was still a tourist after all, just on a bike - and it was nice to stop to take pictures and to take it easy, rather than just smashing out long distances every day to get to an arbitrary distant goal.

We all started our individual cycling adventures solo, and we all finished them solo too. But in the steppe, we were a team; a cyclist family, tackling and traversing this difficult part of our trips. Stronger we were together, for sure, for we made each other laugh, kept each other hydrated and generally just kept each other company in what would otherwise have been an incredibly lonely part of the world to cycle through. Plus, we learned a lot about each other and therefore in turn also about our home nations. It turns out that unexpected "delays" in a trip can create the opportunity to meet others, in ways that may influence a trip significantly for the better.

After a couple days of windy cycling from Aktau, the road took a slight turn and that was the first bend in the road for at least one week straight. In fact, "one week straight" is a particularly apt phrase, to describe that painfully unswerving line. We had no choice but to surrender to this very fact, so we simply cycled in a straight line for the entire day, flat as could be, and camped just off the main road and then did the same the next day and repeated the process. Luckily, we all had company, otherwise it would have been extremely mind numbing to the point of insanity. Some of the Camel Crew were previously considering skipping this part of the route by taking the train, because they had heard about how hard and horrible it was - but all together as a team, it was much, much better. Finally, we reached a small town after which the road took a sharp 90 degree turn towards the Uzbek border. It was such a thrilling experience to see the road change direction, but it then once again became dead-straight, as if it was drawn with an enormous ruler, by a gargantuan giant road builder from days of old. But this time the straight road stretched for double the distance − direct and undeviating for a total of 1,000 kilometres. We had become *really* good at cycling in a straight line by this point. It was vital for our morale, to take regular breaks in the day and even entire rest days to rejuvenate and recuperate.

During one of our breaks in the day, we stopped off at some shops to restock our food and water. Unfortunately for ecology, we couldn't drink any tap water (due to toxicity) so we had to drink only bottled water, all day every day. It was cheap, but we had to carry so much water to get us through until the next shop - which was sometimes a massive distance. I had two CamelBaks which are big water bladders that you can wear as a backpack. I had two because I knew we needed to carry a crazy amount of water, not just for drinking but also for cooking while we camped. This was imperative, for at one point there was only one place to buy more bottled water in a 200-kilometre stretch - which is a rather long time to make your water last...on a bike. I really can't stress this enough − the sheer importance of water. Obviously you all know it theoretically, that humans can't live without it, but it's only in situations like these where you run out of all your water − where you really get to see its true vital importance for living. The entire biological system of the body relies on being properly hydrated, let alone whilst in plus 30-degree heat and cycling for the entire day. In our situation, the body needed water more than ever, and when it was scarce like it was − it became somewhat worrying at times.

Luckily, another way for us to keep hydrated was via watermelon. It is such a useful fruit for the desert because it is so yummy but also so very hydrating, and the locals knew this because they would frequently stop to gift us a fresh watermelon. This was always gratefully received, but you can imagine it was quite hard to carry on a bike, because they can be bloody heavy when they're big. Thank goodness for people's kindness though, especially in 35-degree heat.

One morning we restocked our supplies at a small roadside shop, and we got talking to some locals outside. They asked us where we were going and where we were from, which was the usual conversation starter. They were lovely people and they were trying to give us some cute puppies for free but we kindly rejected their offer, since we couldn't possibly cycle with puppies even if we had wanted to. One of the men had pretty good English so we spoke for some time, and eventually we got onto the topic of his eagle. He whipped out his high-end Samsung smartphone and showed us a picture of him in traditional Kazakh-ethnic dress, with his huge eagle on his arm, both man and bird looking out into the vast open distance. It was as if this image already existed in my imagination before crossing the Caspian Sea, and now here it was, proudly presented to me on a Kazakh's smartphone screen. It struck me how depressingly inauthentic this experience felt, and I pondered how globalization seems to have gobbled up the world's culture and exchanged it for homogenous smartphones. The true Kazakh culture I was anticipating still exists of course, but in this case beneath the veil of a screen, despite being in what seemed like one of the most remote places on earth.

Even right in the middle of the desert in a vast land of nothing, there are still Samsungs and Coca-Colas. The sight of him zooming off on his motorbike instead of a stallion, really reaffirmed the notion of an insatiably hungry capitalist economy gobbling up all cultures in its sight. I had a similar experience to this in Lapland, Sweden when I lived in Stockholm - where I learnt that the Arctic Sami tribes herded their reindeer using helicopters, which is so different from their ancient traditions. But hey ho, this is the reality of the modern world and it is ultimately just a naive preconception to believe that there are still indigenous cultures living in some form of pristine isolation, living true to their roots. The web of capitalism has spread across the entire globe and stuck to everybody it possibly could. But this isn't necessarily a bad thing, because everybody should have the choice to engage in modernity or not. It is definitely not the Western World's place to dictate who should be able to "progress" or who shouldn't, just because we've already had our glory days. In fact, it is countries like Kazakhstan, with their huge oil and gas reserves, that will be the next emerging economies gliding alongside China in their pursuit of wealth and fortune. This naive image of nomadic warriors will only become more and more a distant memory of the past.

Chapter Eleven

Ancient Silk Road Cities

Still on the dead-straight road, we continued towards the Uzbek border, where we would face more desert but also some incredible cultural gems - the ancient Silk Road cities. This part of the "road" was the bumpiest ride imaginable, utterly uncomfortable for one's backside and crotch, constantly getting battered by the bumps from below. It was a bloody long ride, but after an entire day of getting knocked around from underneath and struggling not to fall over, we eventually reached the border.

We converted our Kazakh money into Uzbek Som, and we became millionaires in the local currency. Every pound was worth about 12,000 Som, so we had a huge wad of cash that made us feel rich, but in reality we were still poor, homeless cyclists. Not much had really changed since crossing the border, because it was a very similar steppe landscape and the exact same straight road for many more kilometres. The Camel Crew was still tightly knitted together as one group, albeit some people slightly went ahead by a day or so, and some slightly dropped back here and there, but overall we would all reunite and continue as one entity (or "caravan" may be a more apt term for the Silk Road, considering that was the name for groups of traders or pilgrims journeying in groups through this land). We had somewhat naturally divided off into small groups of two: Zach and Alize, already being a couple became a firm cycling pair, Frederic and Gunnar glued together being the strongest cyclists out of us all, and Fredward and I formed a pair too -

bonding over our mutual Englishness. We named ourselves Team Sky after the British cycling team and would sometimes seriously pretend that we were in the Tour de France (desert version), just to make ourselves go a bit faster.

In fact, I say that Fredward and I were alone, but that's not strictly true – because we were frequently in company with the most annoying little things to have ever set foot in the steppe – hitchhiking desert flies. I know you must be thinking "What? How can a fly hitchhike when they don't even have thumbs?" Valid question, please do allow me to elaborate. Well, for starters they didn't even need thumbs because they didn't wait for our consent to start hitching a ride. They simply jumped on our helmets from out of nowhere and then proceeded to do their utmost to annoy us until boiling point. I think we named one of them Eric, because I swear it was the same bloody fly the entire way for a good few hundred kilometres, and even after an entire night of camping he would still pop up the next day and annoy me some more. I know that flies in general are inherently annoying, and it is why God put them on the earth in the first place, but there was something different about Eric the Uzbek fly and his fellow steppe companions that was just so fricking infuriating. They had an obsession with our faces. They just loved to get as close to our face as physically possible, and even sometimes would try to get up our nostrils or into our eardrums. This would have been better if we were stationary, and then our attempts to kill Eric and his friends (sorry, my animal ethics only stretches so far) would have been far easier. However, when you're on a bike, avoiding potholes, and also trying to kill these blood-boiling creatures, it's a recipe for disaster – so we had to focus on the road and simply allow Eric and his mates to continue hitching on our helmets. The most annoying thing was the incessant buzz that they emitted, just constantly buzzing and buzzing around the face and then back around the other way. I'm sure that the flies were having a great laugh, but Fredward and I certainly didn't appreciate their company. But we were glad to have one another. Team Sky were still going strong, despite the flies.

Overall, it's pretty impressive that we stuck solidly together so well and had no big disputes or issues, despite being six tired and smelly people in the unforgiving desert. We essentially did everything together, not just cycling, but also sleeping and eating and everything in between. We camped mostly, because there was always an abundance of camping spots just off the main road either left or right, and a lack of anyone saying we couldn't camp there. We would commonly cook in our pairs, helping to share the ingredients and the cooking, would make a little fire in the middle and after staring at the infinite stars above we would eventually go off to sleep (in our case, not in a pair) and prepare for the next day of cycling. It made us extremely close, when you consider that we shared every single moment together when there is absolutely nowhere to hide in the steppe. Even when it's that time of morning where you must do your toilet business, regardless of how far you walk into the distance to do your poo, the Camel Crew was still able to see. Not that anybody looked, no way, but just the fact that they could, was enough. So, this forced us to become very comfortable with everyone very quickly - and that was nice, to have the social norms between us melted away naturally by the heat and the environment we were in.

One morning waking up from camp, we were greeted by two lovely big camels, and Zach and Alize went to share their breakfast with the big mammals they'd just made friends with. However, there was another interaction that Alize had with a camel which wasn't as kind. It was a sort of teenager camel and must have had some disabilities because it was smaller than the rest and the odd one out. It was behind the shop, and she went over to stroke it, but obviously it didn't want to be stroked because it sharply thrust its leg to the side and kicked her in the shin. She screamed and it was all rather hilarious, bless the poor little camel. Alize was fine and giggled it off.

We didn't camp out in the desert every single night because sometimes we could stay in a hostel, and other times we were even hosted by a family. Previously with all six of us, it must have been quite off putting to Kazakh locals to host us in their homes, and rightly so. But once we'd split off into our pairs, it was a much more manageable affair for someone to put us up for the night. I had missed having that experience, where you have an opportunity to truly get to know the local people and share cultural differences and idiosyncrasies over food and tea. The people of Uzbekistan were incredibly friendly people, always waving at us from their doorways with a huge smile, constantly welcoming us into their country. They reminded me a lot of the lovely village people of Turkey, and it's not surprising seeing as they are of Turkic origin also. One evening, Fredward and I were hosted by a lovely Uzbek family who preferred Fredward over me because his uncle is a butcher and I'm a vegetarian. It seemed they weren't too keen on vegetarians, but I think they respected my choices too. Another time we weren't only welcomed into somebody's home, but we were also welcomed into their wedding.

We stopped for a break from cycling, to check out what type of cultural celebration was occurring in the village hall, because everyone was dressed up particularly smart and we'd not seen this type of gathering before. We started chatting to some of the lads in their suits and not long after they told us it was a wedding in the village, and then they started to sincerely invite us to attend the event. I can only assume that the actual wedding ceremony had happened earlier on, and this was the after party, because it certainly seemed that way. We kindly denied the offer out of respect, but they insisted, finding it quite an entertaining prospect having us there. We were told to wear smarter clothes so we quickly got changed into what we considered our smartest possible attire, but considering we hadn't packed with weddings in mind, we weren't looking our smartest.

We were ushered into the hall where most of the family and friends were already seated, and I'm not joking when I say that every single person present turned around to stare at us enter. Most people were genuinely quite happy to see our random western faces, but some attendees looked rather confused, but they couldn't have been any more confused than we were. We got placed on a large round table with other men (men and women were sat separately on either side of the hall) and the ceremony began. There were speeches, songs, dancing and of course, plenty of vodka. Luckily, I haven't drank alcohol for the last six years of my life, so I politely turned down people's offers of perpetual vodka shots, but Fredward on the other hand wasn't as saintly as I, and was welcomed onto the naughty table. These guys were clearly the troublemakers of the extended family and they had brought Fredward under their wing. After quite a few vodka shots later, they were all piddled and more dancing commenced. Many people found it very amusing how we were dancing and just generally having these two random Brits at their village wedding, and they were all videoing us on their smartphones. It must have gotten to the point where the hosts had enough entertainment from us because they kindly asked us to leave from out of the blue. I think they just wanted a more private affair by this point, but I told Fredward that they kicked us out because he was too pissed (which I knew wasn't the case, but it was good fun pulling his leg). They had an outside sleeping area prepared for us a couple doors down, and we really appreciated in every way the relentless kindness from these wonderful strangers.

The absolute highlight of Uzbekistan was the beautiful Silk Road cities that were utterly remarkable! The Silk Road was such an important trade route for a large number of cultures, but namely for China and Europe as it was the path which carried all the silk and spices to the Roman Empire. It is a big reminder for why Central Asia has such a romantic aspect in the imaginations of many. The attention to detail in the blue and cream tile mosaics of the grand mosques are mind blowing, and the perfectly carved wooden pillars are a true example of what the human hand is capable of - creating wonder. We first went to Khiva, which was a beautiful place, albeit slightly Disney-esque in its layout and touristic appeal. It clearly had lots of renovation work done recently to bring it up to scratch, but even then, it was a tremendous sight to see it how it used to be. One can imagine the area in its historical setting, with myriad merchants selling their exotic spices and garments, received from distant lands in the East, and being sold to traders of the Roman world. It would have been a bustling place to say the least, a definite meeting point of East and West, transferring objects and ideas from both extremes of the Old World.

The Silk Road wasn't necessarily one road, as such, but multiple roads linking China with Europe, but undoubtedly the roads that we were cycling on had been traversed for at least two thousand years. This was a strange feeling. One could feel the history oozing from under our feet, and it was amazing to feel a part of it. We also went to Bukhara which felt more authentic than Khiva and was just as aesthetically stunning. Even though none of us identified as religious people, you could sense the religious piety and faith permeating the entirety of the ancient city. Bukhara was a hub for Islamic academia and today is still home to an important religious university. The countless minarets reach high to the sky, and the facades of the mosques were something to certainly marvel at, for hours on end if one so wishes to do so. I am grateful to have witnessed such wonders, before they become too well known and tourists smother the streets, turning them into Central Asian equivalents of Venice or Florence - where you can barely move without getting slapped in the face by a selfie-stick.

Our final Silk Road city was Samarqand which was much more like an actual city than the other two – a lot larger in scale and size. Sources state that this is one of the oldest inhabited cities in the entirety of Central Asia, all the way back to the 7th century BC. There is history literally exuding from its veins, everywhere you look there is a quality of historical richness. It was a city conquered by the famous Macedonian Alexander the Great, later occupied by Genghis Khan, and even later became the capital city of Timur's famous empire. So yeah, it's a city that's been through a lot and has changed hands innumerable times. Rather fascinating if I do say so myself.

But in terms of the actual cycling, I was still on my route to New Zealand and we were now getting ever closer to the mountains. The Camel Crew were still strongly united, however Gunnar had run out of time on his Uzbek visa (due to being a numpty during his application process) and he had to run off to get out of the country before his visa ran out, and before they fined him an obscene amount. By this point we were rather fed up with the desert and having to see the same thing every day without the slightest bit of change, ultimately the exact same landscape for one whole month. We were ready for some altitude and some climbing, just to switch it up. The flatness was fine, but we wanted some challenges. We were about to leave the flat desert of the Silk Road to slowly ascend exponentially upwards into the mountainous desert of the Pamir Highway.

Chapter Twelve

Nomansstan and The Tunnel of Death

Gunnar, our noble wrestler, had rushed to the border to avoid said fine, and Frederic had also shot off ahead. With Zach and Alize slightly behind, Fredward and I kept our momentum, and cycled from Samarqand to the Tajiki border. It felt like we were crossing borders very frequently as of late, and the amount of new cultures and countries coming our way was somewhat overwhelming. I think that Fredward may have felt this way too, because we had a minor squabble that evening as to whether we should cross the border that night or wait till the next morning. I'm not sure why, but I was quite anxious to just get the border crossing over and done with that evening. On the final stretch, we were waved at with so much compassion by the Uzbek locals, essentially wishing us well on the road ahead. This was used as an argument from Fredward as to why we should stay and camp one more night that side of the border, because the people were just so lovely here. I agreed, but still wanted to push on.

Fredward eventually gave in, and we aimed for the border. It was getting late, and it was dark for quite a while by this point, but we kept going regardless. Eventually when we made it to the border crossing - it was the easiest border control we had ever had. It turned out that the man behind the desk didn't even look at our passports and just simply stamped a piece of paper and let us through. It seemed too good to be true, but they were just super relaxed. Fair enough! We asked if there was anywhere for us to camp on the Tajiki side of the border, and they said: "not for quite a while because it is all military land". To get to the next village that night would have been a rather unkind mission, so the border guards suggested that we just set up camp within the border. We found this to be an absurd suggestion, but we accepted the offer firmly. We were essentially in Nomansstan (another new country we made up). It did not belong to Uzbekistan nor Tajikistan, so we were residing in the middle between the two - and thus "Nomansstan" was born. We set up our tents and they even brought us out a huge watermelon which was very warmly received by our parched and exhausted selves.

We slept incredibly well in our new nation, and in the morning crossed the other side into a real country - Tajikistan. Although it was still rather flat at this point, we could see in the misty distance the sight of huge mountain peaks and we knew what was coming. We were both excited and nervous, because we knew it would be hard work to say the least, but beautiful nonetheless. Off we pedalled!

Something that certainly stood out instantly was the sheer amount of interest that we received from the local children. We could literally hear them from a mile away, a chorus of cries from the village children shouting "helloooo". It was a really strange experience, being bombarded with such an epic multitude of hellos coming from all directions. Sometimes the hellos were literally coming from the centre of the road, as the kids sprinted into the middle of the two lanes in order to get an all-important high-five.

For sure, we had lots of beeps and waves in Uzbekistan throughout the country, but our first two days in Tajikistan were rather crazy with how excited these kids were to see us cycle past. Some shouted "tourizt, tourizt!" as if to alert their fellow youths, prior to the subsequent machine-gunning of hellos. It was hard to explain to them that we were in fact intrepid "travellers", not tourists - so I didn't bother trying. As well as this, some groups of Tajiki village kids asked for a moving high-five, of which we happily adhered to. But, unfortunately some school boys found it funny to slap our hands as hard as humanly possible in order to inflict pain, so we banned high fives for groups of school boys and chose to "sike" them all instead, by lifting our hands up at the last moment. The schoolgirls were generally more respectful, so we still allowed them a high five here and there.

On one particular descent where I had to dodge lots of kids, one of them proceeded to throw a large stone in my direction, which only narrowly missed. I was not happy about this at all but there wasn't much that I could do, considering that I was going so uncontrollably fast down the steepest of hills. And even if I did confront them about it, what could I say or do? They are only kids after all, so is it just kids being kids, or are there potential reasons for a distaste for Westerners? It brought suspicion within me, because already twice before this incident, one kid had kicked my back pannier, and another tried to grab hold of one and pull it off whilst running next to us. I didn't take this as malicious, but these certainly weren't friendly gestures. I mean, when I was a small boy running around Aldershot, if I saw a Tajiki man cycling through my town, I wouldn't even think about throwing a stone at him. I suppose I'd got so used to friendly encounters that this greeting struck me as concerningly curious.

This hostility felt all the more striking considering the recent event with cyclists in Tajikistan, where four cycle-tourists got killed by five radical terrorists. They ran them over with their car whilst going forwards, then reversed back over their bodies and proceeded to finish them off with knives and an axe. Despite warnings not to come through this country by worried peers, we decided that it would still be safe because it was merely a one-off attack. And due to the attacks having been so recent, the police and military presence in the area was higher than ever which arguably made this route safer than ever. And it really was a one-off, when hundreds of cyclists have taken this route before over the course of many years and only had pleasant experiences. Considering how staggeringly beautiful the mountains were, it would have been a shame to skip the Pamirs entirely because of only one event. After the monotony of the steppe, these stark, scraggy mountains towered over us with promise.

As we imagined, even within the first few days of being in Tajikistan the mountains were proving difficult. Regardless of how much you prepare psychologically, there is always a part of you that thinks "ah, I'm sure it won't be that hard". But it was, and I'm pretty sure they will always be that hard to cycle up forevermore into eternity. By car or motorbike, then for sure, what is all the moaning about? But by bicycle, climbing to monstrous heights, on bloody awful stony sandy roads, will forever be a mean feat.

The biggest imminent challenge was the climb to 2700m high, which we were slightly worried about, for Fredward had heard rumours of the so-called "Tunnel of Death" at the top. He said he wanted to hitchhike through the tunnel because he'd heard such awful things about it, but I brushed off such rumours because I'm the biggest manly man to have ever walked this planet. Just kidding, I may not be Hercules, but I was adamant that I was not going to hitch a single inch towards New Zealand (unless I was forced against my will by Police) because my challenge was to cycle the entire way with no assistance on land. It was a big part of my trip. If I say I'm going to cycle the length of the world, then I bloody well will cycle the whole way. A lot of other cycle tourists aren't as strict with their trips and will take a train here and there when things get tough, or hitchhike. But for me, it felt like cheating myself, for it's these difficult stretches and challenging moments which make the bicycle such a great tool for learning and growing. Of course, I could understand Fredward for placing the safety of his life over that of an arbitrary cycling goal which ultimately means nothing. So yeah, he had the upper hand in logic and sensible reductionism, and I had the upper hand in illogical stubbornness.

The high altitude started to mess with my resolutely stoic attitude, and I started to wonder if this tunnel really was as awful as the rumours made out. The highest I'd ever been before in my life was 2000m in Turkey, so at 2500m I was really struggling. I had a headache, probably due to both heat and height and simply had to take refuge in the shade of some trucks. One by one, a truck would leave, and I would have to painstakingly force myself to move into the shade of the next one, before that one would bloody move too. I was even shaking a bit, but the honey and dried chickpea combo saved the day. Who would've thought it? The power of sugar, eh? With the pace of a sedated snail, I painfully inched further up the mountain road, bit by tormenting bit. Finally, we were at the summit, and the infamous tunnel revealed itself. It looked like a normal tunnel...but the dark void inside didn't supply us with much confidence.

It was power-nap time for me, before I tackled this ominous beast. Meanwhile, Fredward stuck his thumb out and waited for a lift. To no fruition initially, but almost simultaneously with the ringing of my nap alarm came his white van lift. Off he went, safely, but slightly cheating (I'm only joking). He left me his high-visibility vest and I prepared myself for what really did look quite unforgiving. In preparation for the chilly downhill after the tunnel, I put on my mid-fleece and in the glimmer of the burning sun, I saw a pendant. It was the St. Christopher from my French auntie. He is the patron saint of travel, and this was her way to keep me safe on my trip. It might sound somewhat airy fairy, or just downright dumb, but I really do think that this pendant is what protected me even more than the high-vis vest through the tunnel.

Without further thought, I leaped gallantly upon the back of Rasta Bike and started through the Tunnel of Death. It all became instantly evident as to why it had been given such a nickname. It was breathtakingly dark, void of all natural light, and had the stinkiest stink that you ever did stank. With so many trucks passing through every minute of the day, a permanent black smog lingered menacingly in the enclosed air. I simply cycled as fast as I possibly could - which is difficult when it's 5km long. And if you've never cycled through a tunnel, it's impossible to understand how awfully long this really is. At points I had to seek refuge in the little galleries in the side of the tunnel, for the tunnel only had two lanes, and at times there would not only be one truck-dragon raging towards you, but also one surging towards you from behind. Maybe it would see my flashing lights, but with such a tight gap it's not worth the risk of being squished like a ripe berry. Thank goodness for these spaces on the side to hide from the fire-breathing machines. The experience was slow and almost felt like a never-ending journey, with my head almost bubbling over with adrenaline and survival hormones, bursting at the seams.

But, oh my, the sight of the light at the end was overwhelmingly sublime, and the feeling of elation when exiting this doom ridden space was unmatched in magnitude. Utmost joy. Wow, I was still alive, and so much more of a man having lived through this sub-journey of my big one. The endless mountain-scape view was glorious. My body was rushing, as if I was at a rave. And now the prospect of a 70km downhill to Dushanbe, the capital, felt like an endless breeze, and so it was. With the prospect of a shower and a bed at the bottom, I glided down the opposite side of the mountain I had just laboured up without a care in the world.

When I finally arrived at the hostel and saw my face in the mirror it was black like a chimney sweep's, but looked more learned and wise. The shower resembled how showers in paradise must feel like. I was alive, healthy, washed and now had a bed to curl up in. And even better, I had beaten Fredward to the Greenhouse - the hostel where we rested for the next few days. We washed clothes, maintained our bikes and prepared ourselves for what was now officially the start of the Pamir Highway, starting in Dushanbe and finishing in Osh.

Chapter Thirteen

The Pamir Highway

T he Pamir Highway ("Pamirsky Trakt" in Russian) is a main road that spans four different countries: Afghanistan, Uzbekistan, Tajikistan and Kyrgyzstan. It snakes up and down through the Pamir Mountains, and at its highest summit - it is the second highest road in the world outside of the Himalayas. Although the specific M41 route is only 100 years old, roads taking a similar route have been used for millennia, as it's the only main option to get through these epic mountains, and it would have been one of the major trading routes of the Silk Road also. People can't agree as to where it officially starts, but many people state that the cycling route begins in Dushanbe, the capital of Tajikistan.

Upon leaving the capital, we gradually went up, up, and believe it or not - up some more. The urban residential buildings slipped into a part of our past, and the road winded this way and that way, sometimes turning into tight hairpin bends. We essentially followed the main river the entire way up, with it mostly on our right. It was usually flowing against us, which meant that we were ascending, perpetually. The deep valley was constantly being cut by such an unforgiving river, which soared rapidly at an extraordinary pace. Well, something must cut a valley, and one can see how this particular river managed that - with its tenacious velocity. It was a transient body of transparent crystal-clear flowing water, moving faster than any river I'd ever laid my eyes upon prior.

The mountains themselves really were incredible. Everywhere I looked were striking stark spikes, absolutely monumental in stature, capable of bringing even the sourest fellow to a state of awe. The mountains of the world truly are a sobering sight, especially the Pamir Mountains - for they are ever so brutish in their grey and brown colour palate, ascending tirelessly towards the heavens. It's fascinating sometimes when huge skyscrapers in the city make you feel insignificant or small, and these mountains do the exact same thing if not more - because it shows you really how powerful nature can be. As we traversed further into the range, and further from the city, the scenery gradually became less civilised and more overwhelmingly beautiful. Occasionally there would be huge herds of goats, in the hundreds passing us by on the road. We would have to wait for them to pass, because bicycles and goats don't really mix all too well on an extremely narrow road. Most evenings before sundown the Tajiki locals would be walking with their donkeys on a lead, and this would always confuse Fredward and I. Was it like a dog, in the sense that they were taking it for an evening stroll? Who knows! And although we had finally escaped the grips of a never-ending flat road, we were still technically in the desert. Other than the odd oasis of green next to the riverbanks, it was still incredibly dry and there weren't all too many trees in the slightest. As we got higher and higher in altitude, the amount of green reduced even more. Browns and greys and silvers and yellows now dominated the landscape, and multitudinous greens in all their lushness were now a mere memory of home.

It didn't take us too long to reach the part of the Pamir Highway that travels alongside the Afghan border. The ferociously fast flowing river was the only thing separating us from this mysterious country across the water. We waved at Afghan kids who seemed happy enough playing on the banks of the river on their side. We saw small settlements of simple earthen housing, and we could even see local Afghan people working the crops and seeing to their animals. It was educational and quite reassuring that the lives of these particular people looked quite peaceful and nourishing. But we were later told that beyond those mountains behind their villages, war was still tearing their country apart, as it has done on and off for centuries. And although these small settlements looked peaceful, there were still rumours of the Taliban possibly coming to the river.

In fact, it was only after this part of the trip I found out that an Australian friend of mine had been shot at across the river during this part of his trip by car, but luckily the bullet missed him. It may have only been a warning shot, but he quickly fled regardless. I'm glad I didn't know that at the time, otherwise it would have been an unwanted addition atop my other worries. We were still building our trust in the Tajiki people after the recent murders, and the road safety in and of itself was enough to worry about. It was awfully surfaced, and not sealed at all. It took utmost attentiveness and focus the entirety of the time, because with so much sand and rocks, one wrong move on the bike could lead to one falling off the edge into the ravine. Without any barriers or the like to the right, one would be inevitably tumbling to their doom, into the beautiful but violent river down below. The possibility of this was heightened by the occasional Motor Monster that would zoom past us on the left-hand side and it would be a pretty heart-quickening moment while the monster passed.

I knew it was all going to be a big challenge to say the least, but one thing that I didn't account for, was an uncontrollably sick stomach. Bloody hell, some of the days of cycling in the Pamirs were almost that itself - hell. Well, I guess it could have been much worse, say, if I was cycling with fiery burning scorpions in my lycra shorts whilst trying to cycle with newly decapitated legs or something. So not exactly hell, but it was pretty flipping bad.

With all these individual issues mixed together into a cocktail of complications, it made the Pamir Highway an ultimate test of willpower and determination, towards what was essentially a very arbitrary and odd goal - the other side of the world. Pushing yourself to your physical and mental limits, climbing up a seemingly endless protruding rock spike, is really quite the

105

peculiarity. Especially considering that there's no sensible or obvious reason at all to be doing it, other than for the completion of an utterly crazy trip, configured by an utterly crazy person - me. It's funny that when you're cycling the flat coastal roads of southern Greece, you can't help but mentally applaud yourself for designing such a wondrous idea of a trip, and for putting yourself in such a paradise, atop a liberating freedom machine. Yet, when you are unforgivingly climbing, in headwind, with a gravel road slipping beneath your tyres, you really do question everything about your sanity when you planned such a ridiculous expedition. But saying this, it doesn't mean that the challenge of the Pamirs wasn't an absolutely stunning challenge, because everywhere you looked there *were* breath-taking images. This was the reason so many cyclists still take this route despite the challenges, because it is simply so gorgeous. And the other reason ultimately, is the sense of achievement that everyone in the Camel Crew wanted - to successfully cycle up and over the highest point of the Pamir Highway.

The highest summit of the Pamir A41 was 4,655m above sea level and if that means nothing to you, well it's pretty bloody high! It's over half of the height of Mount Everest, so it's not just a wee hill that's for sure. To get a gauge for the scale, my previous maximum height before the Pamirs was 2,700m - so this was nearly that, and that again. Although the summit wasn't super close by, it was always on our mind. But we had a while to go yet until we would reach that ultimate climb. We stayed following the Afghan border for one week, cycling every day. I must say, it was a relief to eventually leave the river, because it eliminated the risk of the Taliban. Although we were never fully sure of the severity of said risk, it was one less thing to worry about nonetheless.

We eventually arrived at the sanctuary of the Pamir Lodge, which is another famous haven quite like the Greenhouse in Dushanbe. It wasn't too dissimilar to Portistan, in the sense that there were travellers from all over, all travelling in different ways. Some people we met were traversing the Pamirs by motorbike,

106

some by shared taxi and we even met a couple of other cyclists who were going the opposite way to us. It provided an undeniably well needed rest - the rejuvenation and the lack of cycling was certainly overdue, for it had been pretty full on as of late. The Pamir Lodge consisted of multiple different wooden buildings, filled up with bunk beds for weary travellers. They had a couple of ping-pong tables which was how we occupied the majority of our rest days, and they even had Wi-Fi (albeit, with a pretty terrible speed) so that we could finally message our loved ones back home and let them know that we were still alive and in one piece (albeit just about).

The main summit we were heading for was the AK-Baital pass which was going to be the highest point for all our trips. As we got closer, we spent quite a lot of time above 4000m, fluctuating up and down around that altitude. This brought its own hardships, for most people know that the higher up you go, the less oxygen there is, and we definitely experienced this scientific fact. One day in particular I was pretty bloody ill, but against my pleas for a rest day, the Camel Crew insisted that we kept moving and I blindly followed, for we were nearly at the end of our time together and I wanted us to remain as a solid unit until then. So off we went, with an ill Cody struggling at the back. The Americans surged forward, with high hopes of getting to the top of one particular pass. Fredward had an issue with his rack, and I had a relentless issue with my stupidly ill stomach, so we dropped back. Team Sky was well and truly struggling. Well, I was struggling at least, which meant that Fredward had to struggle with me because we were a team, and that's the very nature of a team. Unfortunately, at the hardest part of this climb, the road turned to sand, which meant the bike slipped every time I stood up to pedal the steepest bits. And because we were nearly at 4000m, ridiculously high up, we struggled for breath, which was troubling for an endurance sport which already makes it hard to respire even at sea level. I had to stop for a ten-minute powernap every hour, and that was the only thing that got us up that god-forsaken mountain. All in all, it was probably one of the hardest days of mine over the entire journey.

We spent quite some time above 4000m and stayed in guest houses pretty much every night at this point because it was simply bloody freezing. But, one night, the Camel Crew decided it may be a good reason to try out the tents, to really see if it was too cold to camp at such an altitude. Yes. The answer was yes. It was too fricking cold, and I could have told them all exactly that before the silly experiment, and in fact I did, to no avail. Actually, my torso was fine and warmish due to good clothing, but alas my feet were ridiculously cold - to the point of pain. Shock, I knew that would be the case. Ever since my wet shoe experience in the Alps kindly damaged the nerves in my feet, long term. Yes, the whole European winter was disastrous for my feet in my tent, and I knew deep down that the approaching winter would be equally harsh on my tootsies! Hooray!

Unfortunately, it seems like there is a lot of moaning in this chapter, but I'm wanting to be authentically expressive with this book - and I felt authentically shit at times during the Pamirs, hence the authentic moaning thereby. There's no point in painting the trip unrealistically as a glorious time, the entire time, with no hardship at all - because ultimately, life is hard...and this trip being a microcosm of life itself, was inevitably hard. We kept pushing pedals regardless and made it to our next rest stop at Murghab.

It was a curious little town, with small bungalows all painted the same homogeneous colour of white, with a small market area with shops made out of old shipping containers. It was a nice aesthetic, and the town had a good vibe to it - quite quaint. There were a few traditional yurts also scattered around the town, and all in all, it felt like a quintessential Central Asian settlement. By this point we were getting closer to the border of Kyrgyzstan, and we were told that Murghab had the highest numbers of Kygryz nationals in the entirety of Tajikistan - which we could definitely see. Some of the Kyrgyz people wore their traditional attire, and it gave us a glimpse into the country we were soon to enter. The most prominent feature that stood out was the beautiful kalpak hat. It was quite tall, coming up like a top hat, but was white and made from felt. They were usually embroidered with a swirly pattern on the side in black and were a symbol of common unity within that particular people. They were a different ethnic group to the Tajiki people, once again looking more Mongolian like the Kazakh populace that we saw directly after we crossed the Caspian Sea, whereas the Tajiki people were more Turkic in ethnic origin. Ultimately, this difference was not readily important, and the two groups mixed well in this peaceful little town. We were happy to be there, and stocked up supplies, ready for the main ultimate AK-Baital pass which was now very nearby.

We dressed in all our warmest cycling clothes and left Murghab to keep cycling upwards. It took us a couple of days to get up into that area, and before we knew it the all-important summit was in sight. For the first time since last winter - we saw snow. The tops of the neighbouring mountains were white as white could be, and it was a clear sign that we were very high. It was the same white as the houses of Murghab, and the kalpak hats alike. Possibly there was a relationship between all these things. We were merely at the end of September, which is basically the end of summer in the Northern Hemisphere, so to be seeing snow at this time of year was quite the oddity, and a sure sign of our sheer altitude. I'm not exaggerating when I say that the final few hours of climbing were utter agony. There were hairpin bends all the way up, and we kept on pushing despite the wincing of pain painted across our faces. Being so close was helpful, because we knew we couldn't give up now. With each agonising pedal stroke, we were inching closer and closer. Eventually, many pedals later, we had all gotten to the very top of the summit and were standing at the highest point we had ever stood, and probably the highest point for the rest of our lives too.

It was a monumental moment, and one that is unforgettable, for the sense of achievement was overwhelming. We had finally done it! There was also a huge feeling of relief within all of us, that we wouldn't have to go any higher than this, and that it will mostly be downhill from here onwards - meaning more oxygen, more energy and generally more fun. We didn't wait around for dark, because we would have absolutely frozen to the core. Thus, we got back on our stallions and smashed the steep downhill, being careful not to die in the process.

Chapter Fourteen

The End of the Camel Crew

It was amazing to realise that we weren't going to be in the mountains forever, luckily, and that they would eventually come to an end. What a magical moment it was, finally descending at the extent we deserved, with good roads, watching the monstrous mountains slowly diminish around us. After passing through another Nomansstan, we eventually reached our final country of the Pamirs - Kyrgyzstan. At this point, the official end of the Pamir Highway was in sight, the city of Osh. After descending for a couple days, we had to climb slightly more before we were able to descend 2000m downward in one afternoon, which was invigorating to say the least. On the way down, the landscape gradually transformed itself from stark mountains, to hills and flat meadows. The transition was slow but oh so refreshing and revitalising. You can't help but feel miniature when looked down upon by such gigantic rock spikes; when the world opens up with space, however, you feel so much more psychologically comfortable. It's like spending weeks in a very confined room, and suddenly being able to stand in a huge banquet-hall. The spatial contrast around me suddenly smashes into smithereens any previous sense of claustrophobia.

So, on the one hand, coming from the mountains into Osh was really relieving - but only to begin with. On the other hand, having spent so long away from cities - cycling into one, at night, was a nightmarish shock. It was absolute mayhem. Motor Monsters were pulling out from all angles, seemingly ready to kill their prey. After having cycled the entire length of Kyrgyzstan after Osh, it's safe to say that the Kyrgyz people were the worst drivers in the world (that I saw, at least). They don't look when pulling out. They overtake when they know it's life-threatening. They don't care. And it's strange how cities completely alter the way you think and act, at the flick of a switch. You only really notice this when you've spent so long away from them. In this case, I was turned into a savage animal in road rage. To survive, you *must* adapt, to meet them at their own level, and avoid getting squished off the road. Coming into a city on a bike always makes me both dramatically less empathetic and more selfish - this is what happens in a jungle, and these cities are certainly concrete jungles.

I first noticed my own transformation when arriving into Athens by bike towards the start of my trip. It was survival of the fittest. The natural world is far less aggressive than these sprawling metropolises, where people are crammed on top of one another. The outgrown monster of economic growth, infinitely proliferating, forever seeking "progress", yet catapulting us forwards towards its complete opposite. A strange exchange, it seems, to take economic progress for social, ecological, and ethical decline.

Yet, regardless of how much I could sit here and critique cities, one is always so encapsulated by their myriad distractions and temptations. Especially after having been in the middle of nowhere for so long. By this point we were quite fed up of Central Asian cuisine which was just sheep meat and oily rice (for me, as a vegetarian, this meant merely oily rice), so we were excited to finally be in a city where we could eat all types of international food. We ate pizza, Indian and Chinese - marvelling at the sheer choice and abundance. Osh was the official end of the Pamir Highway, which we were very pleased about. Unfortunately, however, it also meant the end of the Camel Crew.

By this point we had been as a group on and off for two whole months, giving us time to bond and solidify friendships. Imagine going on a random holiday for two months with a bunch of strangers. People simply wouldn't do it, and that's the awesome thing about cycle touring: it pushes you into strange experiences which are authentic in every way. But now, Frederic decided to stay back on his own, with Zach, Alize, and Fredward all heading straight to the Chinese border. I planned to take the northern Chinese border crossing because I heard it was a better crossing and I wanted to remain north for Korea and Japan, whereas the others were heading south straight away to reach South East Asia. We had one last party at a football stadium that had Kygryz national singers performing, and which ended with some electronic music. We had a proper boogie for the first time in a long time, and the last time for a long time too. We said our goodbyes, and off I cycled, alone once more, headed for the capital of Kyrgyzstan, Bishkek, where I would finally reconnect with a familiar face.

It was a week's worth of cycling from Osh to Bishkek, and it was strange to be cycling alone again after becoming so used to two-wheeled company. But I was soon comfortable again being very weird on my own, singing at the top of my voice (although I still did this with the Camel Crew). There weren't many noteworthy situations during this week, apart from nearly plummeting full speed into the side of a cow as I descended in the dark one day. Shit, that could have really, really hurt the both of us. Thankfully I saw him at the last minute. Silly moo should have been wearing a high-vis jacket or something.

I arrived in Bishkek and, believe it or not, I reconnected with Gunnar who had previously been part of the Camel Crew! It was amazing to see him again. He was still with two members of his "Pamir Pack" and they were lovely people down to the core. Me and Gunnar planned to cycle the majority of China together and take the northern border. I was excited for the prospect of spending more time with him. We spent a few days in Bishkek together, doing a bit of light-hearted sightseeing and relaxing.

Bishkek was an interesting city full of brutalist Soviet architecture, with domineering and intimidating flat facades.

While we were there it snowed heavily, settling on the cold pavement like a thick white blanket - winter was on the horizon. The white-laden streets matching the white soviet buildings felt visually very cold but certainly novel. Gunnar and one of his friends from the Pamir Pack (a 40-year- old Swiss doctor, and one of the nicest Swiss doctors I've ever met...and the only one) decided to take a detour around some lakes to get to the Chinese border where our Swiss friend would fly off. I wanted to take the most direct route because I didn't want to add any unnecessary distance - I was just simply so knackered still from the Pamirs. I also wanted to check out the city of Almaty, Kazakhstan, which had a reputation for being quite trendy and stylish. Either way, we had to pass through Kazakhstan once more to get to this particular Chinese border. So counterintuitively, Gunnar and I split up once more, knowing that we would see each other again in a mere ten days' time.

The cycle from Bishkek to the Chinese border was rather noteworthy for a number of reasons. Even though I'd escaped the Pamirs specifically, I hadn't yet escaped the mountains all together. Kyrgyzstan is a country predominantly made up of mountains; there is very little flat land there at all. Indeed, 90% of Kyrgyzstan's elevation is over 1,500m, which is considerably higher than Britain's highest peak. Imagine the entirety of the UK looking like Snowdonia with London as the only flat area and the rest of the country being composed of huge mountain peaks and valleys. It's difficult for us to imagine this because Britain is part of the Northern European low countries, which is essentially what it says on the tin - low and flat. Kyrgyzstan is quite the opposite: it is literally a high country. With this in mind, I still had my work cut out for me now without company to push me up the hills.

The drama started soon after leaving Bishkek. It was probably the coldest experience of my life. On this ghastly afternoon, I was absolutely soaked from head to toe from the relentless snow plummeting into me and the cars perpetually splashing me. I was beginning to panic about my fingertips which were, by this point, proceeding from numbness into utmost pain. It was as if lots of tiny elves with tiny knives were in my gloves, constantly stabbing my fingers. My feet had reached a similar place.

What would a sensible person do in such circumstances? I really don't know, because I am not a sensible person. But it wasn't my fault as such for there had been no prior warning of a monster snowstorm, until cars started coming towards me with layers of snow on their fronts. We had stayed an extra two days in Bishkek to see out the worst of the cold weather, departing on a day when the weather was supposed to have improved. And behold, the weather was totally fine, at least for the first half of the day.

I crossed the Kazakh border once again and it was only when I started climbing slightly that the light rain turned into white, frozen flakes. But it wasn't even winter yet and I wasn't at that high of an altitude. Whilst I was dry, I was totally fine. But as soon as the cars began soaking me with their side-spray, the pain of the frozen rain started to kick in. My plan was to just soldier on through and keep going until I arrived at the town I'd seen on the map before I left. Because of this plan, I carried on cycling past some smaller settlements in the promise of a larger town to warm up in. But this was a decision that I really regretted an hour later, still climbing, getting even higher and even colder, now with absolutely no sign of warm, human-inside-places. At this point, I was sincerely worried about the condition of my fingers. The word "frostbite" haunted my head and worsened the panic. Usually I'm an advocate of pain endurance, as it can, in turn, make you stronger. But it's times like these where my stoic philosophy goes flying out of the window, marked by my squeals and wincing in the unavoidable discomfort. I honestly could not go two pedal strokes without squealing in agony with a gripped jaw and the noise of a tortured man escaping my clenched jaw.

I resulted to sticking my thumb out, with the hope that someone would at least let me warm my poor hands in their car. Nope, rejections en masse. Some even splashed me as they ignored my shivering pleas, making matters worse, thereby. I saw an ambulance coming towards me with its lights on, and in my semi-deluded frozen state, I thought it was for me. The paramedics looked at me with my quivering thumb out like I was some cycling nutjob, and I then looked at myself in the same way - like an idiot. I should have stopped earlier which most sensible cold humans would have done. Most would value their inner warmth over bizarre targets and goals. But not me - as the same avid determination that takes me to faraway places, can also hinder me greatly and put me in actual, physical danger. The cars weren't willing to help so I just continued riding, painfully so. There was no imminent sign of warmth. I was dreading the nearby downhill as well, which may seem counterintuitive for most normal cycling situations. But no, this could have been seriously dangerous. Whilst descending, velocity increases, and with this additional speed comes additional resistance against the wind and with already frozen hands this can do some proper damage. Not to mention the freshly ploughed hard shoulder was ridiculously slippery, already nearly causing me to faceplant multiple times. The forthcoming descent was a recipe for disaster.

"But wait, what's that? A tractor...Okay, well, you better bloody stay there tractor and not leave me to freeze!" I thought, out loud. The tractor turned around and went back into the work yard. It was a wind farm, with hundreds of wind turbines perpetually spinning. My eyes lit up with unbounded elation when I could finally see buildings dotted around the wind farm, of which almost definitely had some form of heating in them. My face was completely wincing and squished up in pain whilst trying to do the normal polite greeting process in Russian. Thank goodness this place existed and thank goodness the people working there were as kind as they were. A heater, warm tea, some food and a warm bed. What legends! Luckily my hands *did* warm up with time, because it honestly felt deep down that they were never going to get back to their normal temperature ever agin. God knows if any long-term damage has been done, but regardless, I knew I was in a drastically better position to be in that warmth, than to be hurtling down that potentially murderous mountain.

One worker showed me the forecast for the following day - sunshine, and much warmer temperatures. The descent could wait till then. Yeah, it meant that I probably wouldn't arrive in Almaty for Saturday night for the possible prospects of a party, but at least I will arrive alive, and with some feeling in my extremities. There's no point putting yourself in danger for silly arbitrary goals, even if it was my main reason for visiting Almaty in the first place. Still, I reiterate - being alive was infinitely more important. There's no way of dancing if you're not breathing.

I couldn't be any more grateful for that safe-haven wind farm, really. I expressed my utmost gratitude to the staff as much as I could whilst I was there, and it may have been a bit annoying for them in the end: "harasho" they would reply, meaning that "it's all good". I was gifted with the priceless lesson that I needed to buy a new top-of-the-range pair of gloves, and find a way to properly waterproof myself, because otherwise it was surely going to be a long, agonising winter in the forthcoming desert of Western China. Luckily the angelic wind farm staff offered to give me permanently the bright blue overalls which they'd leant me for the evening. They were toasty warm, and the most practical winter cycling garment that one could imagine. I was to wear those overalls every single day for the next five months after this worrying event.

Chapter Fifteen

My Cycling Highscore

O kay, so it turns out that, despite everything that I wrote above, I completely went against my newfound logic. The next day, after seeking refuge in the ever so friendly Kazakh wind farm, I catapulted myself once more into another arbitrary and unnecessary goal – to arrive in Almaty by that night! It was my original plan when leaving Bishkek, and a totally reasonable one at that - 230km overall to Almaty, in two days, doing about 115km both days. Possible, if not simple, compared to the Pamir cycling with little oxygen, awful dirt roads and ridiculously steep inclines. Honestly, comparatively, I felt like an absolute athlete when cycling on flat, well-made asphalt roads with normal levels of oxygen. Yet regardless, it didn't make my new goal any less ridiculous. The original plan was flipped upside down by the awful snowstorm and agonising pain in my poor little fingers and toes. I was forced to stop, thereby only having managed to traverse 65km that day - leaving about 175 km left to Almaty. Okay, well that was my two-day plan down the drain. Not possible. For sure, I would have to add another day at least. Even then, the wind farm workers were insisting it was too cold for me to leave the next morning. Nonsense - it was toasty warm compared to the day before, and now no slush on the road to endanger my life.

I was leaving for certain, but unfortunately would have to arrive in the city on Sunday - which kind of grinded at me, for a large part of the incentive to take the Almaty route, was to check out its apparent underground music scene, and cool, trendy Kazakh hipsters having it large out on the town, painting it red, so to speak. This was a fascinating prospect for me to witness, for Central Asia is mostly made up of barren desert wasteland, camels, and lovely old buildings. Seemingly, murmurs of a techno scene (albeit a small one) felt out of place in the land of the nomad steppes. I think that it's fair to say at large, that most people don't have a God darn clue about Kazakhstan as a nation, other than a misguided and incorrect conception provided by the fictional character Borat (though, it is undeniably a hilarious film), let alone, knowing much about Almaty specifically as a city. It's a massively uncharted territory, and this presented a novel opportunity to not only find out about this fresh and exciting place, but to also participate in it.

Unfortunately, I had read online that this aspect of Kazakhstan only comes alive during Friday and Saturday night. Shit. The article said that other than these two nights, the phenomenon is invisible. I was now to be arriving on Sunday due to the stupid snow and might as well have been going towards any other boring city. "But it is *still* Saturday. So it is *still* Saturday night tonight, and you could *still* make it there by tonight..." I pondered to myself, while starting the day at lightning speed surging down the descent, covering more ground than I thought I would, early doors. It also just so happened that I started the day unusually early, as I was woken up in order to have breakfast with the good Samaritan wind workers. The road was flat, wind in the back, and it just so happened that things were in my favour. Then, whilst buying all-important snacks, I asked a rural local: "how long to Almaty from here?" In return, he looked at my bike setup and casually said:

"One day."

His friend confirmed that by bike, it should take only one day. Of course, they knew absolutely nothing about cycle touring, and the sense of distance on two wheels, but this was all I needed to make the final decision, that - sod it - I will make it to Almaty by tonight! 175 kilometres in one day, let's bloody-well do it!

This meant that, not only would I be able to witness what I wanted from Almaty, but I could make a new distance high-score for a day's worth of cycling! My current record at that point was about 160km, when I painstakingly cycled Rasta Bike for the very first time ever (actually this was before he became a Rasta) from the shop where I'd bought him in Bristol, back to my home near London. That was a very, very hard day to say the least. But I was ignorant back then, unaware in all aspects of the art of long-distance cycling - a mere infant to the cycling world. But by this point, I was a fully grown cycle-adult, engulfed in the lifestyle, matured like an expensive cheese. I was to beat that high-score, and with less hardship. Maybe so, but it was still unbelievably difficult. I started the day's pedalling at 8am, and arrived at 9pm. Yep, it was most certainly a lengthy one - not for the faint hearted, or those with genuinely dodgy hearts (I would like to say at this point - don't try this at home, kids). But for so many hours on the saddle, it went by surprisingly smoothly, as I was just ever so determined. I'd stop occasionally to stretch and snack, but otherwise I simply pedalled, relentlessly - reminding myself to stay single minded and one-pointed in my focus, like that of a resolute Buddhist monk.

Lo! I successfully arrived in Almaty, albeit absolutely shattered - fully cream crackered. But I couldn't afford to be too tired, otherwise I would miss out on the Saturday night that I'd made my unwavering focus. So, I shook myself out of it, lying to my own brain about being fatigued - "of course you're not tired, you've barely done anything all day you silly billy!" I said to my own brain, deceivingly. I checked into the hostel, and had an all-important power nap, two energy drinks (once again I don't recommend these lifestyle choices, children) and then I hit the town, for once and for all, without any further ado!

120

I was up since 7am, and after a day filled with the most exercise that I've ever done in my whole entire life, naturally I ended up raving from midnight until 5am. Wow. I was up and moving (a lot) for 22 hours straight, almost one whole day. It was great! Actually, it was an incredible day, and one I shall remember wholly, for it reminds me of what we are capable of achieving physically - which will prevent me from ever falling into the disease of laziness.

It was an epic night. I was recommended to go to the only actual place playing underground music - which sounded legit. I was told by the source that it had no sign outside, merely a red door that I'd have to find. It was an old converted Soviet factory, now a temple of music - which sounded quite up my street. I found the building, entered and was pleasantly surprised to be witnessing a good sound-system, with thumping industrial techno surging out of it. Interesting Kazakh youth were moving their bodily spirit-carriers in rhythmic ways to the bass, in unison, creating that sense of oneness that dance floors usually do in such places. There were youngsters with dreadlocks, some with brightly dyed hair, and a few purposefully dressed entirely in Berlin black. I was loving it, nearly hugging the right speaker and losing myself in dance, to celebrate my new cycling high-score and life-at-large. It was nothing new to me, having witnessed the infamous Berlin techno scene, and the booming music culture in Tbilisi. But this was certainly new to Kazakhstan, and was thereby exciting and fresh. People expressing themselves in such a jubilant way, in otherwise culturally conservative Central Asian countries, is a promising sign for the future. I danced until I could no longer, and then went to sleep.

But despite Saturday night being over and done with, the city didn't stop being interesting. It had a very "European" vibe, as such, and even had a falafel shop which is always a good sign. I hadn't had the pleasure of eating falafel for many months, so my taste buds had a jolly good boogie too. In my hostel, there were some interesting characters. One being an old English man driving around the world in a converted truck, who held every

121

British stereotype possible - wearing a rugby shirt, sporting a red nose from drinking too much beer, and a crude yet stomach-tickling sense of humour. That Sunday was spent how God intended for it to be spent: resting and eating falafel. I also purposefully-aimlessly strolled around the modernist, creative architectural buildings, which were complemented by the jagged snowy mountains behind them.

The following day, I met up with a mutual friend that I knew online - Anita Shanti. She was a Kazakh national, with Russian heritage, who'd been living in Goa, India, for seven years as a psytrance DJ. Quite the mix of influences, I do say. She's a fascinating woman, who is a mother to her half-Indian child, and currently undergoing a divorce whilst pregnant with another baby from another boyfriend. A bit of a whirlwind of a life, of which most would probably crumble under the pressures of. But not Anita, she was fascinatingly strong in the head, and unconditionally accepting of her position – making the most of what she had. Her positive attitude was contagious, and we laughed all day, being silly and happy. In a city that was actually full of wealth, due to the huge sums of Kazakh oil reserves, it could sometimes feel somewhat up its own ass, for want of a better term. Mercedes, BMWs, Range Rovers everywhere, it was basically the rich city in Central Asia, with posh little coffee shops and designer boutiques. So, it was quite amusing to have two chuckling hippy types whirling through it. She was great, although she certainly did love to talk, and non-stop too. Mostly it was about herself, and her story, which I was luckily interested in, because otherwise I couldn't get a word in edgeways. She showed me her music, her art, and even her new singing project. After my day with Anita Shanti, I felt inspired to create and smile, and it was exactly these types of idiosyncratic individuals that I'd hoped to meet in Almaty. Thus, I was ready to move on. My thirst for interest in this place was satisfied, for now, and anyhow, I had to reunite with my good friend Gunnar the American, as we were about to cycle through China together!

Unfortunately, on my route from Almaty to the Chinese border, I had a bit of a confrontation with a local Kazakh man. This is how it came about: off I went from Almaty, back on the velo, albeit feeling relatively well rested. It's crazy how beneficial three nights of proper sleep in a proper bed can be for your body, when compared to achy restless nights in my stinky tent. Anyhow, I was off again, with Gunnar and the Chinese border in touching distance. Headwind was a threat, according to my wind-app, and luckily, I was only on the peripheral edges of an otherwise very harsh headwind. The traffic was pretty heavy, and with no hard shoulder it was kind of difficult to navigate, but nothing new. It was manageable. But, not only do you have the moving traffic to contest with, but you also have the flipping idiots who are stationary, parked, and wishing to join their moving counterparts. With their wish in mind, they do so, reversing into the road, but without bloody looking! This is one of the most frustrating and angering things as a cyclist, when they just don't check their mirrors. In fairness, they probably aren't used to random cycle tourists being on the road, but you can't help yourself from getting annoyed. When they narrowly miss knocking into you, it's natural to say something in your mother tongue, along the lines of: "watch where you're going you absolute knobhead!" This generally has no negative repercussions, because, well...they don't understand a word of it. But for sure they sense the tone, as they glare back at you, rightly feeling antagonised.

But this particular Kazakh bloke, after nearly smashing me off my bike whilst reversing mindlessly out of his parking space, wasn't so pleased with my tone, to the point of cursing me back, in his own language, to which I obviously wasn't so pleased to receive back. "You're the one in the wrong here you silly bugger" I thought, and outraged, I subconsciously and uncontrollably allowed my right hand to swing upwards, with one particular finger separating from the rest.

He clearly understood what I meant by my single left hand and the single finger being aimed towards him, as it's a universal sign, unlike my prior angry words. The middle finger, the world-over, is a sign which is not ambiguous at all and clearly says "screw you."

"Oh poops," I thought, as soon as I brought my left hand back down to my handlebar, "what did I just do?" Prior to this, I'd made it officially illegal in Cody Law (which is an unwritten list of stuff I ban myself from, like alcohol and dead animal flesh) to give the middle finger during brief spats of road rage. I'd made this new law, after hearing stories of cyclists giving the finger, and then getting hit by metal poles by drivers. Not for me, I didn't want that, therefore I banned myself from middle fingering and this was a sensible move, even though sometimes you are just oh so angry and really want to. I made some alterations and instead usually resulted to just throwing a hand up in distress, as to say: "what the hell are you doing, putting my life at risk?" This was much less confrontational than the universal "screw you" symbol. But on this occasion, Cody law and order had no control over the all-important finger, and it flung up nonetheless.

The driver was fuming. He zoomed past me and skidded to a stop, waiting for me. Oh no, actual confrontation! I was taken by surprise, because only moments after realising that my naughty autonomous finger had broken sworn Cody Law, I was in the middle of actual conflict. He got out of his car to confront me, and I stopped my bike for the same reason. He was a short but stocky man, with a muscular build. He had clearly gotten up on the wrong side of the bed that morning, because his glaring scowl could have evoked fear in even the heartiest of men. Possibly even Braveheart himself would have been taken by surprise. We met face to face, squaring each other up, as such, both shouting at each other in foreign tongues (which was kind of pointless), then from out of nowhere, he stabbed me in the heart. No, I'm joking, he didn't do that. But he did sharply swing his arm back and pretend to punch me. Of Course, I flinched, due to something called "instinct" and he saw that as having won this spat of road rage, and pathetically kicked my front wheel before driving off.

Look, guys, I just want to reassure you that I'm genuinely a nice young man. Anyone who knows me personally would confirm that I am a peaceful individual who doesn't go about looking for conflict. When I was a youth, yeah maybe it was slightly different and I enjoyed a fight here or there, but what else are you going to do when you're 13? Cinema, bowling, or bare-knuckle fighting - it's a no-brainer (I'm kidding again by the way). I'd never go looking for it back then either, just dished out a few blows in defence. But at this point in my life, I'm anti-violence, clearly a hippy in values, all about pacifism, meditating and smelling roses on the wayside. I'm on this earth for joy, elation and beautiful moments, not to be scrapping on the side of the road. But believe me, there's something peculiar about drivers nearly killing you with their negligence and audacity which really boils one's blood, like a screeching kettle telling you it's finished. Even Gandhi, in all his equipoise, would surely have blown up when confronted with this stuff (well, if he was cycle touring through Kazakhstan). Out of the thousands of encounters I had with locals during the Full Power Bike Ride, a vast majority were an exchange of compassion and love, and this exchange of anger was an absolute one off. I'm a nice person, but everyone can lose their temper from time to time, even our hypothetical cycling Ghandi.

The drivers were worse in Kyrgyzstan, as I briefly mentioned before. I previously thought that Turkish drivers were rather outrageously dangerous, but they were no match for the Kyrgyz maniacs. It was funny, that when I was united with three other cyclists in Bishkek, we all shared the same experience, and we related in feeling absolute anger towards these reckless men, wanting to inflict violence on the faces that nearly took our lives away all day every day, with their disgraceful driving. Strange as it is, you find yourself genuinely wanting to fight these people, like some foreign warlord from the 3rd century. You find yourself transforming in an instant from a nice person to a raging warrior. At so many points during this large cycle ride, I wanted people to get out of their car and confront me, for I was so, so angry and wanted to show them this in the form of force through fists. Luckily no one had stopped, for their sake and mine. But this guy *did* stop, and it took me by utter surprise, as I was not feeling the same anger as usual (as I was having a lovely day until then).

But thankfully it didn't erupt into anything volcanic, for it would have either ended up with me hurt, or in prison. Just a thought, but they do say that Genghis Khan, the relentless conqueror (and consequential sperm donor) had 16 million male descendants in his direct lineage, and you can certainly see this in parts of Central Asia, particularly in this man. He was an angry individual, of Mongol heritage, wanting war, but I'm glad I didn't give it to him. You can see how some cycle tourists end up getting into fights with these people, but I'm happy to be one that hasn't. I henceforth banned myself once more from giving the universal finger curse and ensured that I finished the trip without scrapping with any locals, as it's certainly not what I was cycling across the world to do. After all, my aim is to be a part of the love generation, not the hate generation.

Anyway, I carried on unscathed, albeit a bit shaken up with adrenaline rushing around the cranium. But I soon laughed it off and thought of myself as a silly billy for getting myself into such a childish situation. The rest of the day was a good one, and I forgot all about it. The next few days were painless, with a little bit of wind, but a brand-new highway to stick on and just keep pedalling. Nothing too exciting to see, and nothing too boring either. There were some lovely sand dunes at one point, marking the return from the mountains back to desert, and a rather beautiful Muslim cemetery with large mausoleums devoted to passed loved ones. But there was also a not so lovely sight of a horse, decapitated in two bloody halves with its guts sprawled out across the road.

It was quite a sobering sight - seeing this destroyed animal, who was once freely leaping around the vast steppeland, now squished into the asphalt. It shows the type of drivers and their driving standards in this part of the world, and how, all in all, I don't think they view us as cyclists as being all too different from horses and the suchlike in our road status. So I cycled past this squished majestic creature and felt thankful that it was not me lying there in half, because there were many, many times where that could have been my fate - due to these careless drivers of the steppe.

Eventually, a few days later, I made it to the border town of Zharkent, and so had Gunnar! We were both now ready to enter yet another enthralling country - China!

PART FOUR - A TWO-WHEELED ODYSSEY THROUGH EASTERN ASIA

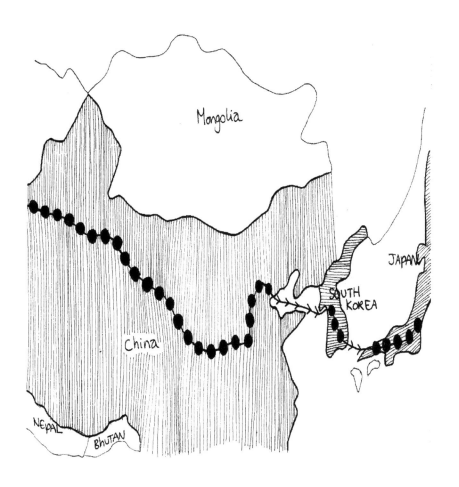

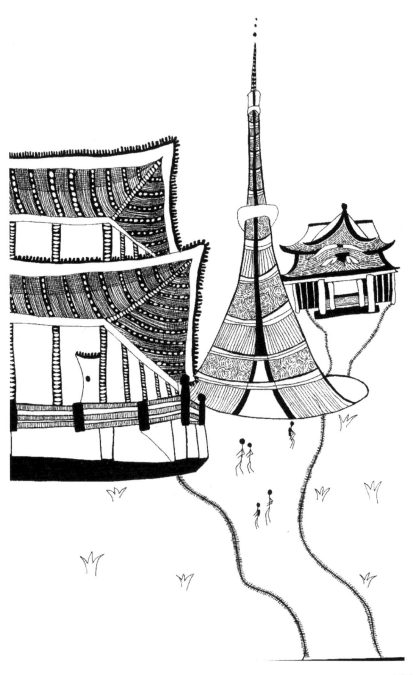

Chapter Sixteen

From Central to Eastern Asia

Τhis was an uber exciting point for me! Not only was I about to enter China - the true marking point of being in the Far East, but also to be back with Gunnar to cycle together a long way through this ancient culture! I met Gunnar where I met all the other Camel Crew cyclists - in Portistan. However, I felt something special with Goondog, and the conversations we had while cycling always ended up diverging into DMC's (deep, meaningful conversations), yet we also had lots of fun together. It was all a rather strange experience cycling with others, after spending so many months cycling alone to get to Azerbaijan, and in some ways, it was hard to adapt my personal routine with other people's ways of cycle touring. But Gunnar's way seemed similar to mine, in fact we shared many similarities, albeit he was four years older than me - which was great, because I love learning from people with more experience than myself.

Thereby, when we both decided to cycle through the supposedly challenging Xinjiang region - we both knew it was a great idea to do it together! We had lost each other a couple times prior, firstly during the Camel Crew days, because he was the fastest out of all of us and zoomed off ahead (while me and Fredward were being silly doing Italian accents and frolicking around), and when we looked up, Gunnar had vanished into the distance. After he ended up finding a new cycle crew to do the Pamir Highway with, I thought I would never see the friendly

American again. But how wrong I could be! We made the China plan and reunited in Bishkek. Then, by this point we were officially at the border to China and royally ready to rumble.

We had a day's rest in the border town of Zharkent, as we had some things to sort out - namely, getting the back of an earring, and a new zip for my jacket. Therefore, we went looking for these bizarre objects in the bazaar, because where else could you find seemingly useless, miscellaneous things? There is a strong bazaar culture in Central Asia, as huge conglomerate supermarkets are yet to have undermined them as they have done in the West. And, looking through the bazaars was one of the joys of our rest days in this area. It also sustains a strong "mend-and-make-do" culture, where, when something is broken you can simply take it to the specialist bloke whose job it is to keep that thing alive. This lies in stark contrast to our own cultures, where we just throw it out and get a new one without a second thought.

This fixing culture is one I had only just started properly practicing thanks to these bazaars and I want to keep it going throughout my life. So with this pursuit in mind and with the help of a lovely young Kazakh lady - boom, we found both the things I was looking for! Now, my left earring could stop falling out of my ear, and my jacket could zip up properly (the latter was still screwed, but oh well). We did a big food shop and said goodbye to Central Asia - of which we were both very ready to do. We had been in the region since we set foot on the land over the Caspian Sea - our first time in Kazakhstan. It had been about three months overall, which really did feel like a long time - almost too long. Of course, we had seen some amazing things: plentiful camels, breath-taking mountain ranges and fascinating nomadic ways of living. However, it also meant three months of unhappy stomachs, agonising uphill cycling in the mountains and simply boring national cuisines. In all honesty, we were just fed up of the food! We needed something new, and just over this imaginary border lay the promise of the world-famous Chinese cuisine. We were ready, and off we went - heading for China!

Slowly, we approached the border, wheels spinning freely beneath us, both harbouring that butterfly sensation in our stomachs - the same feeling you get as a child at parent's evening, when you just know your teacher will tell how naughty you've been. We bloody struggled to even find the border prior to this, because not only had they made a new one recently, but they also have this special "Free Economic Zone" thing with its own trade border. So, this resulted in a miss-match of misinformation and constantly going back and forth. Eventually though, before we lost all hope - we found the right one.

We had heard so much chitter chatter from other cycle tourists about the gloom and doom of the Xinjiang region of Western China and had also heard of tumultuous experiences crossing the border with the Chinese police. Amongst some of the accounts were stories of the police taking people's phones, in order to download all of their personal pictures onto a big database, and even sometimes uploading spy software onto their device to see what future pictures they will take. In preparation for this complete and utter breach of liberty, I ensured that my phone was drained of battery, and thanks to its smashed screen - I was going to say that it was broken. We had also been told of police confiscating knives, of which we also weren't looking forward to - because we needed them for cutting vegetables when camping. All in all, we had prepared ourselves for a blooming long wait, as some people accounted that they'd waited hours and hours till they finally got through to the other side.

In our experience, we had a very different version of events. Surprisingly, the border crossing went suspiciously swimmingly. It didn't take very long at all comparatively and they didn't even ask for my phone at all. Although, yes, we still did have to go through the process of a full-body X-ray, a logging of our fingerprints for their national database, and to look into a camera for their new facial-recognition technology. It's hard not to feel somewhat violated through this process and a bit incriminated, but at least it was a speedy violation. We still managed to keep our phones untapped, kept our knives and even managed to not have my cooking petrol confiscated, somehow.

Although she did look back and forth from my passport photo to my actual face several times and asked for her colleague's opinion as to whether the photo was genuinely me or not. They concluded that it *was* me - fabulous decision! It's funny, growing up, kids share jokes about how all Asians look the same, and sometimes people back home suggest that they might think the same about us, albeit this is usually dismissed right away. But it turns out it's actually also true in the reverse! The amount of times that people looked at Gunnar's passport photo and pointed to me was crazy. To ourselves, we look clearly different, but to them we were just both two white, blonde guys and looked very alike. Curious, isn't it!

We received the green light to go ahead, which signified that we weren't terrorists, or offering a significant threat to the Chinese regime.

We left the customs building and officially made our first step on Chinese soil (well, Chinese concrete - but you know what I mean, there was probably soil somewhere underneath). The building itself was quite a striking image, rather futuristic in its imposing grandeur. Now we were free to explore China at our own will. We knew from our research, that this wasn't exactly going to be the case - free will is kind of a thing of the past in China. However, regardless of this, you can't help the feeling of wanderlust provoked by unchartered territory when you cross into a new country, and specifically by a land border. You feel that this country is your oyster. And maybe so, but this region of the country, Xinjiang, is an oyster that is heavily, heavily controlled by the police force, who are of course controlled by the state - a state that is watching your every move.

We heard rumours that this region was comparable to Orwell's 1984 "Big Brother" scenario, or even said by some to be one of the worst police-states in the entire world. Well, I guess the truth is not so far from these claims. I have never been to North Korea or

Turkmenistan, so I can't quite compare, but I'm sure they are both equal to the situation Xinjiang. Upon leaving the border into our very first Chinese city, Horgas, we were bombarded with a ridiculous amount of flashing red and blue lights, literally everywhere. Honestly, you wouldn't want to be cycling through these places if you were epileptic! On every corner of every block stood a police booth with Chinese officers fully armed with riot gear. They all had big riot shields and these peculiar black spears with a blunted end, of which wouldn't necessarily cut you if you touched it, but for sure would go through you if it was shoved hard enough into your torso. Curious, but not particularly threatening, mostly because our prior research of the region prepared us for these sights, and because these weapons weren't intended for us.

All this puffing of the police force's chest on behalf of the state is not to threaten tourists, but to pose as a threat to the Uyghur Muslim population, of whom this land used to belong to. They look clearly different from the Han Chinese, appearing more Central Asian, whilst also have a language which is Turkic, entirely different to Mandarin. These lands have been of specific interest to China for millennia due to their amazing strategic positioning on the all-important Silk Roads. Yet, it's only relatively recently that China took the colonial plunge and have taken it under its imperial wing, officially making it also "China".

It's a similar situation in some ways to the happenings in Tibet, and how the Tibetans have lost their nationhood under the umbrella of China. Tibetan monks *did* protest against this conquering, albeit in a way that didn't bring violence to Chinese authorities, mostly due to the non-violent nature of Buddhism. However, there were cases of self-immolation, where monks set themselves alight in flames and burnt to death whilst meditating throughout their final minutes, not moving a bone in their body. So one could call this violent, yet it was only self-inflicted. With the Uyghur population on the other hand, there has been some armed resistance against the Chinese occupation, which has supposedly been the reason for such a mental extent of surveillance and police control.

Yet, we found out on our Silk Road audiobook that the Chinese had originally trained the Uyghur people some time ago, in Jihadi tactics in order to help the Afghan Mujahideen in resisting Russia. Oops, just another example of how a country's Frankenstein comes back to bite them in the ass. This is comparable to the recent situation with ISIS who received weapons and training from the West whilst they were still being called "Syrian rebels" in the media, but then oopsy daisy, they became dogmatically radicalised and then used exactly those same Western weapons and techniques to bring terror to their maker. So, the situation in Xinjiang spoke with a great deal of irony - a sticky one that the Chinese authorities created for themselves. Anyhow, that's just a little bit of historical context, necessary to explain why things are the way that they are in this region with the otherworldly amount of police presence.

Eventually, in Horgos we managed to find a hotel which hosted tourists. We had heard a lot about cyclists struggling to find "tourist approved hotels" in Xinjiang, because most of the hotels are only for Mainland Chinese citizens. But in Horgos this caused no issues and boom, the second one we tried accepted us and was a reasonable price as well. The price of these special hotels was one of our major concerns, because if you have limited choice and they cost an arm and a leg, what can one do? But so far, so good. We settled ourselves into our room, then headed out into the city, excited - with the prospect of our very first Chinese meal, in actual real-life China! As I previously mentioned, we were rather fed up with the monotony of Central Asian cuisine by now, and were more than ready for a new type of food.

We rushed down the main street, excited like little children on Christmas morning. There were oh so many places with Chinese signs we couldn't read but which probably sold food, with some Western looking places in the mix, which was definitely not what we were looking for. The signs were mostly written in bright red flashing LED Chinese characters, and all the bright lights together were quite the sight. The smell of freshly cooked food and stir-fries was oozing out of every corner possible, and was luring us this way and that way, and then back this way again. We couldn't pick where to go, because there was so much choice! It was relatively noisy when compared to the steppe or the mountains, and hearing Mandarin for the first time was rather strange, because it's usually spoken at a very high volume, and the phonetics were particularly sharp. All in all, our senses were fully awakened, and it was almost like being at a theme park, both Gunnar and I eagerly anticipating the most important thing in the world – food.

Finally, we found an authentic local restaurant which had all their ingredients out on display for us to choose. It was a strange set up, but we knew we had some cultural adaptations to make and we were open to it. They gave us a metal tray and we just chucked loads of different veg and tofu on our tray, and they subsequently went and stir-fried it all and it arrived back on our table, hot and bloody ridiculously delicious! It was the best meal we had both had in what felt like aeons! Happy bellies and happy minds.

Everything around us was so strange and novel - we were so very happy to finally be in China. We left the restaurant and popped into the little shop next door. There were boundless new products that we had never seen before and our food related excitement shot through the roof once again. In our elated state, we bought these tubes of jellybeans that were essentially in the body of cute little adorable inanimate animals. I bought the panda one (Sad Panda, named thereafter, due to his solemn facial expression) and Gunnar bought the little green bunny one (Sleeping Bunny, named as such due to his constantly closed eyes). We went back to the hotel and had a celebratory party for making it so blooming far - by bicycle! We scoffed all our newfound sugary snacks and played some classic party tracks from SoundCloud, for example "Rock this party" by Bob Sinclair, an undeniable banger. The internet was a bit dodgy, so every time the music stopped and buffered, we stood stuck completely still and turned the party into a game of musical statues. It was liberating to feel like proper children, once more. Ultimately, in my opinion this is what true travel should evoke!

The next day we had a slow morning, trying our very first Chinese breakfast - which consisted of noodles and dumplings and suchlike. Having only savoury things for breakfast was another new thing to us, but I'm not complaining - as it was all super scrumptious stuff! Much better than a full English breakfast, that's for sure. All the Chinese grub was bloody brilliant for vegetarians due to a long cultural history of vegetarianism and this came as a huge relief. After breakfast, we got back on the road, to start traversing the huge region of Xinjiang, which in and of itself is not so different from the geographical size of Mainland Europe. We straddled our Surly stallions and began the pedalling.

By noon we had done a solid half-day and had started a little bit of the climbing that we knew we would have to do the following day. The drivers were considerably more courteous than in the previous countries that we'd marginally survived, and the roads were absolutely sublime - not a pothole in sight. Once again, the road quality contrasted starkly to what we'd had to endure the previous months in the Stans. At around 5pm it was getting dark, and at this point we were preparing to find somewhere to sleep. By the way, at this point we were working off of a different time-zone to the rest of China because Gunnar and I had decided to distinguish "Our Time" from "Beijing Time" which was still a whole two hours ahead of us. It makes absolutely no sense to have merely one time zone based on the capital, when their peripheral territories are thousands of kilometres away. Our plan was that when we got to the middle of China, we would go an hour forward, and only when I got to Beijing would I be functioning off actual Beijing Time.

In terms of finding a place to sleep, we knew that it was illegal to camp in Xinjiang, but equally, we knew that our friends had managed to do it before. Along with the complete absence of tourist hotels in this area, we literally had no choice *but* to camp.

However, the worst thing we could have done is to make the mistake that plenty of cycle tourists do at this point of the day - to cross the police checkpoint. The likelihood is usually that they will force you and your bike into a car and take you to the nearest town with an official tourist hotel. This was a somewhat scary prospect for me, as I said from day dot of this trip that I would cycle the whole way across the planet's landmass solely with my own leg-power, and taking a car would certainly undermine that. I had already made the shitty mistake in Paris, forced into a police van for five kilometres, and I wasn't willing to do it again. I am not a cheat and certainly not a wet flannel.

Saying this, we were very lucky to spot the flashing lights and big sign saying *"POLICE CHECKPOINT"* before we hurtled straight into the spider's trap. Our map had said it was due to be further ahead, so it took us by surprise. We quickly slammed on our brakes and spun ourselves around. We were in code red, and as Gunnar said at the time "we've gone from being in the frying pan to falling into the flames" - things were getting hot.

We found ourselves in a relatively urbanised rural village and were faced with the challenge of finding a discreet place to sleep. Finding good camping spots was never my strong point, so I let Gunnar take hold of the reins. We were very lucky to stumble upon an orchard full of already harvested apple trees. We and our stallions had to jump over a little stream, but then we were in our own private camp site. Or so it seemed, for a few minutes. We heard some kids playing in the orchard and they looked at us in silence as if we were green aliens. We thought, for sure, that they would come back with their angry Chinese daddies telling us to leave instantly and to never come back. Or even worse, we imagined the sirens of the police coming to collect us and chuck us in their evil monster cars.

Much to our shock, nobody came, not even a whisper from the neighbouring people. We were able to relax finally and cook, albeit we remained quiet as mice throughout the evening, in case we roused suspicion. We felt naughty, mischievous and almost in danger when the thoughts of those shields and spears would come into our minds. This was the start of our Xinjiang bandit career and we were loving it. Just like when you are a child, the stricter the rules imposed on you to behave in a certain way, the more fun they are to break, and this was merely the beginning.

The following morning, we got to the checkpoint down the road which we'd narrowly avoided the night before. They asked us a myriad of questions about where we came from and where we were going - and we answered accordingly. They asked where we slept last night and we said the hotel in Horgos, where we'd actually slept two nights prior. The thing is with the bicycle, is that they really didn't have a clue about how far you can travel on one, and how long it takes. We knew full well that it's almost impossible to do 60km in one morning on fully loaded bikes by 9am unless you begin crazily early, but to them it sounded perfectly reasonable.

We survived the initial interrogations, but our hearts sunk when we looked down at Google Translate on the officer's phone. It was obviously an awful translation, as always, but it said something along the lines of us: "you are not possible able to cycle over the following stretch of motorway – you must have to take bus". We laughed it off and told him that this was impossible because we are only cycling and never ever take cars. We argued back and forth over Translate for a long time and I was beginning to get frustrated. I was treading on a thin tightrope, acting harshly in my role as Bad Cop, and it was only when Gunnar took over the translator as Good Cop, did we progress anywhere.

He told the officer that we had cycled 15,000km by bicycle without a single car, and just like that, as if the Fairy Godmother had swished her magical wand - off he went, impressed, to convince his senior to let us cycle. He came back with good news and we cycled past them, extremely happy bunnies! Freedom, now on the open road ready to climb our final mountain pass for a long time to come. We felt ever so empowered, not only having slept with our own autonomy intact, but we had also now managed to remain on our bikes and not give in to their blind and illogical rules. He tried claiming that it was for our safety, but this motorway, the G30, had the hugest hard shoulder on the side which felt big enough to be its own bicycle lane, in and of itself. There wasn't much traffic at all, and the trucks that did pass left ample amounts of room. We felt ourselves to be in the safest cycling conditions that we'd been in for a very long time - maybe even since Greece!

The climb up to 2000m was kindly gentle, and the road very gradually moved upwards inch by inch. It was an easy climb, when contrasted to some of the ridiculously steep passes in the Pamirs. We even chatted all the way up, sang songs and had lots of fun, which is the first time I've had a jolly good laugh when climbing a mountain on a pushbike. Before we knew it, we were near the top. Just ahead of us was an astonishing feat of human engineering. It was a massive white suspension bridge and a series of tunnels which made an enormous curl around the mountain - hugely impressive in its size and scale. We reached the top, and began the descent, both as happy as Larry.

We'd spent the entire day going upwards and then it started getting dark. We hadn't gotten as far as we'd planned (probably because we spent so much pedal energy on singing at the top of our voices) and darkness was rapidly approaching. In the Stans, when it had gotten to this point of the day, we could just look either side of the road and see an abundance of places to put up our tent, chuck it together, cook and sleep. In the Uzbek desert for example, the whole desert was our free camping ground. But here, on the G30 motorway in Western China, it wasn't quite that easy, even though the landscape wasn't all too different, and we were still surrounded by nature. The difference here was that the road on both sides was laced for miles with indestructible barriers to prevent cars from falling off the road, and behind these was an endless huge fence, lined with barbed wire to stop anyone entering or leaving the motorway.

The road travels for 4000km west to east, all the way to Shanghai, and had these barriers on both sides of the road the entire way across the gigantic country. The scale and cost of building this road must have been monumental. But for us, it was a big problem, as it made it incredibly hard for us to find anywhere to camp. We were essentially trapped, imprisoned by the road itself. With slightly ironic tones, the road that we had fought hard to cycle with our freedom intact, was now taking away from us our very freedom to sleep freely. It was frustrating to say the least - for we had just climbed up a mountain on a bicycle, it was dark, and we were extremely tired. We were prepared to cycle in the dark until we found a gap in the fence. And almost just as we had put on our night lights for safety, we were very lucky to find a brief end in the first barrier. As if a gift from above, one panel of the barbed wire fence behind had been undermined somehow, and we were able to pass straight through. It was quite a tricky surface to push our bikes on, and wasn't the best ground for camping either, but beggars can't be choosers in these situations. We were happy to be ultimately free from the motorway prison.

The evening was quite chilly, yes, but not too bad and not particularly windy at all - nothing noteworthy. We cooked, ate, and listened to the end of the Silk Road audiobook, and then entered our tents when it became too cold. As always, I didn't put the pegs into my tent, because it was free-standing, and I never had to. Only when it was really super duper windy, did I need to stick the pegs into the ground. But, unfortunately for me, this coming night *was* windy, and not just a little bit but otherworldly wildly windy.

I was already asleep when I was forced awake by the storm surging its violent gusts straight into my home. I woke up with half the tent resting on my face, with the flysheet flapping spastically, relentless. Realistically I should have gotten out and sorted it out, but it was far too cold and windy, yet it was so noisy that I could barely get back to sleep anyway. Things suddenly got worse when I sat up to get some water, and the ground sheet - the actual tent itself - went flying upwards, taking me with it. The beastly gusts of wind were almost taking me and my tent flying into the distance. I heard a loud *snap* and instantly the other half of my tent then flopped onto my legs. I managed to wrestle myself backwards back into some form of a sleeping position and tried to imagine that none of this had happened and wasn't happening. The entire tent was lying on me and I somehow fell back to sleep, solemnly surrendered to the traumatic situation.

I woke up to a windless morning, the calm after the storm, with Gunnar laughing hysterically and taking pictures of my broken tent lying on top of me. To be fair, it was an amusing sight when he showed me the pictures. I had at least three inches of snow sitting on my weary face, on top of my broken home, and my tent poles had snapped in two places (but he reassured me that they were fixable). A few things had flown away in the wind, forever (one notable object was my pink bucket that I had only just bought, with the purpose of hand washing my clothes in it. I bought it after we struggled to find a washing machine in Horgas, and Gunnar suffered a hefty £7 bill to wash his clothes at a dry cleaner. A bucket was a long-term investment, but now it was flying away somewhere in the Chinese desert in the ghastly wind) but at least I was alive, and ultimately all was fine. So rightly so, we hit the road again.

Every morning when I painfully threw that right leg over the steel stallion and locked foot with pedal, post-sigh, I got this unavoidable feeling of "still going" and being "back on the road", because such a journey of this magnitude in length is relentless in every way, so it's a feeling of fatigue yet excitement, for what this new day might hold. But after a storm of such magnitude, it does feel even more challenging to swing that leg over the saddle once more.

In this case, the day held for us more harsh gusts of wind, but this time we were awake, on our bikes, and the wind was directed into our faces. To begin with it wasn't such an issue because we still had lots of downhill to do and it wasn't particularly harsh at this time of morning. But suddenly, once we turned the corner and things flattened out - it hit us. It continued to hit us, perpetually in the face for the entire rest of the day. We had planned to make it to the next major town, Jinghe, by the end of the day, which was a mere 110km away. Yeah, of course it's still a long distance regardless, but on a normal weather day, with a lot of downhill to begin the day - it should have been an absolute breeze (excuse the pun). It in fact, was not a breeze at all, not a walk in the park, or any other way you may wish to phrase an easy day. It was the opposite - bloody excruciating. Gunnar and I are pretty similar in our level of stubbornness, and you kind of have to be a stubborn and determined person to be a long term cycle tourer, but to us, when we said we will make it to Jinghe, it meant that we will do *exactly* that unless something huge stopped us. In this case, the headwind wasn't enough to stop us, but it was enough to slow us down massively. It's hard enough already cycling for a whole day with heavy baggage, legs aching, bum sore - not easy. But when you add harsh headwind into the equation, things start to become that tad bit more challenging.

I'd say, in general, that cycle touring is half a travelling experience and half a sporting experience - the days that you're on the bike at least. However, on days like these, the travelling aspect somewhat goes out of the window entirely and is lost in the gale force conditions. With your head down, body in an attempted streamline position, staring at your front wheel and wishing it to keep rolling forward at a decent speed, things suddenly turn into a full-on sporting experience altogether. At least in my experience, you forget where you are, what there is to see or learn, and simply focus on moving forward. It even surpasses that of a fun sport and feels more like an endurance sport or extreme sport at some levels.

I feel like I became a much stronger cyclist, and a much stronger individual at large, due to the Pamir Mountains. The steep climbs, lack of oxygen and awful road conditions made for some hefty development. I noticed it a lot during the stretch towards Almaty, my biggest day yet, having done 175 km, but with flat riding, plenty of oxygen and perfect roads. I felt invincible, strong and as if I could do anything on a bike at that point. Yet, despite this, headwind turns things upside down, and despite us only doing 110km comparatively, due to the wind it had to be one of the hardest days I've ever cycled and probably one of the hardest days of my life so far (I know I've used that term a lot during the last few chapters, but there's a reason why - because it's true). This was harder than the Pamirs, harder than the hot days in the summer heat of Azerbaijan and even harder than desert riding.

I've done many sports in my twenty-four years of life where I've had to push myself to the limit of my drive and energy potential: played football at a competitive level, trained in karate until brown belt and have even ran two half-marathons. Thus, I know endurance, I know pain, but this was something else as a sporting experience - the top of the game, the hardest of the hard. For sure this trip has brought me to new heights in travel experience and worldly living, but now it was bringing me to new places in terms of physical endurance also, and this prospect was exciting and inspiring - showing me what I can do with this body of mine. Albeit, it is a slightly broken body, due to my slightly out-of-straight spine thanks to mild Scoliosis, and my innumerable football injuries along with my previously dislocated shoulder - yet it's a working body nonetheless, and for this, I am an infinitely grateful young man. It's amazing what this body can do despite its flaws. Frequently, I let my mind wonder as to what would happen when I return home if I put myself onto an ultra-lightweight road bike and put equal endurance energy into a full day of cycling on one of those, the same as I was doing on the heavy long distance set up - and I wondered how fast and far I could go.

We pushed and pushed, pedalled and pedalled, perpetually pummelled by said headwind. Alas, it got dark, and alas it got cold. We put our headlights on, and we continued into the unforgiving evening. The sign now said 13km to Jinghe and what a pleasant sight to see it. Unfortunately, the road signs weren't always factually accurate, and in this case, it couldn't possibly have been, because it felt like it was an awful lot

145

longer than a mere 13km final sprint. We could see the many lights of the city to the left, but they just didn't get any closer.

At this point I think I began hallucinating purely from fatigue. We knew we had to take the next overpass and I kept conjuring up unreal fictional overpasses above, subconsciously just simply wishing that the exit would come already, essentially tripping out from tiredness.

Now *that* was a level of physical exertion that I really had never experienced before the trip. It's not just the exercise that makes the cycling-touring experience extraordinarily exhausting - it's the entire lifestyle. When you train for a marathon, you ensure that you sleep and eat very well the night before, and when it's finally over, you ensure that you do nothing but rest.

However, quite the opposite could sometimes be the case on this trip. It's completely possible that you may have the worst night of sleep ever, due to camping on a hard surface in freezing temperatures, eat food that doesn't fulfil the nourishment needs of an adult human, not have much time to stretch properly and then have to engage in physical exercise which pushes you to the literal limit. And unlike the modern marathon runner living in the normal modern world, it's not possible to sit on the sofa the following week, because we sometimes had to repeat the same routine the following day, again and again. So, in that sense, it could sometimes feel like we were running back-to-back marathons every day without proper rest and nourishment. This, along with pooping in holes, being perpetually ill in certain countries, and being totally out of our comfort zone the majority of the time - are just a few reasons why cycling across the world shouldn't be seen as one long joy ride, because it most certainly is not.

Chapter Seventeen

The Forbidden City

That harsh and hard evening, after that harsh and hard day of painstaking wind, was in fact made even harsher and harder by, (you guessed it!) the fricking Chinese police. Essentially, because Xinjiang is one giant prison as previously explained, it means that absolutely everything is ridiculously monitored. So, it's no surprise to have your very whereabouts watched intensely and ever so closely. One area of intense monitoring were the police checkpoints before every small town and city. Every single time we were going into any form of settlement, we would have to go inside to have our details registered and sometimes this would take an awfully long time. Most of the time they didn't know what to do with us, and our very being there confused the hell out of them. At times, we'd have to wait for over an hour while they dealt with their silly bureaucratic rigmarole.

There is also the issue in Xinjiang, that you can only sleep in specific hotels that accept foreigners, so usually the police would usher you to the one that does. However, this night, they put a spanner in the works, by saying that the city we had worked so very hard to reach - did not even have *any* tourist hotels at all and we were forbidden to enter.

Well, actually, *I* was allowed to enter, as I was a noble English gentleman (sort of) but, Gunnar on the other hand, being born to the land of 'Merica, was strictly forbidden to enter the city. We

147

really couldn't work out why, but they said that these were the rules - and "rules are rules"! Not only US citizens were banned, but also Swedish and Japanese. It seemed a peculiar mix and no explanation was given as to why. They tried to relocate us to a neighbouring town 20km away, but no way in hell were we taking *that* much of a detour when we were already so blooming spent - to the point of hallucination. We were going to give it our best shot to convince them otherwise that "rules aren't rules", and in fact that rules are impermanent, malleable mental constructs that are to be changed when they are damaging people's rights to freedom of movement.

This is what we'd been doing all the way since crossing the border, and it had never stopped since. Luckily, we finally found a decent English-speaking policeman so that we could argue our case with our mouths instead of the awfully inaccurate Google Translate. He was a tall and skinny officer, wearing glasses and clearly had a history of being studious in his English classes at school. It was also lucky that he turned out to be a nice guy too because he could see how tired and broken we were, and how the arbitrary rule of banning Americans was silly and unnecessarily hindering. He showed empathy and argued to his senior in our defence.

The first time he came back it was a hard no, with the explanation of "we are doing special things here in Xinjiang" to which we replied "we know!" as we'd done a lot of research before we even entered the country, about the modern concentration camps and so on and so forth. We sent him away again, not budging from our equally hard stance, and the second time he returned he said that we *could* stay in the Forbidden City, Jinghe, just only it was only for one night maximum. Knowing that we'd broken the loophole called empathy in this otherwise unbreakable legal system, I tested the waters further by asking "how about two nights, so that we can actually rest?" to which he replied "erm...okay but only two maximum!"

Yay! We were truly victorious once more. This meant not only that we could genuinely have a proper rest day, as I'd said, but also that we had an entire day to explore the strictly forbidden city, of which must have to have some pretty epic things to hide, considering they'd gone to such an effort to protect us from it.

Turns out that it didn't, and it was actually incredibly boring with no juicy gossip to be found, not even in the nooks and crannies. For sure, some dodgy oppressive imperial things were happening somewhere, just not within our eye view. We felt like journalists in jeopardy abroad, and despite tribulations in the hostile foreign land, returning home empty handed without headline news. Okay maybe that's a slight exaggeration, but we did nearly get speared through the chest that night - which is kind of juicy, I'd say!

Well we went to the allocated tourist hotel, which looked very nice as usual, but much to our dismay, it was way too expensive. Having cycled through Central Asia for so long, paying £5 maximum for a guesthouse, it came as a shock when they slapped us with a £40 bill...each! China was slightly more expensive than Central Asia, but for proper hotels we were doing well capping ourselves at £10 a night, and we weren't about to end that winning streak with quadrupling it.

"Sorry, we just simply can't afford that," exclaimed Google Translate, speaking on our behalf. We asked them to call the same police dudes we'd just been talking to, in order to see if there were any other cheaper hotels that accepted foreigners. We had to wait a while, and to our surprise, about ten policemen came storming into the hotel with riot shields and wielding the infamous big black spears of doom. To your average Westerner, this would evoke a heart-wrenching shock, but to us, it was just a normal day in Xinjiang - thus we didn't flinch even an eyelash. The receptionist clearly hadn't gotten through to the same police dudes from before, but instead must have made a fresh new call-out to their 999 equivalent. I think that the ten young officers were a bit disappointed that they wouldn't have to spear either of us in the chest, because we were clearly innocent tourists who merely wanted to sleep somewhere cheap. So instead of ending our lives, they simply escorted us to the other, cheaper tourist hotel and everyone was happy in the end. We slept, finally.

But yeah, Jinghe, the Forbidden City was certainly underwhelming and a big anti-climax to our curious minds. We were left baffled as to why Americans were banned, but probably something to do with Trump and his boundless arrogance. But we were also left feeling triumphant once more, confirming that rules really aren't concrete things, and even in one of the strictest police-states on earth, you can still bend laws if they are genuinely unreasonable. For example, "You can't cycle on the motorway", "yes we can", "oh okay". The police there really were just acting mechanically, enforcing laws that they saw as concrete, but as soon as one disagrees, it's such an unusual occurrence for them, that it makes them question the moral fabric of the law and the framework of the police state itself. If you can tickle their humanity and spark within them a sense of moral reasoning, they usually side with you over the law they're meant to be enforcing: "You really can't stay in this city!" "nope, we can, and we will", "oh, okay". I feel it to be a victory, not only for the sake of our own convenience, but also for helping these police dudes to question the social conditioning that is otherwise so strong and suffocating.

Well, ironically, we thought we were doing oh so well at winning against the corrupted police state, but in one day alone, our victory came crashing down on our heads. We had planned a half-day, just a mere 60km to bring us into the next town and sleep, leaving the following day to accomplish the big stretch into Urumqi. But of course, nothing is allowed to be that easy in Xinjiang. We cycled out of the Forbidden City and after half a day we decided to go into the entrance of the next town along to have a late lunch. As usual, we got pulled over to the police checkpoint to get checked in - nothing new here.

The particular bunch of policemen in this town were a strange assortment, all of them being the type of people picked last for sports class when younger. One was an absolute giant, at about 7 feet tall, and another had eyes pointing in opposite directions. Each had their own idiosyncrasy, and I'm not saying that's a bad thing at all - but it was just an interesting choice of policeman, that's all. What made it more interesting was the chief of police in this town - a young officer, seemingly newly graduated, with fashionable glasses and a very cocky demeanour. His pinky fingernail was notably longer than the rest, which Gunnar thought was in order to sniff cocaine from (which apparently is a common thing in the States), so this made us feel like he was even more dubious of a character. But what made his uneasy and uncertain personality all the more disconcerting was the grenade launcher sat firmly around his neck, with one finger always resting on the trigger and the other hand always on his iPhone. He acted harshly to his assorted police crew and ruled over them with an iron fist.

We were told to sit in the office, where they all smoked cigarettes together, and sometimes there would be a minor confrontation between the strange cops - like young apes asserting themselves and testing the strength of the others. Meanwhile the boss just played a game of Tetris intensely on his phone and chain-smoked incessantly. We were waiting for a response from his senior or something, to find out where we could sleep. It was getting close to two hours of waiting when I started getting agitated. We'd waited for long durations for most cities but come on - this was too much. And to make matters worse, we were told once again that there was actually nowhere at all for us to stay in the town because, yet again, they were doing "special things" there, and that we would have to be taken to the nearest city 30km away.

We were infuriated. To have to wait so blooming long just to be told we couldn't even sleep there, which was more than a joke. And now they were going to try to get us to take a lift in the car with our bikes. Of course, we straight up refused, stating once more that we'd cycled every inch from Europe, and we weren't about to stop there. Eventually after some back and forth, they brought some reluctant officers to escort us by driving behind.

You could tell that they weren't keen, because 30km is a long way to go when driving behind two bikes going 10km an hour.

Just as soon as we left, we had to have a toilet break. After coming back from a wee-wee, I looked down to my handlebars and something didn't look quite right. I couldn't put my finger on it, until it hit me - Peace Bear had disappeared! Oh my God, I was utterly distraught. I'd already nearly lost him once when he ran away in Turkey and swam back to the UK (yeah, he met a lady-bear-friend at the festival in Fethiye and tried jumping off the handlebars to go find her but then he got swept up in a storm and ended up swimming back to England, so my mum sent him back out on the next flight when she found him. Anyway...) but now I had a bad feeling that I was going to lose him for good. We told our escorting officers that we had lost an invaluable item, and we went back to go search for him.

There were some kids playing nearby and the officers interrogated them, but they honestly said they didn't steal my best friend. The only option left, was that one of the police guys must have taken him while we were waiting for those frustrating two hours. My bet was that it must have been the stupid grenade launcher leader, because he clearly didn't like us and clearly didn't want Peace Bear to be spreading his infinite peace and love around the totalitarian dictatorship of modern China. Although the officers didn't confirm this, both Gunnar and I knew this to be the case, and it was a sad moment having to leave Peace Bear, knowing that he would be in prison at least for the next 20 or so years. Once he's out and a free bear once more, I will go back to China to find him. But for now, we were forced to push on forth by our escorting policemen - who couldn't see the priceless value of a mere tie-dye teddy bear.

They painstakingly followed behind us, inching along like a fatigued tortoise on a blistering summer's day. We tried to go as fast as we could, but this is still awfully slow by a car's standards. We were passed on from person to person as we reached multiple different checkpoints. The escorting officers were finally free to go back to their post, and it was the unfortunate responsibility of new officers to escort us further. We naively thought that we may have been able to sleep at the next checkpoint somewhere, but to no avail, and instead we had to keep on going till the next town. We downed a strong coffee and kept going. When we finally reached the next town, we had the same awful situation as before - the only allocated tourist hotel in the whole place was a five-star fancy affair, and far too pricey. Gunnar was not giving in and became quite annoyed, dropping his role as Good-Cop. Somehow, we managed to convince our escorting officers to bargain with the stubborn hotel staff and try to bring the price down to a reasonable amount, and we even offered for them to exclude breakfast.

By this point it was already 1am, and we were so ridiculously knackered. We tried to reason with them that we would only be in the room for a mere 9 hours, nearly a third of a day, therefore we should have a discount due to that fact. Bless the cotton socks of the officers, because they genuinely tried bartering with the receptionist for a solid half hour before they literally gave up and abandoned us. Not only did they abandon their bargaining, but they abandoned their job entirely, because they were absolutely not meant to leave us until we had firmly booked a room. Knowing that we were free (somewhat) from the unwavering eye, we then weighed up our options.

Realistically, we didn't have many. There didn't look like an abundance of places to camp in this town, and even if we found one, we didn't want to risk being woken up at 2am by sirens and lights. We decided on doing the undoable, and to arrive to Urumqi (the capital of Xinjiang province) that night. We knew it was still an awfully long way to go, but we also knew there were significantly more places to stay and at a massively cheaper rate. Either way, we would be cutting out another day of cycling and substituting it for another day of rest and exploring, which is always wanted. So, we did it, now without an escort, playing games and singing songs. At one point, we even had the audacity to run a police checkpoint by hiding behind a row of trucks, by cycling to the left of them and weaving through the barrier. Luckily, we went unnoticed, because we couldn't bear the idea of another escort.

Thankfully, at around 7am we finally made it to Urumqi, the capital of Xinjiang. Once again, it was a humongous day of around 170km, nearly matching my high-score and we went to check in to an affordable hotel, struggling to keep our eyes open. We checked in and slept like babies, for an outrageously long and restful period. This part of the journey was absolutely nuts and we jolly well knew it. Although it was ridden with conflict and drama, we were loving it deep down.

Urumqi was great. It was a relatively large city with skyscrapers that glowed in different colours. We visited big supermarkets and bought lots of supplies and went into malls to visit arcades filled to the brim with all sorts of cute and cuddly toys. There were many mosques still intact there, although the Chinese Communist Party are doing their best to slowly eradicate them all with time. There was an equal split in the populace of local Uyghur people, and Han Chinese, and all in all, considering the circumstances, it had quite a good vibe to it. Our hotel was rather luxurious when compared to some other places that we stayed when we got back on the road.

With only three months in total on our visas and a ridiculously long way to go, we knew we couldn't rest for too long in one place, and only had a maximum of one or two rest days in each town. This did create a feeling of non-stop pursuing and striving, but it was necessary if I wanted to get to New Zealand eventually. About one week down the road from leaving Urumqi (bearing in mind that a week may sound like a long time to you, but in terms of cycling the entire width of China, it's really not that far down the road), we were lucky enough to have the honour of sleeping in a rather unusual place. Namely – the men's toilets.

So, yeah, we slept in the toilet block of a Chinese truck stop - no lie. This genuinely happened. Overall, if we had to review it

154

on Tripadvisor we would probably remark: "bloody good laugh, would do it again" - and we felt surprised as to why people don't sleep in toilet blocks more frequently. Of course, I'm only kidding regarding that, but I'm being totally honest about where we slept that night. Xinjiang was one constant surprise of newness and spontaneity. For I slept in many, many obscure and strange places during this trip, especially during my first seven months where I banned myself from paying for accommodation, but not once had I slept in a place where people poo and wee, until then.

I can reassure you that it wasn't the decision of Gunnar nor I, for it was the decision of our new Chinese friend, Molo. But before I add the totally necessary context about our new mate and his peculiar choice of sleeping arrangements, I should first probably bring some context to the weather outside at the time - it was flipping freakingly freezing! Literally freezing, and way below it, probably about -10 degrees. There's absolutely no way that we could sleep outside in our tents and sleep properly, due to our feet being in a painful, constant cold state of misery.

By this point, we were literally a stone's throw away from the infamous Gobi Desert. In fact, you could argue that we were actually cycling through the very edge of it, because the borders of it are pretty ambiguous. Regardless, it was a humungous, dry and arid region – therefore summer temperatures soar to around 35 degrees, but winter temperatures can plummet down to minus 30 degrees. So, it really is the home of both extremes, and we were certainly experiencing the lower extreme. With this in mind, we banned ourselves from sleeping outside, and rightly so.

In this region, it just so happened that the day before, from afar, we saw a small, slowly moving blob which could only be another cycle tourist, surely? Lo behold! It was! We were excited to meet another Westerner and were shocked that someone else was equally insane to come so far from home in order to cycle in this hostile and dramatically uncomfortable environment. We eventually caught up with the blob until it was a human, but they weren't a Westerner after all (and before, I was half hoping it might have even been a beautiful young cycle touring lady...but this would be very unlikely, so I quickly dismissed the lonely sailor thought) and they weren't a lady, unfortunately. It was a local Chinese man! A very worn out cycle-touring Chinese man, looping around the entirety of his humongous nation. This sounded epic and unbelievable until we remembered that we were cycling across the entire globe ourselves. He was wearing a sleeveless leather vest, with plenty of layers underneath, a mop of hair atop his cranium and a tripod around his neck. A tired, ragged looking fellow, but totally intriguing nonetheless. We'd never met a fellow cycle tourist who wasn't an interesting character, and Molo wasn't about to end that streak.

Only 3km after we met him, there was a truck stop which we would have eaten in anyway, but now that we had a fluent Chinese speaker with us, he was able to ask if we could sleep inside the complex. Of course, they said, because it was simply insanely cold outside, beyond reason. We slept on some benches in the lobby and all was great. Well, it was greater than our tents, that's for sure! The idea was to replicate this plan the night after at the next truck stop complex, 97km further on.

We smashed the 97km, albeit it was mostly uphill, but we knew the reward would be more noodles to warm our bellies and benches to lay our bodies - or so we thought. Instead, it turned out that we found ourselves lying on the bathroom floor in our sleeping bags and the whole affair felt fully surreal. But it was new, novel and I will never do it again so why not enjoy it while it lasted - a thought that I'd never thought I'd have in such a situation. I would have maybe asked the food shop next door first, but Molo showed me a translated sentence on his phone saying: "I found us a place to live" and this was joyous news to my eyes. I trusted him fully after his success the night before, but baffled I was, when we walked our bikes into...the toilet block.

Well, it's not *all* bad - at least we weren't far at all from the loo if we got the urge to sprinkle in the night. There were also taps in the morning for a sink shower. Bloody luxury! Well, it was starkly contrasted to the place we stayed in the previous town before we met Molo - a swanky five-star hotel. It turned out to be only £12 including breakfast and was totally top-notch quality. And this is exactly why I love the randomness of cycle touring, for the absolute unpredictability of where you're going and where you will sleep at night. It's mad how one can go from sleeping in a five-star hotel, on the 15th floor, to the actual floor of the actual toilets a couple days later. Good times!

We slept surprisingly well, on the tiled floor of the washbasin room, in the truck-stop toilets. Although, I was grateful to have had my earplugs in, because Gunnar said that lots of loud and obnoxious Chinese truckers came in early morning yelling and shouting (clearly showing no respect for the pop-up hostel we had created). The benefit of the earplugs is that they turn these annoyances into mere murmurs that find it hard to disturb your sleep. But he did say that he still slept better than the night before on the benches.

We were abruptly woken up at 7am by the confused and slightly annoyed cleaner, who turned the lights on sharply. The artificial white light burnt our poor little eyes, as they were suddenly adapting to their first visions of the brand-new day. The sun hadn't even risen at this point, so the light was super-duper bright. But to be fair, we did need to wake up sharply anyway, because we had a big 140km day ahead of us to get to the next city, to enjoy the warmth of an actual room and an actual bed. The cleaner was dressed in a full camouflage military outfit, so at first, I wasn't sure if it was an army man coming to arrest us for sleeping in the loos.

It's peculiar in China, how just about everyone in every role of the society dresses like the police or army whenever they want to. For example, the waiter the night before was wearing an armoured vest with the word "POLICE" written on the back. Surely, he couldn't have been a police officer, as he had only just served us noodles and tea. It begs the question, if it works the other way around, vice versa? So, do the actual military men wear cleaners' outfits and waiters' clothes when they go to war? I don't think so, but it is a very strange phenomenon nonetheless.

It's kind of like the "boy who cried wolf" in a way, in Xinjiang, when you are so used to seeing flashing lights and police clothes absolutely everywhere, it desensitizes you to these things and they don't evoke the same fear as they used to. But you never know when someone genuinely has the authority to act on the law. So, can you tell the waiter that the food is mediocre, or will he just arrest me? Who knows? China is weird. But so were we, therefore it was a great mix. In said restaurant with said waiter/policeman, there was a big X-ray machine that beeped every time someone walked through it. You would know the ones, like those you'd see in an airport. And even in an airport it's somewhat frustrating and you feel kind of violated. But there, they have them literally everywhere. Every single hotel you walk into, you have to go through the beep beep machine, put your bag through the X-ray conveyor belt, and then you may even get an additional rub down with those weird hand-held beep beep devices also.

It was a bit ridiculous to say the least. One time for example, we wanted to go into a Carrefour supermarket (which is actually a French supermarket...I know, in China - proper globalisation stuff, I'm sorry) but it happened to be in a complex which had a mosque nearby. Therefore, we had to go through the whole checking-we're not-a-terrorist process, and they even demanded to check our passports too. This was one of those moments where all the surveillance really did feel utterly ridiculous - we were just trying to go to a supermarket for goodness sake to buy huge quantities of sugary European snacks! I can understand the logic of these anti-terror measures, if it was in an extremely crowded place where a terror attack was likely to occur and would cause maximum casualties, like a concert or sports game for example. But then later, whilst with Molo, we had another insane moment where we received the entire terrorist-check rigamarole simply to enter a park. A bloody park! There wasn't even anyone inside it, other than a man flying his little pink kite (and not doing a great job of it, bless him. Not that I could do any better). Just crazy. We only wished to go for an afternoon stroll, not blow up the trees and park benches. It was all just a bit silly and hyperbolic if you ask me, but we know all too well that it's essentially an excuse to heighten police presence in order to expand The People's Republic of China's imperial frontiers and oppress any minority groups that wish otherwise. It's poo, and we were very excited to finally leave Xinjiang to hopefully see the end of such poo.

To be fair, once we had finally left the Xinjiang border and entered a new province, Gansu, it *didn't* stop being poo. The police-state situation was still poor, and it still felt like a totalitarian dictatorship (oh wait, that's because it is one).

Geographically speaking, by this point we had cycled the equivalent of the entire width of India, and only just entered another province. I still had to cycle that distance two times over again, until I got to Beijing. We were actually very close to the border with Mongolia at this point, and hence so close to the Gobi Desert. It was almost a combination of the Central Asian desert and the Central Asian mountains in one, because sometimes we would have lots of climbing and at other times it would be extremely flat for weeks on end. Regardless, it was still very barren and there wasn't much life around us at all.

But at one point, in Gansu province, we reached a high plateau where we had climbed up to over 1000m and had gotten to a flat expanse. It was late November and we were slowly crawling into the height of midwinter. Thus, the snow came down from the sky, slowly but surely. It was peculiar, that at the time a "snow day" meant something very different to what it used to mean to me, back when I was a child. Back then, in the good old days, a snow day was a magical prospect, a glorious opportunity and a day filled with fun loving snow. Essentially, it would mean a day off school, where you could freely frolic in the delights of lots of compacted

159

water molecules in a solidified state, otherwise known as snow. But something you probably, if not definitely wouldn't have experienced, is what a snow day meant to us at that point in time. For during that period, we were not at school, and were in fact cycling through China, towards New Zealand, so the opportunities for building snowmen and having snowball fights were few and far between (although I was tempted to start a snowball fight a few times with the awful Truck Dragons). Instead, snow meant for me danger more than anything, adding further hardship to what was already a pretty difficult challenge in a pretty difficult life - cycling the entire length of the planet.

Although we'd been cycling on the highway, we'd had a giant hard shoulder which had essentially been our very own cycle lane, and It had felt incredibly safe thus far. In fact, the G30 motorway spanning the entire width of China, is one of the safest roads we'd both ever been on, with two lanes on both sides - we thereby very rarely felt endangered by passing cars. Well, that's until winter hit us in full force and the snow came plummeting down from the frozen white sky. Then it became a different story altogether.

The previously safe and sound hard shoulder became but a slippery slide with a sprained elbow waiting to happen, and in avoiding this, in order to cycle on the non-iced surface, I had to move onto the slow lane of the road itself. This, as you can imagine brings its own dangers, considering there are hurtling trucks going 100km an hour, narrowly avoiding you. So, on your right is an icy lane holding the prospect of slipping and hurting yourself, and on your left is the prospect of, well...death. It's not a great choice to choose from, thereby I tried my best to stay safely in between the two, and I neither fell nor died - great job Codz! Gunnar chose to stick to the snowy hard shoulder for want of completely minimising the risk of, well...death. It was probably the most sensible option, although he did slip twice in one day, thankfully not hurting himself all too badly. Yes, I didn't slip nor die, but the likelihood of me slipping under the wheel of a truck was much greater than usual on these, no longer magical, snow days of new. And this had been a point of contention between me and Gunnar, resulting in a discussion one night about whose snow-day-cycling-position was right or wrong. We concluded that neither was right, nor wrong, as such, but that *my* choice was much more life threatening at least.

This opened a whole new can of worms, and catalysed many different offshoots of the conversation, into our philosophical thoughts on danger, death and our overall spiritual beliefs. Gunnar suggested that he was generally conservative in the way he approached life, and wanted to minimize risk where possible, thus he chose to ride in the snowy hard shoulder, and this does make perfect sense, right? During my turn, I had to discuss why I chose the path with maximum risk of fatality, and this was certainly a strange thing to do - in turn, revealing a lot of things about myself that I didn't previously understand.

Danger - being a scenario that could lead to death, and death - being the cessation of one's physical body. That's my understanding anyway. And with this understanding in mind, I'm not scared of death, which thereby means that I'm not scared of danger, because of course why would I fear the cause of an effect I'm simply not scared of. But this is only the case due to my spiritual beliefs.

I believe that we *have* a body, yes, it's somewhat impossible to deny that, but just like a lightbulb, the outer casing is not the *only* part of it. The lightbulb has glass to keep its shape, but really it only serves to allow electricity to pass through it. I feel that it's the same with us. The lightbulb has the glass body, but the most important aspect is the electric current which makes it glow, and likewise, us as humans have a body, but we also have our own electric current which I'd call "spirit" - and it's that which makes us live and glow too. I believe that this part of us doesn't ever die, just like when the lightbulb falls and smashes, the glass shell may be dead, but the electricity has just gone elsewhere. Electricity can't die - it is energy, and energy can't be given or taken (so said Einstein who was a pretty bright bloke) it just changes form, goes back to the void - the nothingness and anythingness. So, in keeping with the original analogy, when our physical body dies, our spirit does not, it just goes back to the void, ready to be catapulted into the next form which needs life. And that, I guess, is why I was cycling in the lane of the highway during our snow days of new, because I know that "*I*" will never truly die. And after all, although we didn't have a referee for the discussion to decide who was right or wrong – the proof was in the pudding, because Gunnar fell twice and I didn't fall once (I'm honestly not competitive at all...honestly!).

Danger has never really scared me during my lifetime, hence my many injuries as a child doing silly things that one probably shouldn't be doing. And clearly, I still don't have much fear of danger, possibly because of my spiritual beliefs, but maybe because of other factors. Me and Gunnar discussed what those might be: maybe due to my innate personality type, being very outgoing and adventurous, or because of my age - as I'm still quite young, I may still be suffering from the "invincibility complex", where kids think that they are indestructible. It's probably all these things put together and also being in a position where you're not supporting a family - kind of means you have less to lose. Of course, dying would still be a massive loss, as in the rest of my life, but in terms of not having a wife and children, it may have been a factor making things less of a scary prospect for me.

Although, when I thought of my mother and how she would react to the loss of my life, it was certainly a sobering thought and one that made me very upset just at the thought of her reaction. The rest of my family, and all of my beautiful friends would likely feel a similar level of pain, and it was these thoughts which made me act considerably more carefully in life and forced me to be more conscientious to avoid unnecessary danger and unnecessary death. It was hard though, because this trip was intrinsically dangerous, in and of itself. Cycling across the world is not easy by any means, and avoiding danger is almost impossible, mostly because you spend the majority of your life on a road, and in uncharted territories with unknown cultures and peoples. The most dangerous points were probably the long dark tunnels and these snow days of new. So, although it was absolutely stunning with white laden hill tops, and snow-capped mountains as we descended down huge declines, with the Great Wall of China to our left - it was still, unavoidably a cycling scenario which brought forth the highest likelihood of death.

Although the G30 motorway became increasingly dangerous due to the snow, it was our only option because the other option, the G312 was far, far worse. We'd tried it before, and with only one lane going in each direction, it made for some incredibly hairy moments when an oncoming truck would overtake another oncoming truck and you'd then have two fire-breathing-truck-dragons hurtling towards you with unthinkable velocity. Plus, the amount of traffic was much more than the G30, so we decided to abandon that road, completely disregarding it entirely as being a possible option - meaning that we'd continue to have to illegally sneak onto the highway.

Usually we had next to no issues when sneaking ourselves through the tollbooths. Every time we came off the highway to sleep in a town, we would have to re-enter through a tollbooth the next day, where cars pay for access. We'd had quite a few people shout at us telling us to stop, which we conveniently didn't hear (wink wink) nor act upon and had only one unfortunate moment where the police redirected us. But never, not once, did we have someone stop us forcefully with their own might, until "The Wall".

Gunnar re-named this man "The Great Wall of China" due to his epic grasp on preventing things to pass through him. Quite akin to the real Great Wall, we concluded that he could have probably kept out an entire invading Mongol army solely on his own. So, we had slept in a town called Yongchang, and over breakfast we had made our usual plan to sneak onto the G30, for it was still the safest road. When police told us it was not safe, we would usually tell them that they didn't have a clue where's safe to

The Full Power Bike Ride

cycle, but that we did, having cycled so bloody much. As usual, we hit the road, the toll being 5km down the line. The wind was on our backs and we had built up a good pace, so the 5km went by in no time, and boom, there was the toll to the right, so off we went. But shit, it was up a hill.

These were the worst tolls, for you can only approach them slowly because that's simply the only pace you can go uphill on a fully loaded bike - there are no medium or fast options unfortunately when climbing. Along with this, they had a long time to spot us and react accordingly to stop us from entering the strictly forbidden motorway. But the majority of the time they just panicked, not having a clue what to do with cyclists (because no other cyclists in China would ever try to be on the motorway, because they were not nutcases like us), and they usually just ended up staying in their little booth and meagrely shouting for us to stop.

But on this unexpected occasion, it couldn't have been any more different. We were inching towards the toll booth from all the way at the bottom of the hill, still a long way from the barriers which we'd planned to slip seamlessly through, and the door of the booth was opened aggressively. "Oh golly gosh, what is this?!" I thought to myself. The rest all happened in what felt like a split second, as the man came charging out of his booth and stood firmly in the gap between the barrier and the wall, with his arms fully spread either side of him - showing that his intention was to block, block and block. Not for one minute did I think he was seriously going to stand in the way of us indefinitely, especially considering that we were now moving at a decent speed, reaching the top of the hill. I thought he would move in the last second as we approached the barrier, and then we could just zip straight past him onto the highway, victorious. Yeah, of course the police would have got called to come tell us to get off, but this happened every time and we knew how to deal with it by now, and most of the time they would let us continue, because they also knew it was safer than the other road.

But not the Great Wall, it was his job to stop us and it was his job he was always going to do, even if it was the last thing he would ever do. He stood there, slightly fat (but to be fair, this is advantageous when acting as a wall) and he stood and stood without budging an inch, even when I was a couple metres away telling him to move. In fact, he not only successfully blocked me but also managed to push me over to the side, almost making me fall off my bike entirely. I was shocked. "What the hell?!" I said to him a couple times, but then I realised he couldn't understand it, although I'm sure he understood the tone. I wasn't angry, just seriously shocked. And he didn't seem angry at me either, even though I basically ran into him with my bike. He had only a look of sheer pride on his face that he had sufficiently been a noble Great Wall of China and protected the all-important law of the People's Republic. Bloody hell, he had won the battle fair and square, and there was nothing else to say or do at that point, other than to bow my head in shame and take the other road - the infamous, ominous G312.

Well, after all that heightened drama, it turned out that the G312 wasn't all too bad, and probably the better option for this part of the journey anyway. Gunnar had a front-row-seat perspective of the whole morning ordeal and said he'd found the battle with The Wall to be utterly hilarious, and once I'd gotten over my shock and adrenaline rush, I shared the same opinion. It really was so ridiculous and funny of a thing to happen on a Thursday morning. Fair play, The Great Wall scored a point for Chinese authorities but at that moment we were still winning the motorway rebellion game 10-2 and were completely thrashing them, so really it was merely a consolation goal and we didn't care about it. At least that man will grow old happily, knowing that he is the one and only human Great Wall of China. Fair play to him.

So, on we went, on our new road which we both felt more comfortable on. Turned out that the following day we had a humongous climb up to 3000m where the highway had two long tunnels which would have been super-duper dangerous. So, it ended up that the wall man did us a big favour and did keep us in a safer position - so, cheers for that mate!

As an afterthought, after mentioning the Human Great Wall of China, I guess I should speak a little about the actual Great Wall of China too. We were cycling right next to it for a long time without even noticing. We visited the westernmost point of the Great Wall which was impressive but quite touristic and modern. But at times, we would see a long something going up and down the hills continuously and it was only when Gunnar pointed it out, we realised that it was *the* Great Wall itself. All the glorious images of the wall on Google are quite recently renovated parts near Beijing, hence why it's in perfect condition. It's more of a tourist attraction than a historic masterpiece of literal blood, sweat and innumerable tears. But in the far west of the wall, where we were, it was a kind of nondescript mud mound, just about still alive. This part of the wall was over 2,000 years old and although it wasn't as stunning as the Google images, to me it was much more epic - because it was the original, and not just a replica. At one point, we cycled straight through the middle of it, as they had to cut a hole in it, in order to build a road through the middle. On the one hand, it was a shame they cut that hole, but on the other hand it's pretty amazing to be able to say that I cycled *through* the Great Wall of China, as if I was some ethereal cycling ghost.

Chapter Eighteen

The Only White Men in the Village

We had another hilarious moment that morning, the same day as the toll booth drama, prior to the big climb. All we wanted to do was to get a couple of drinks from the village shop, in order to get some liquids inside of our bodily systems before all our water inevitably froze.

Just to focus on the cold thing for a little bit here - who would have thought that mainland China would be so excruciatingly cold? Not me! At times, in the mountains, it got down to -18 degrees Celsius, which is just ridiculous. To illustrate this level of coldness, imagine your eyelashes being at such a freezing state that they start gluing together, sticking your eyes shut - because this is what happened to us! I literally had to keep pulling my eyelids apart to unstick my icy glued eyelashes, in order to keep my eyes open. I'm not sure if you've cycled much before but having your eyes open is quite imperative. For the first time ever in my life this frozen eyelash phenomenon started to happen, and hopefully for the last time in my life too. The moisture from the air or our breath froze on our facial hair and our heads just ended up as one big snowball - very strange! The worst of all, was going downhill at a fast pace and having headwind, ripping fiercely through our layers of clothing. At this point, in this sheer extent of coldness, there's not all too much one can do to guard against it, other than of course not being a nutter in the first place and deciding to cycle across the face of the planet.

And our water, the very stuff keeping us alive and moving, would quite quickly transform from its nourishing, refreshing liquid state into a useless block of solidness faster than you could say "ice". Even my trusty CamelBak would freeze to a point of uselessness. The hose connector which I drank from would just harden and solidify, but sometimes if I tucked it under my armpit, my body temperature would keep it unfrozen and useable. Pretty gross though, right? Even parts of our bikes were freezing! Sometimes, going uphill, my gear shifter would get stuck and I realised that it was due to a block of ice forming around the shifting component rendering it stuck, so we'd frequently have to stop and dislodge the ice to free up its moving capacity.

But being in the height of winter in Western China wasn't all tears and numb extremities (although it *was* mostly that). We got a little bit of consolation considering the novel beauty of seeing frozen waterfalls in mid-fall, the icicles slowly dripping, and what would usually be powerful free-flowing rivers, stopped frozen still by high winter in all its might. Everything was thick and solid, and it made for quite a white sight, to say the least. But it was hard for us to enjoy these things when we were in utmost pain - but we managed it.

So, on our way into the shop to buy non-frozen liquids, we must have picked the absolute worst ten minutes to pass through that town for it must have been break time from school for all the kids, and we found ourselves surrounded by innumerable little nippers all gawking at us wide-eyed, not having any idea as to who we were or what the hell we were doing in their tiny town. There was a huge mob of kids by the end, when Gunnar was in the shop buying the drinks. They had their heads pushed against the door of the shop seeing what he was doing inside, and they were so excited that they were almost breaking down the door. This certainly must be what it feels like to be famous.

We quite frequently alluded to a running joke from Little Britain, the comedy sketch show, where there's a gay man, Gavin, who lives in a tiny Welsh village and quite enjoys being "the only gay in the village" - and when he is introduced to another gay in the village, he gets very angry because he's lost his USP. And this situation was quite akin to our own, but instead - in relation to our whiteness. I know this is a strange line of thought but bear with me.

We had shared a sobering thought after being mobbed by the kids, that we really could be the first ever white people that a young Chinese child in a sleepy remote town may have ever seen in their entire life so far. Some of these villages really were so small and quiet that there is absolutely no reason to visit them as a tourist, because nothing at all is happening there in a touristic sense, therefore no tourists go - apart from cycle tourists, because we have no choice other than to pass through everywhere big or small, interesting or not. This is one of the major benefits of cycle touring for me, as you get to see everywhere and not just the major tourist attractions, but you can also pass through some incredibly non-descript quiet places too. And in those places, the locals really are shocked to see you - and rightly so, what the hell are we doing there? And what the hell are we doing in general? We didn't really know ourselves!

We stopped stationary in a village at one point and shared the thought of "how many cycle tourists do you think have passed through here?" And the collective answer was not many, if any at all. China is different to Central Asia in that regard, because it's just so flipping huge in scale, and there are such an innumerable multitude of roads to choose from. In contrast to Tajikistan for example, in the Pamir Mountains, yeah the kids were still excited to see us because we looked and acted differently to them, but in the summer, it is full of cycle tourists, all taking the same one road - the Pamir Highway, so the sight of us wasn't all too shocking.

Yet in China, there are just so many routes and options with the roads that it already reduces the amount of cyclists passing through villages, let alone the fact that generally much fewer people cycle through Western China anyway because they think it's far too challenging (rightly so), and they just fly to Thailand or suchlike instead. We met many cyclists in the Pamirs who just skipped China entirely.

So, with this in mind, we really could have been the first Westerners that these young children had *ever* seen. And this explains their absolute awe at the very sight of us: the fascination with our eyes, our clothes and even our earrings. Me and Gunnar both had an earring in each ear, which we wore for swag and "because we are total badasses" in the words of Gunnar, (in his thick American accent) but to them it was such an alien phenomenon, because surely only girls wear earrings, no? We had times in supermarkets where the mum would point us out to the child by slapping them enthusiastically on the back of the head, and the kid's jaw would drop in utter bewilderment and shock, along with much subsequent pointing and giggling. Sometimes entire villages came out of their homes simply to stare at us and work out what on earth we were, and whether we do even come from Planet Earth itself. The parallel to aliens was sometimes somewhat fitting.

The celebrity comparison though is not necessarily so accurate. Gunnar suggested that it's more like people staring at an exotic animal like a panda or something, working out its behavioural patterns. And in a way I agreed, especially when it came to meal time - because without fail, in the restaurants, whether it be the staff or the customers, they would stare at us very closely, in order to study how we used the chopsticks. They were crazily fascinated at our ability to use their domestic eating utensils. It's as if they were watching monkeys in a zoo, who for the first time were trying to use a toothbrush to brush their teeth. They didn't realise that we do actually use chopsticks back home when we eat at Asian restaurants, or the fact that we'd already been in China for two months by that point, and had managed to not die due to lack of food in our mouths, due to not knowing how to use chopsticks. They watched ever so intently as if it was our very first time, all collectively giggling under their breath, waiting for us to screw up. It was nerve-wracking as if performing a song on stage to millions, and we always got butterflies during mealtime, in front of our village audience. Usually they would just come over and hand us a spoon, even though we were doing just fine with the chopsticks. We often entertained the thought of us doing this back home to a Chinese person in a fast food restaurant and handing them a pair of chopsticks to eat their McDonald's cheeseburger with. For sure we'd be called racist if we did that, but not in China, the other way around. Yeah, it's not malicious for sure, just uber curious, but it still doesn't remove the race element, that our race really was the odd one out there.

It's funny that we both never thought we'd be in that position. For white, middle class men in the West, it's very hard to be the subject of any finger pointing or abuse, and you can blend in easily. But not there, certainly not. It's lucky that we are both drama queens and love the attention, because otherwise it could've been a bit overwhelming and one would wish to crawl up into a ball in the corner of the restaurant if they are naturally shy. Luckily, we were not, although I must say, the whole being-stared-at-the-entire-way-through-your-meal thing, was not so enjoyable to begin with, but like anything - you get used to it. After a while, I became a little bit too used to it, to the extent that it was simply a sign that all was in order and the universe was working just fine. If I ate a meal in China and somebody wasn't staring at me and analysing how I used chopsticks, then it was a sure sign that something big was wrong and broken. I felt that it would be very strange to be in a country where this wasn't the norm, and that I maybe wouldn't be able to eat properly again without the staring. Luckily this wasn't an issue, but yeah, we *were* surely seen as obscure tropical animals on bikes, in some senses.

However, sometimes it really did feel like we were seen as celebrities too. On one day I had to post some Christmas letters back to the UK for my family, and it was a bit of an ordeal, so it ended up with a female member of staff from the "postal bank" escorting me to the actual post office to send the letters. It was

171

quite a sight, us two, with me towering over her tininess as we walked together on our letter mission. We happened to pass a bunch of schoolgirls, who as per usual looked surprised by my very being there, but as they passed they let out a collective group squeal of giddiness, the type only heard in relation to boy bands and Justin Bieber. It was undeniably a reaction of "oh my god! Did you see him? Oh golly" (obviously in Mandarin) and even the bank worker seemed to have felt indirectly complimented by being with me. I didn't feel flattered however, because I know full well that I'm a normal looking bloke back home and no supermodel, but there my foreignness in and of itself, was enough to make the schoolgirls blush. So, in a way, we also felt like famous pop stars sometimes. All in all, I guess the most accurate way to describe it is that - cycling through China as a Westerner, you're likely to feel like a famous popstar panda.

Back from the tangent to the actual cycling narrative - Gunnar and I shared an interesting experience one evening, in the middle of China, trying to get to a hotel. A combination of dark setting in earlier than usual, only being able to stay in certain tourist hotels, and forgetting to charge our bike lights created this experience. We were right in the midst of one of our huge distance days, which had become the norm, and it was only when it became dark did we realise that our lights weren't working. Before it got dark, this obviously wasn't an issue, but now that the sun was hiding its body from this part of the world, it suddenly became one. Things were fine for a while, still feeling moderately safe while the sun still left glimmers of its last rays, and as the car's headlights came on, we could see them, and they could see us. But just like everything in life, this was impermanent. Soon, the dark got darker, until the horizon was black and lifeless. All was still fine, until we realised that we had forthcoming a huge descent, zigzagging down the mountainside before we could arrive at our hotel. Uh oh, now this could certainly be an issue.

So, we'd descended at night before, but of course with our lights on, like any sane human being. But even still, even with these little illumination devices, descending is a whole different ball game in the dark. Writing this brings me back vividly to the time I nearly went flying full pelt into the side of a cow in Kyrgyzstan one night. The cow couldn't see me, because it was a cow...and they happen to be hopelessly haphazard when crossing roads, and I couldn't see it either, despite having lights. Because until you're in that situation, you can't fully know that the side-profile of a strolling bovine mammal doesn't have any reflective properties at all. But yeah, turns out it doesn't, and that cows aren't particularly reflective animals in the slightest. So, I nearly went flying into the side of it very, very full power - literally.

Imagine, if that was *with* lights, the risks of us descending *without* lights, were far greater. We had no choice, it was far too cold to camp up there at the summit, and our hotel was just down at the bottom, really not too far in terms of distance, but we just had to be oh so careful in getting down to it. We were incredibly tentative, inching slowly down the hill. The bends of the mountain were only revealing themselves at the last minute, so we couldn't approach them too quickly as we risked flying straight off the side of the mountain. Occasionally a car would go past, but they didn't really cause any problems. Gunnar was in front, but suddenly, he must have seen me whizz past him speedily which must have come as a great shock. He shouted something about me being crazy, and I shouted back for him to follow my lead. I had a plan, and I was about to execute it.

Luckily, one of the vehicles that went past was a huge truck, of which must have been holding some valuable contents, for it was also very careful in its descent. This was perfect for us, because it meant that if we went fast enough, we could surf the back of it, by cycling very close behind - gaining the benefit of seeing the road clearly with his bright red backlights, and also just following his turns thereby knowing where the corners were. It was incredible! It had the added benefit of blocking all the wind because we were so close to it, therefore we ended up going very fast down the hill, and comparatively very safely in contrast to our situation before. The only downside was that we were entirely obligated to go as fast as possible to keep up with the truck in order to retain our gains, and not end up back to square one. I didn't look around once, because the descent required my absolute attention at absolutely every single moment to stay safe and alive, so therefore I thought Gunnar must have dropped back. It was only once we'd successfully finished the descent, that I turned around and saw him a few inches behind me, surfing me, surfing the truck. Boom! We smashed it! And did so safely. But oh my, the adrenaline was sky high, and one can only know the feeling of being glad to have survived, after going through something as risky as that.

That night, we couldn't find the hotel that we'd pushed ourselves so hard to reach. It's difficult to feel as frustrated as we did at that moment. So tired, so cold, and simply needing to sleep - yet having no place to do so within. We went into a little shop to ask for the nearest hotel, where they proclaimed that they *themselves* were actually a hotel, as well as a shop. We were gleeful to receive such news, and we could've fallen into a deep sleep there and then, probably even while we were stood up. But now came the price. "How much?" we asked, in Chinese, although it was one of the only terms we knew in Mandarin, because it's one of the most important - in all countries for that matter. The husband looked at the wife, and they had a strange exchange where she suggested something and he bit back at her almost aggressively, as to say "that's far too cheap, let's get a little bit more out of these rich white guys".

We could smell the situation from a mile away, and they weren't even discreet, as they didn't quite realise that we were travellers and not tourists, and that being on the road for ten months straight, ensured that we had our heads screwed on for matters such as these. A *tourist* is someone who flies from place to place, sees the main attractions, stays in the big cities, and experiences the country as an outsider. Whereas, a *traveller*, especially a bicycle traveller, witnesses all places big and small, eats with the locals, sleeps with the locals (not in that sense, you dirty minded people! I

174

mean in the literal sense, of sleeping in bunk beds with local truckers, or sleeping in the toilets of a truckstop) where you would never find a tourist. You experience the country from an insider's perspective - sharing the local's lifestyle. Yet time and time again, people confused us with straight-up tourists and tried to charge us an arm and a leg. We'd been there before, and we will certainly be there again at some point.

So, it didn't come as much of a surprise when their price was way too high. We just chuckled at them, shaking our heads, showing that this was a ludicrous asking price. Using Google translate at this point (our Chinese wasn't at a point where we could barter effectively) we told them that their price was far too expensive and that we could only pay half of that price, maximum. They agreed straight away, without flinching, and knew they were in the wrong by being that cheeky in the first place. Many times by then we'd been able to slash the asking price considerably in a split second, showing that the initial price must have been a long shot. To be fair, China was pretty good with people charging the same amount for locals and travellers alike. Regardless of the colour of your skin, if the meal costs £1, they will charge you £1, even if you look like you may have more money to your name. The irony is, most of the time we really didn't have more money to our name than they did, especially in the cities. Maybe our countries did, or our families may, but we personally were poorer in monetary value than most of those people. Yet, of course, our opportunities and scope on a global scale were much greater for us to even be cycling through their village in the first place, and for that I am extremely grateful.

So, China had been generally okay with prices, but in Central Asia it was very common to leave a shop with a feeling that you'd just paid a lot more than what the items were worth. With no prices written on the products, the shopkeeper is thereby free to make them up as they go along, but they walk a thin rope as they can't make it too obvious that they are ripping you off. So even though you know he's imagining a more expensive price on the spot, the multiplication of your currency to theirs being by the thousands, makes it very hard to convert the price quickly enough to argue your corner. Generally, I just paid the price, and later worked out that they had slightly taken the micky. Oh well, you win some, you lose some. But in this case, we won, and paid a decent price for a decent night's sleep, although the room was nearly as cold as outside. Like I said, you win some and you lose some.

Going to sleep that night, I couldn't help but consider how lucky we were to have not fallen or collided with anything. But speaking of falling and colliding, it hadn't been all plain sailing. Of course, I'd had my fair share of falling off a bike in the past, most famously when I was an eleven-year-old and a car essentially ran over my head after I fell into the road off my BMX bike. If I'd have been a few inches further to the right then that would have been an early game-over for me, but obviously it wasn't my time to go. I learnt to be much more cautious after that experience, but naturally you let some complacency slip in as time goes by, enough to allow another fall to happen. The most recent bad one being at university, going downhill, no-handed in the rain (I know, flipping stupid) and colliding with the road so hard that I dislocated my left shoulder, which took a meaty chunk out of my right knee that looked as if someone had spooned out a part of my flesh. But luckily no car was behind me, and once again I came out lucky.

Nothing as severe had happened on this trip, apart from a few minor falls, but it was nice to know that I wasn't the only one that makes errors, for Gunnar also made a few himself. But the two that happened in my company, happened to involve colliding with people - Chinese people. To contextualize, cycling through any Chinese city is an absolute nightmare for a cyclist, and although they usually have a "cycle lane", it is absolutely overrun by these awful meddling mopeds and little electric bikes and scooters and all sorts of moving objects which aren't cars, but also aren't bikes! They make the entire affair an absolute hardship. If you go in the road, you have the awful Motor Monsters to deal with - buses overtaking taxis, taxis overtaking buses, and the odd boy-racer going way too ridiculously quick. They are not prepared to spot a cyclist and they don't even care if they do see you, they will pull out and endanger your life regardless. But if you want to risk the bike lane instead, you have to battle through the hundreds of scooters dangerously weaving in and out of you from all angles, with a bunch going in the wrong direction also, just creating a load of awful factors. The amount of beeping horns was enough to bring a headache to anyone, and the sounds and smells of hundreds of engines was bloody intense. So, bear this in mind when considering Gunnar's collisions.

It got to a point where I was a fricking expert at surviving in these situations and getting through a manic inner-city quite rapidly. You have to meet them at their own level and play them at their own game - in a doggy dog world, sometimes one must act like a big barking Rottweiler and be abrupt and rude in your driving also, in order to not get smashed into. Yet, Gunnar, being more conservative in nature and trying to keep up with me, ended up in a couple of bad situations. One of them happened after a bus pulled out in front of him to pick up some passengers, cutting him off and acting as a hazard - therefore his thinking was to skirt around the right of it before the passengers got off. But alas, in perfect timing, a lady got off the bus as soon as he passed the bus door and boom, he hit into her. All in all, they both were relatively unharmed, just a tad shocked.

The same thing happened the very next day, when he skirted around the right side of a parked car in a bus stop, and boom, a surprise opening of the door, in perfect timing left him flying towards the floor and knocking over a lady's fruit stall. This time however, he *was* harmed, and he suffered a nasty bruise on his leg. He didn't stick around long enough to see what damage he'd inflicted on her brand-new car door, but ultimately, it *was* her fault for not looking when she slammed it open. I didn't see either of the incidents first-hand for I was in front whizzing past hazards myself, but always on the left-hand side, because I knew this could happen, from already having cycled through huge cities like Paris and Istanbul.

I took the piss a few times about him being a dodgy cyclist and being haphazard, which we both found funny because the irony rang loudly, considering that I'm one of the worst cyclists alive for agility. This irony was well illustrated a week or so later, when I fell off my bike trying to headbutt a passing branch of a tree. Yes, that's right, you'd read it correctly the first time. If you needed any more proof that I'm a weirdo, then, there you have it. Well, it's not *that* strange, I mean, it's actually a rather fun game that I'd invented.

The game's rules are as follows: you pass a bunch of branches on your bike and you headbutt as many of them as possible (with your helmet on of course) and the amount of branches that you successfully headbutt without hitting yourself in the face, is the amount of points you score. So, I thought that I was rather brilliant at it, considering I'm the creator of the game, but it turns out that it can be very dangerous.

Me and Gunnar were in mid-conversation, and out of nowhere, a perfect headbuttable-branch came into my vision a few inches ahead, and without even thinking, my natural reaction was to hit it with my helmet and win a point for myself. Unfortunately, multitasking with speaking and headbutting branches and cycling all at the same time must have been too much for the frontal cortex of my brain to comprehend, and the cycling part was compromised, as I accidentally mounted the nearby curb to my left, and thereby slow-motion fell to my right dramatically, as if I was a stunt double straight out of Hollywood. To avoid hurting myself too much, I had to perform an equally dramatic barrel roll for several turns and eventually laid there, still and stiff in the middle of the path. Luckily, this time we really were on a *legitimate* cycle path with only bikes and we were the only ones there, so the accident was in a safe place at least. I looked up and Gunnar was absolutely bent over in hysterics, having found it oh so funny, even though he didn't understand how on earth I'd managed to go from cycling normally in a straight line to barrel rolling off my bike like James Bond. Of course, I had to tell him about my secret little game and his laughter grew even louder and stronger henceforth for many minutes more.

Okay, so it was actually quite embarrassing and it led to me not being able to make any more comments about his collisions, and I subsequently banned myself from ever playing that game again during the Full Power Bike Ride for health and safety reasons. But I still continued to get that strange giddy childish feeling I used to get before I banned myself, when I saw some perfect branches up ahead, longing to give them a good solid headbutt, so I'd have to stop myself at the last second. You could've compared me to a heroin addict coming off heroin, I guess? Oh well, I survived.

Chapter Nineteen

The Longing for Greenery

Gunnar sporadically made clear his longing to get back to a landscape of greenery and living nature. It hadn't yet dawned on me that we had essentially been cycling through desert landscape, since way back in Azerbaijan. So for four months straight, since August in Azerbaijan until December in central China, we had been in the midst of a dry and barren landscape with very little living things surrounding us: a lack of mammals, a lack of green trees, a lack of anything really living at all - even a lack of people. Of course this is natural, for when an environment has the harsh extremes of being either extremely cold or extremely hot, it doesn't make for a particularly easy place to live and thrive (and you can extend this further to it not being a particularly easy place to cycle through either).

The Pamir Mountains were in a way a nice rest for the eyes from the extreme flat planes we'd adapted to, for it made for a much more interesting view, but as Gunnar rightly pointed out - it was still desert, technically speaking. It may have been mountainous, but still incredibly lifeless (in terms of biodiversity). I hadn't really dwelled on this fact, because I take things as they come and was clearly stimulated enough by changing culture, cuisine, and everything else to not notice the homogeneity of our environment. But Gunnar had certainly noticed, and it was beginning to eat away at his nerves. Frequently his mind would wander off into a dreamlike state, considering getting further south so that he could finally see green trees once again. He suggested that this largely stemmed from the lush green mountainous forests that he was used to, having grown up in the north-west state of Oregon in the USA. And it was only once we started speaking about the matter did it also start to affect me, and looking around, I also started to miss trees and greenery and it was quite an upsetting realisation, that the place we were in was quite lifeless and boring. This sullen mood continued for a solid week or so.

But suddenly, one day cycling in the hills, things started to get a bit more scenic and eye-pleasing. We passed through a very small settlement, turned a corner, looked upwards and lo behold! - the entire hillside was full of lush evergreens, creating a sea of green beauteous flora. It evoked a peculiar feeling in us both, and I never thought that I would ever feel *that* happy to see trees for goodness sake, but it really was a wonderful sight. It marked a pleasant checkpoint for us, that we had dealt with the highest altitude we would have to endure in China, so now we were on the downward straight into a lower altitude, closer to sea level - meaning less cold and more nature! It was a pleasant moment for us both.

Cycling with Gunnar was an absolute pleasure, from the moment we met in Portistan at the beginning of our chapter with the Camel Crew, until the moment we left each other in Xi'an, Central China. Xi'an had always been our planned separation point, as the ancient imperial capital was the end of the Silk Road, and thereby resembled the end of our time together. It was also a good location for Gunnar to start heading south to Thailand, and for me to continue east towards Korea. Our friendship and conversations had been good during the Camel Crew days for sure, but naturally, being seven of us meant that it was a different relationship to when it became just him and I, one to one, all day every day, in the desert. This breeds a very special type of relationship, if the two people click. If they don't click, and end up in conflict, then it can be the worst type of relationship. So, these set of circumstances can lead to a very bad situation together, or a very good one, and luckily, we were on the pleasant side of the spectrum. Of course, we had our minor disputes, or certain little things we didn't totally agree on, but in general, we were both very glad to have had one another for company all the way throughout Western China.

Even together, China was one of the most troublesome countries to cycle through, in terms of authorities, language barriers and harsh wintery conditions. I can only begin to imagine how much harder all these things would have been if we were completely alone. Luckily, being together meant that we could jump these hurdles usually with a smile on our face, with intermittent giggling. It wasn't infrequent that we'd be laughing about something, and joking around, which isn't always a natural response when in minus temperatures and constantly being irritated by the totalitarian police state, but we did very well. And it wasn't a relationship that was *only* about joking around, for Goondog has a sense of depth to him which stretches deep below the surface level, allowing him to consider and reflect upon issues which take a level of astuteness and attention to detail. We shared many similar philosophical beliefs and were interested in similar spiritual traditions, which thereby stimulated conversation. As time went on, we became closer and closer, to the point where he started to adopt certain British idiosyncrasies of mine, and vice versa. I taught him all the verses to Robbie Williams' "Angels" and he taught me the verses to "I Want It That Way" by the Backstreet Boys, and I can't think of a more valuable exchange possible from an American and a Brit abroad.

So, considering this, you can imagine the inevitable struggle of saying goodbye to someone who you've spent every waking hour with, and every sleeping hour with also, for two months straight. We traversed thousands of kilometres side by side, witnessed every breath of each other, and even every fart (if they were loud enough to hear that is). We had a pleasant last few days together, going to see the incredible Terracotta Warriors (which were utterly mind blowing, considering that someone went to those extreme measures of building an entire earthen army, simply to protect themselves in the afterlife), went to a Chinese opera, and then had a final party the night before our separation where we found some interesting alternative locals who took us to an underground techno party - which was superb!

So, spirits were high, but nonetheless it was a challenging goodbye and a sense of sadness was present. Of course, this is natural, as social animals, separating from a friend is always difficult. But I think I can speak on behalf of both of us, when I say that half of the feeling of sadness came from leaving a new friend, and the other half came from the realisation of imminent aloneness, of which isn't necessarily "loneliness", but certainly aloneness was now on the cards. Having been in company for what was now five months, the prospect of cycling alone was a strange one.

Luckily, I enjoyed my own company and think that I'm a very obscure and comical person to be around, because otherwise the separation would've been even harder. And in some ways, cycling alone is actually better as you can culturally and socially find out more about a country as you're more inclined to meet local countryfolk when alone, compared to when you're in the company of other travellers.

It's also an opportunity to introspect and look inward in order to learn more about oneself, and I certainly did this after leaving Gunnar - which I'm glad for having done. At the end of the day, everything in existence is impermanent: all friendships, relationships, objects, feelings and emotions are essentially fleeting and will one day leave. Cycle touring definitely teaches you this lesson in regard to friends, as you have many short but powerful friendships with many people, and then leave them to maybe never see them ever again. I believe that learning this lesson of impermanence is one of the keys to a happy life - and I think that the Buddha would agree (if he could). No matter how *"bad"* something is, it shan't last forever, and no matter how *"good"* something is, it shan't last forever too.

Despite how bad your situation may be, there is always somebody *"worse"* off, and despite how good your situation may be, there will always be someone *"better"* off. Everything is relative. It is all in the mind. Stay humble and stay positive, for it's our choice at the end of the day, is it not?

So, the separation for us both, was somewhat sad but somewhat liberating. Goondog is an incredible character and we made a very good cycling duo if I do say so myself, and I sincerely look forward to seeing him one day at his stoming ground in Oregon.

My very first day back on the saddle after leaving Gunnar wasn't the greatest start to solo cycling again. I'd made an absolute rookie error by leaving my pump in the hostel in Xi'an and I couldn't have been more aptly punished for my incompetence.

It's quite ridiculous sometimes, as to how these things work out. Everything comes together to create a conglomerate of seemingly unrelated events, which turn out to all culminate into one big poo-pie-bonanza. In this case, this particular poo-pie came to the climax due to these factors: having a puncture, having left my pump at the hostel, having separated from Gunnar thereby not being able to use his pump either, having been on the motorway, having been breaking the law by doing so - all in all, leading to me getting caught by the police while I was painstakingly pushing my bike, in the dark, on the hard shoulder of the highway, a mere 1km from the nearest exit. Alas, they beat me this time. The Chinese police finally were victorious over my stubbornness and relentless disobedience. I deserved the defeat and felt like an utmost willy wiener.

It was the second time in the trip that I was forced into a car by authorities, and both times I deserved it. Although luckily it was only for a tiny distance, and hardly cheating because I certainly didn't choose that outcome. They just put my bike in the back, put me in the backseats and drove me to the nearest town. No major drama.

It wasn't the last puncture I got, in fact, I went on a bit of run with getting at least one puncture every day, sometimes two if I hadn't repaired the first properly. It's not the most fun activity to be doing on the side of the road in the freezing cold - that's for sure. A few days after that, I had another strange but scarring experience with the police when I nearly ran over a motionless corpse. Honestly, for a moment I thought I had literally nearly run over a dead body.

Essentially, I was hurtling along in the dark going at quite a decent speed. My plan was to get to Beijing for New Year's Eve, making it for the one-year anniversary of the Full Power Bike Ride. In order to do so, I had to cycle a little bit each night too. I was on the hard-shoulder and I narrowly avoided what I thought was a bag full of rubbish or something. I didn't think much of it, other than it being a bloody dangerous obstruction and that I nearly smashed into it. But a split second later I had the urge to turn around and find out what it actually was. Upon returning to the obstacle, it wasn't a heap of trash after all, but it was a heap of human...what?

I was downright confused, but instantaneously a surge of adrenaline sped through my body, upon thinking that I'd just found a dead body. I rushed to check his pulse to see if he was alive, and thank goodness, he was. That calmed me down a bit, but still I was alarmed by the situation - what the hell was he doing lying in the road? His leg was literally in the middle of the road, and I really didn't know how it hadn't been crushed into tiny pieces by the constant stream of unforgiving Truck Dragons.

I was cautious not to move his body in case he had any serious injuries, so instead I decided to stand in front of him with my flashing lights on, ushering the trucks to go around him to the right. This, ultimately, was putting my own life on the line for the sake of his, and I'm not boasting as if to win some morality competition, like a self-proclaimed Good Samaritan, I'm just saying - the situation was now bloody dangerous for my life, as well as his. I asked a truck to pull over and luckily it did. The driver rang the police, and they eventually arrived. They spoke to him and moved him off the road, and the outcome was that he was just drunk as a skunk, pissed off his head and had fallen into the middle of the road unconscious. Honestly, I don't know how his leg managed to stay in one piece. I was happy to have helped in saving his life, although he was an absolute careless idiot and I was really quite angry at his drunken (and certainly disorderly) self.

Regardless, I moved on into the night, still cycling to Beijing. But luck wasn't on my side that night, because the exact same thing nearly happened again, but this time with a decapitated tree trunk. With the man, I am ever so grateful that I saw him, because if I went flying into the side of him at that speed, there was only one outcome - utmost pain and utmost danger, for him and for me. The same was true for the tree trunk, for if I hadn't seen it in time, I would have truly gone flying over my handlebars into a painful ball of misery - that's for sure. The tree wouldn't have felt much pain, but I certainly would have.

Luckily it was a one off and it didn't reoccur, and days became easier alone as I adapted to the aloneness once more. However, Eastern China wasn't the most pleasant of places on the eye. It is where the majority of the Chinese population live, and with the largest population on the face of the planet, you can only start to imagine how busy that really is. Along with the largest population comes the largest amount of pollution too, and there are factories and fumes in every corner of Eastern China. I even resulted to wearing a face mask to try to curtail the amount of fumes entering my system, although I doubt it helped very much. But when in Rome, do as the Romans do, I guess. But with this in mind, it made it even easier to keep my head down and just keep going towards Beijing.

As planned, I made it there for New Year's Eve and was relieved to have made it to the capital of China in the space of one year. One year to cycle from London to Beijing isn't too bad, although I could've done it much faster and could have done it much slower too. It was just right, and I was happy to be there.

I had a great party with some others from the hostel I was staying in, to celebrate the huge milestone and had a jolly good look around the capital for a few days. There were actually much fewer skyscrapers than I'd imagined for the capital city, but I guess I was naively thinking of the famous cityscape of Shanghai prior. In contrast, the centre of Beijing was full of low buildings and many historical sites, including the world-famous Forbidden City (this was the real one, not the little town that me and Gunnar forced our way into). It was incredible to witness how the Chinese emperors used to live, in unbelievable grandeur. There was also the infamous Tiananmen Square, which became well known due to the deadly 1989 protests that saw tens of thousands of student protestors shot down to their death, due to pro-democracy beliefs. It had a brutally eerie feel to it and was a profound reminder of the potential evils capable of The Chinese Communist Party. But overall, it was an enjoyable city despite the dismal air quality.

Cycling through China was an absolute rollercoaster to say the least, both physically and psychologically. It's a country that lays firmly in my memory as somewhere I really hate, and really love both at the same time. It's an incredibly weird place in that sense, how you can feel so strongly about both extremes, at the same time. "Extreme" was a word and a feeling that I encountered from start to finish of my traversing of the huge landmass of modern-day China. From extreme police presence in Xinjiang as soon as we crossed the border, due to their extreme suppression of the Uyghur Muslims, mixed with the extremely extreme cold temperatures we were forced to endure in mid-winter while climbing mountains, countered by the extreme beauty of traditional Chinese culture and extremely nourishing and tasty cuisine!

I still hold true to the belief that seeing a country by bicycle is the best way, because you are on the ground and at a pace at which you can connect with the locals. But over a land mass this huge in scale, it could become truly unnerving to see such a lack of progress across the map despite putting in everything. In response, Me and Gunnar decided to smash huge days and relentlessly push pedals all day every day regardless of weather conditions and any bureaucratic barriers we faced. We did well, we moved quickly and for the most part kept smiles on our faces. We danced an awful lot, partly to keep warm and partly to celebrate the gift of life. Whenever we took a snack break on the side of the road, we would always do our distinctive "snack dance" which was triggered by our body's excitement for more sugar and insulin. Also, when we were in towns and cities, we would frequently join in with the old Chinese ladies doing their evening dance routines, and it would both warm us up and put a smile on our faces simultaneously. Being in such a harsh environment taught us a lot about ourselves and we definitely grew stronger in the head for sure.

Saying all this, China was still a wondrous land in some respects. The food! Chinese food is famous worldwide and with good reason, for it was always so bloody yummy, naturally rich in vegetables, thereby perfect for a vegetarian, and always so affordable. When you leave a restaurant full, happy and the food having been delicious, yet only having to part ways with one dollar for the entire meal - you naturally can't help but feel happy. The tasty food definitely kept us going along with how hugely different the culture is to our own. You can't help but feel constantly stimulated by these new and exciting features - old ladies all dancing in big groups in the parks to electronic music, little kids staring at us as if we were aliens, and big teddy bears walking around every city. Chuck in a big huge Great Wall to cycle next to, thousands of warriors made from mud, an ancient Forbidden City and you do end up with a very interesting country! Mix this with a myriad of wonderful natural phenomena and China becomes very great in the memory of men!

But then, we must smash these aspects once again with all the awful aforementioned extremes which made it so arduous to cycle through, and then you have a very strange mix of really good and really bad. I guess it's sort of like Marmite, in that you either love it or hate it, but in fact it's hard not to both love it loads and hate it loads at the same time. China left me with many things to think about, but I did my best to summarise it in this small bunch of stanzas:

Taking a Few More Gasps

China, China, China
The place where all roads lead
And also happens to be the place
Where all the seas will reach.

"Made in China",
"Made in China",
Everything is made in China.
This confuses one, when one is young
Really?
How can this be?
My sofa, bed, telephone and even our T.V,
All the clothes on my body,
and every DVD
But when you cycle through the country
This can totally be seen.

Factory, factory, factory
Never have I seen so many factories
Actually,
if we think about it practically
Every machine needs some batteries.

A machine that is 1.4 billion people
Eating, driving, sleeping
The largest country by population
Feeding, fighting, dreaming -
Requires batteries according to the size
of the breathing machine itself.

Hence, in any Chinese city
It's very rare to pass
A group of Chinese people
who aren't all wearing masks.

An inevitable outcome
An invariable conclusion
Of a machine this large,
Taking a few more gasps.

Chapter Twenty

Cycling the Four Rivers of South Korea

After three months in China, cycling from the western border to as far east as I could possibly go - I was ready to leave. 4,500km of cycling on Chinese soil was enough for me, and even if I had wanted to do more, my visa only had a couple of days left on it. It had been a valuable experience, and in some ways, it was amazing, but it was a hectic place in many regards, and I was very ready to move on. I jumped on a boat at the nearest port to Beijing, and after floating over the Yellow Sea, I started my new year, 2019, in South Korea.

I arrived into the port of Incheon, which is essentially the western edge of the capital city, Seoul. But as soon as me and Buddha Bike touched the land of Korea, conflict was already in my face. Typical.

Oh wait...maybe I haven't explained yet, and you're all still thinking that my bike is called Rasta Bike, right? Or maybe some of you may even be considering that I bought an entirely different bike. But no, it is the same bike I left my home on, but he happened to change his religion. It's true, that when we left home, he was a fully blown Rastafarian with long blonde dreadlocks on his handlebars, but with time, he slowly started to shed his dreads one by one, until he became fully bald. This mostly occurred back in China, and it dawned on me that this act of slowly shaving his hair must have been a religious one. It was clear as daylight that he'd changed his faith and converted to Buddhism after spending so long around lovely Buddhist temples, and enjoying the peaceful Buddhist sentiment. Therefore, I bought him some Buddhist prayer beads from a lovely old lady in a Tibetan community in rural China and thus - his name became "Buddha Bike". Anyway, now that that's explained, let's get back to the troublesome situation at hand.

I'd just had to wrestle my painfully heavy, fully loaded aforementioned Buddhist bicycle down four winding flights of stairs to get it down from the boat to the ground, so I was unavoidably worn out. But before I could say "hello Korea!" a port official came striding over to me. In perfect English he said: "please put your bike onto the bus and head towards customs sir". For goodness sake, I should have guessed it: more health and safety bureaucracy forming a hurdle in front of me once more, threatening my only cycling, no vehicles rule.

"I'm afraid that I can't, I'm cycling the whole way to New Zealand and I can't take a bus with my bike…" I attempted, but he butted in and wasn't having any of it. Like always, I'm not quick to give up on my challenges and I fought my corner for as long as possible. He called his boss to ask, and after finishing the phone call he paraphrased the response:

"Basically, my boss said: 'Tell him that if he doesn't want to get on the bus with his bike, then he can get on the next boat straight back to China.'"

Well, okay, screw that - I was not getting deported back to China, especially after how glad I was to leave the crazy country. I tried a couple last-stitch attempts, like asking how much trouble I'd get in if I just point-blank disobeyed him and cycled off there and then, and the answer was dismal - it would have done me no good. So, I begrudgingly obliged and waited for the next stupid bus. It was a three-minute drive and would not have been dangerous at all to cycle, which certainly got on my nerves, but I bit my tongue, took a leaf out of Buddha Bike's book - did some deep breathing and continued with my life.

Essentially, I don't count these blips as failures. If it's forbidden by law to cycle on that land, then it's technically out of bounds and doesn't count - especially if I faced deportation or potential arrest. I always said that I would cycle every inch possible, and that remained the case - the law makes certain parts of land impossible to traverse by two wheels. And my main concern was with my intention - for if I intended to cycle the whole way to New Zealand, then my integrity is retained - but when parts are banned, that's that, with no use for any back-chat. It's quite different to just giving up and getting trains through "hard parts" or hitchhiking south when it gets "too cold". To me, this would be a failure of my mission. But as it stood, it was still all good, and I was still on track to cycling every *possible* inch from England to New Zealand.

Korean customs went fine, although I'm pretty sure the man thought that my souvenir Terracotta Warrior for my dad was a bunch of cocaine, and was slightly upset that it wasn't when he opened it up - no drama for him that day, again. They checked that my double-A batteries weren't for making bombs, and they let me pass freely. Suddenly that strange feeling came to me once more, of being in a totally foreign land of which I knew barely anything about. I didn't understand the Korean language and didn't even have any local currency. It almost felt like starting from scratch once more, having to adapt again, and retain equilibrium in a brand-new nation. So, I had to get started in doing exactly that, no point bumming around.

I had to change some money into Korean Won and find out how to get to the centre of Seoul. I also didn't know where I was staying. I had two Korean friends in total - one I met two summers prior, on a boat to France, and one I met more recently in Beijing - both really lovely fellows. Unfortunately, none of their friends could host me in Seoul, so I had to book a hostel. I was kind of relying on them somewhat to pull through, because my money was running out rapidly, and it was unclear as to when the next opportunity would be for me to rejuvenate some of that money. So being hosted then was more important than ever, because I had to live as cheaply as possible - especially now that I was back in "first world" countries, and people were always warning me about how expensive Korea and Japan are, and they were not fibbing, it really was pricey there. Especially in contrast to China and Central Asia, where you could leave a yummy hearty meal having only spent one pound, to now having to pay at least eight for the equivalent satisfaction.

But alas, no host for me in Seoul, so on I went and booked the cheapest hostel, and on from there - I jumped on Buddha Bike and cycled the 40km into the city centre. The first striking thing I noticed amidst the Korean inner cityscape, was the vast number of buildings with big red crosses above them – "I wonder what they are?" I pondered to myself, whilst cruising through the traffic-ridden streets. They were churches! Many, many churches everywhere I turned my head. It's actually something Gunnar and I heard about whilst in China, that there are a large number of Christians in Korea and that the numbers attending churches have actually risen in recent years. This was a surprise to both of us, but if I hadn't watched that video, it would have really been a shock to see so many churches in the far outer edge of Asia. But I guess it's not so weird, considering that America is equally as far away from Jerusalem as Korea is, and it's globally known how much the Americans love good old Jesus. Maybe it's just because we normally associate far East Asia with Buddhism and temples, that it's strange to see so many seemingly "Western" religious symbols in one place. But that's what's what in Seoul, and it's not right nor wrong - it simply is as it is. I went into one of the churches to charge my phone and they gave me a free tea. Good people, the Korean Christians.

I was recommended to stay in Itaewon, because it was a trendy and international district. Sounded good to me, and, it *was* pretty darn good! I arrived on a Friday evening, so it was bustling from edge to edge. I was surprised to see so many international people, even though I'd had the heads up. The reason for its cosmopolitan vibe is because there is a huge U.S military base nearby and loads of American soldiers used to hang out there. It's continued from that point onwards into the hip and diverse area it is now. But although the neighbourhood was cool, the hostel really was quite bad - but I guess I should have expected that considering it was the cheapest one available. I mean, I've stayed in much worse places, namely my tent or in abandoned buildings and suchlike, but when you're paying money for it you just naturally expect a semi-decent service. And it would have been fine, if it wasn't for the cockroaches in the kitchen, and people frequently waking everyone up at 4.30am for their morning prayer. It was situated quite near the mosque, thereby attracting lots of Muslim guests, many from North-African countries and Arab nations also. They were all sound fellows (other than the one pesky Moroccan dude who was trying to make me fill in his immigration papers in order to stay longer in Korea). Some were particularly kind, like the Egyptian guy in my eight-bed dorm who gifted me with an Egyptian cotton shirt, which was a very kind gift!

The following day I was hoping his kindness would extend even further, because I'd tried to give myself a haircut which I'd done before and it had never previously gone that wrong. I tried doing the back myself, shaving it into a kind of streamline mohawk style, but I made such an awful job of it, the only option I had left was to ask someone for help, otherwise I'd look like an absolute idiot for the foreseeable future. I plucked up the courage and asked him, mostly using charade moves because his English was very minimal. He understood my actions and hesitantly came to help. To begin with, he was kind of shaking and clearly nervous, lacking the usual firm grip of the average hairdresser but nonetheless he went for it and did a fine job.

He was a particularly interesting character, with one wonky eye, a strong lisp and a huge scar harshly marking his forehead down to his eye. It became clear as to how he came to look like that, during a conversation about Egypt and its current issues. I brought up the Arab Spring and the recent Egyptian revolution, and he and his friend became suddenly jittery. They said that they'd played an active role themselves in the protests, and the reason he looks like the way he does is because he got shot in the head with tear gas by an Egyptian policeman. Pretty raw stuff, and he continued to show me many pictures of dead Egyptians brought to their end by police brutality during the protests. It reminded me of the Tiananmen square ordeal, although comparing such events isn't helpful - for each one should be carefully considered in and of itself. It tugged my heartstrings to say the least, but there really isn't anything particularly constructive nor consoling that you can say in return. But in knowing this, it made his shirt and haircut gifts even more pertinent.

So, by all means, they were kind people, but the only annoying part was that they woke up so early to pray and didn't consider the volume of their chitter chatter upon waking and turned the lights on or made phone calls and so on. It's not cool guys, it's flipping four in the morning! Oh well, it was what it was, and at least it was a cheap sleep, eh?

I stayed a total of nine days in Seoul and became very fond of it. It was a huge metropolis but was a nice mix of everything: with some tranquil parks, good museums and a decent underground music scene. I went to a techno event and a garage night in the space of one weekend, so I had my fix of dance music to last me a while. The capital tends to always satisfy in this regard. Also, while I was in Seoul, I was lucky enough to visit Gangnam, which is where the Korean superstar Psy made his world-famous song "Gangnam Style". According to one of my Korean friends, the song is essentially about showing off and puffing out his chest, because Gangnam is the most expensive part of Seoul - so you can imagine that I didn't stay there too long. It's quite funny isn't it, that Gangnam Style was a song enjoyed by people from countries all around the world, and they didn't understand one single word but still loved the song to bits. I don't really have any further point to make about that, just that it's a curious thing.

I was certainly satisfied with the long rest and prepared myself to start the "four-rivers" bicycle path which spans the entire length of the country. As one may expect from the name, it follows along the four main rivers of South Korea, meandering through the entirety of the nation.

The first day back on the stallion was absolutely glorious. It was a sunny day, not too bitterly cold, and a Sunday, with many people out riding their bikes as well – thereby many nods were exchanged with fellow two-wheelers. I put in my earplugs, blasted the tunes and enjoyed being next to the river, without having trucks hurtling past me at killer speeds. It made for a very nice break from the ever so dangerous roads of China.

It was approaching evening and it was soon time to find my place of rest - a "jimjilbang", which is essentially a sauna house. You may wonder why, and how for that matter, can you sleep in a sauna? Well, I wasn't literally sleeping inside the sweat room as such, but instead in a common area where locals spend the night, after they have their sauna session. I did some research into how to live cheaply in Korea and the fabulous idea of staying in the jimjilbangs came up, for you can pay eight pounds for both the sauna and the sleep. Yeah, you do have to sleep on a mat on the floor, so it's not the comfiest night's sleep, but it's a lot better than paying 30 pounds a night for a hostel and not even getting a sauna session included, so it's a no-brainer. And as a side note, the food in the Jimjilbangs was so incredibly scrum-diddly-umptious in every way possible! It was usually made by an old Korean grandma and it generally consisted of many small plates of food, sometimes with seaweed, tofu and kimchi (the famous fermented national dish of spiced cabbage). With all these small dishes combined into one main meal, it always made for a rather delicious affair, after a sweaty sauna session.

In this particular sauna complex, a few day's ride from Seoul, was a traditional round hot room, which happened to be the hottest sauna I'd ever stepped foot in. There were maybe 20 Korean locals on the floor clearly in pain but strangely loving it, and it sincerely felt like a unique moment unseen by my foreign eyes ever before. It felt peculiarly tribal and primitive, with everyone sat in a circle, zoning in on their own pain. The first words I heard upon entering were "is this not too hot for you?" in good English, sent forth by a young Korean woman, but I said "of course not", thereby retaining my hegemonic manhood and continued henceforth in barely coping with such an unbearably insane temperature. I left soon after, but luckily so did everyone else, so I didn't look like too much of a wimp (by the way, of course I'm joking here - I'm totally fine with feeling pain openly in public, and I don't feel that I have to prove myself as a man).

Speaking about manhood, I had a very strange experience the week prior in a similar bath house. I went with my Korean friend who I met on the boat to France, and he did warn me that you had to go into the baths naked. Of course, I was fine with that, because I'm no longer scared of nudity, since becoming a theoretical hippy during my university years. We are born naked, and we will die naked, so why not live naked from time to time? But I didn't consider anything else about the matter, until I actually entered the baths and absolutely every man inside brought their eyes from my white face down to the important parts in between my legs. Gosh, this was a strange thing to endure. Luckily, I'd gotten so used to people staring at me and giving me weird looks during this trip that I just treated it as a normal situation. Of course, I should have known, that stereotypes really do affect men's sense of self. Most people know the stereotype that Asian men have small dongs, so of course they were keen to clarify the opposite stereotype that Europeans are slightly more well-endowed. I'm not sure whether they received verification or not (this is an uncomfortable thing to write about, by the way), but they certainly took a long hard look (okay...well maybe that's not an appropriate phrase to use in this context, but oh well it just came out spontaneously). But what made it worse was that my Korean friend kept making inappropriate remarks in German about how I had a "große schniedel", which we'd unfortunately been using as a running joke throughout the day, and when his friends asked him to translate it into Korean I was praying that he wouldn't, for it really would have made the whole affair a lot more awkward than it already was. It means "big willy" in German and is a silly term used by children, and luckily, he *didn't* translate it, so that we could all leave the sauna with none of us emotionally scarred for life. Phew.

Other than this near miss, the jimjilbangs were only pleasant and relaxing places to be! I had several further days of cycling which were equally relaxing and fine, doing a maximum of 70km, which made quite a change from the frequent 140km days that Gunnar and I were doing in China. After four days of cycling next to the river, I arrived in the small city of Daejeon where I was hosted by a friend of a friend. His family were wonderful and kept feeding me so much good Korean vegan food! During one of the days that I was there, I went to play ping pong with his parents, and they turned out to be amazing, beyond belief. In comparison I looked like an absolute beginner, almost infantile in my ping pong capacity, even though I thought I was semi-decent at ping pong prior. They had a doubles match with another middle-aged couple and things got very competitive even though they all tried not to show it. Daejeon was an intriguing little city, with many sci-fi looking buildings from where they had held a science exposition in the 2000's, and following this theme - they had an engaging science museum which showed a glimpse into the future of robotics in East Asia, which is a pretty daunting prospect.

Before long, I departed in order to get back to the river bike paths and keep heading towards Busan, the port city which is the second largest city in Korea, and where I was getting the boat to Osaka, Japan where I was soon to be with my beautiful parents for ten days! I couldn't wait for our Full Power family reunion, and it was enough inspiration in and of itself for me to keep going.

Chapter Twenty-One

Sweaty Sauna Dislocation

Okay, so, literally, this has got to have been one of the most ridiculous things to have happened to me during this trip, and even during my life at large. "What on earth just happened?" was the only thought present inside my cranium after it all went down. Essentially, the situation started off relatively normal, as in, I was doing what I did most evenings when cycling in South Korea - relaxing in the sauna in the jjimjilbang, where I was about to subsequently spend the night. The only difference was that this specific time I decided to lie down on my back. But I laid my body down *all* the time, every night in fact so I didn't consider, even for one moment, that doing so would bring any harm to me. But alas, it did, it most certainly did. I laid with my arms spread at my side, like a cross, comparable to Mr Jesus Christ's famous position.

It was comfortable, life was good, I was even reflecting on how smooth and peaceful cycling in Korea was - the relaxing bike paths during the day, saunas in the evening "ah, this is the life," I thought. But only God knows how, I somehow managed to dislocate my shoulder, with the ball of my arm popping out from the socket of my shoulder. It was a re-dislocation from a previous injury two years prior. Absolute agony surged through my shoulder, matched by an equal flooding of surprise of - where the hell has this sudden pain come from? I realised, of course, and tried to do what I've done before and just pop it straight back in, but it induced a sheer shock of pain which screamed at me not to do that again. I denied my bodily instincts and carried on trying, but to no avail, and my ball was still hanging out of my socket - lost, astray and away from home - silly, silly shoulder!

I was unsure of what to do from there onwards, well and truly baffled as to what logical steps I could take to make this situation better. I tried shouting for help of course, although this took a big dent to my pride, even by attempting to alert people, because how could I explain this situation without looking like an utter weirdo? Especially in a foreign tongue, in which I was totally inept at voicing. I tried and tried to get attention with numerous words, both in English and Korean, loudly projected from my mouth. But they really could not hear me, no one, and my helpless words seemed to be swallowed by the sauna itself.

Thus, I was essentially deemed stuck. Not able to sit up due to an inability in dealing with the relentless agony when I tried to do so, and with no help coming my way, I was temporarily disabled with no choice but to lie there and sporadically shout for help like a yelping canine - hoping that the right person would walk by at the right time. Thank goodness that I was only in the medium, benign, hot room, for if I was in the hottest sweat room it really would've been a living hell, in a rather realistic simulation of the underworld. I'd only just came out from the room with the most intense heat, and I'm oh so happy that the ordeal didn't happen inside there. Luckily, it was in the middle grade room, but nonetheless it was still a bloody sauna! I lay there, in utmost pain, with the added distress of being in a room which was certainly double room temperature and at a heat which wasn't comfortable for the human body at all. It honestly felt like I was lying disabled in the middle of the Sahara Desert - and the comparison probably isn't too far off, considering the sauna must have been heated to at least 60° Celsius, like the summer Sahara. Ridiculous, once again, another utterly ridiculous situation that I'd gotten myself into. Full Power Codz...sort of.

I continued to shout from time to time, with the volume and severity rising in alignment with that of my increasing pain. Luckily, finally, the boy from the front desk popped his head in and asked if I was okay: "No!" was my response, sharp, as if to say - of course I'm not okay that's why there was swearing and squeals of pain coming from inside this room. But I took it easy on him for it wasn't his fault in the slightest, so I just gave the one-word response which said it all, in plain and simple English. He got his phone out and dialled a number.

"Finally, some paramedics will come, pop it back in and all will be hunky-dory, right?" Or so I thought. The boy told me to wait five minutes and this reassured me somewhat. But it either felt like an awfully long five minutes, or it actually did take much more time than that.

But eventually in came three people in uniform. It really was a peculiar moment, having three Korean emergency staff ducking into a sauna where a sweaty white English boy was lying, unable to move. I tried to tell them the situation but one of them got out their phone for translation. It must have been the longest wait for an on-the-spot diagnosis that I've ever received, but it's still incredible that Google sorted out the situation. Eventually it must have correctly translated that it was a shoulder dislocation. One man and woman looked slightly baffled nonetheless and their faces weren't reassuring for me, but thankfully the other girl knew what she was doing and slowly but surely relocated by ball into my socket. It hurt for sure, but her gentle motion was spot-on and in it went, boom, back to normal straight away. A shower of relief came crashing over my still horizontal body.

I was finally able to sit up, and slowly shuffled my way out of the sauna like a newly born worm. They had the stretcher ready to take me to the nearby hospital, but I was actually able to bring myself to my feet and my shoulder was already so much better, now that it was popped back in. In the newfound light, I could see that their badges actually said "fire services" so the boy must have called the fire fighters rather than the ambulance service, which explains why the two members of the group looked slightly confused about the medical specifics. Luckily one of the fire women must have listened in her First-Aid classes. I apologised for the inconvenience, said I won't need to go to hospital and that I just needed rest, and off they went. I sat, rested, and reflected on the hot hurricane which had just passed. After some time, I started cracking up laughing in realisation of how utterly ridiculous it was that I was just helped by Korean fire fighters, with my dislocated shoulder, inside a sauna. Thank goodness that I wasn't in the nude at the time. Golly gosh, these things only happen to me, I think.

The following morning, my shoulder felt fine and it was safe to keep cycling. Considering that it was still deep midwinter, we had a fair bit of snow fall from the heavens. A thick white blanket of snow had laden the entire surroundings, but the river continued to flow next to the bike path. It wasn't too much of an issue, although it was rather nippy for sure, and I did have a minor slip up on the icy bike path and scraped my face a little bit, but it was no biggie. Regardless, I was still so glad to have been on the bike paths with barely any other bikes around me, let alone cars. Starkly different from cycling through Chinese cities in the hectic "bike lanes" for example. It was peaceful, and even when I fell over, I could feel rest assured that no car was going to come out of nowhere and run me over. It was a massive relief to let my hair down (not that I had much hair at this point) and to not have to worry about horrible Motor Monsters nor Truck Dragons.

A couple day's ride away from arriving in Busan, I stayed in a Buddhist temple (which Buddha Bike was very fond of, so that he could finally practice some actual lengthy meditation sessions). I had heard somewhere from a local that some temples allow you to stay overnight there when passing through, as a tradition that has carried on from the olden days. When I asked one of the monks at a temple in a small town, he was more than happy to host me for a night. He gave me some temple food which was notoriously delicious in East Asia and gave me my own little room with innumerable books about Buddhism. Quite alike my bike, I was relatively well versed in the main principles of Buddhism and have found them to be incredibly helpful in day to day living. Especially during an incredibly arduous task like cycling across the planet, those principles can come in handy when the going gets tough. I have a particular interest in the concept of impermanence, because I believe this to be one of the most liberating principles possible, if acted upon.

Considering that nothing lasts, and everything must at some point perish, it is much healthier to avoid strong attachment to physical things, because *all* will one day become dust. This may seem somewhat defeatist on the surface, because our egos wish to cling onto the idea of our own permanence and lasting sense of self, but ultimately nothing lasts, so the quicker we let go, the better.

I read some of the books in my room about Mahayana Buddhism specifically, and found the contents to be valuable and beautiful. I enjoyed an hour or two of sitting meditation that evening, releasing the tensions of the day, and simply focusing on my breath. I woke at the normal temple waking time of 4am and I joined in with the morning chanting. It was awfully freezing inside the temple, but bearable. A good test of one's forbearance, I suppose. The monks appreciated my commitment and participation, and I of course appreciated their wondrous hospitality and unconditional kindness. It was everything I needed to keep me mentally healthy, and to give me that final push that I needed to arrive at my final Korean city, Busan.

Chapter Twenty-Two

The Unbeknownst Casino Raffle

usan was a rollercoaster. But one of the days while I was there, I simply felt that "Okay, life is officially weird." Not that I needed all too much verification of that, because my life had already been incredibly strange. But one night I won a lot of money at a casino, in South Korea. No, it's not what it looks like! I didn't turn into a raging gambling addict straight after my wholesome and nourishing Buddhist experience, and in fact, I didn't spend a single penny in that casino, but received an awful lot of pennies nonetheless.

It was a particularly poignant situation for me at the time because of a lack of real money and pretty much all my funds were running out as if the last bit of sand was slowly falling to the bottom of the hourglass. So, as you can imagine, money and the planning of how to make more of it had been a cause of inner tension and angst, but after that night, suddenly these concerns were no longer as firmly in my mind. Something happened that no planning in the world could ever have sorted, it was simply pure synchronistic chance. A raffle. Essentially a lottery, and I won.

To contextualize, I had been Couchsurfing in Busan, and was sharing the space with the Korean host and some Russian surfers. The Russian lads tipped me off about the casino by the beach where they gave out a free coupon every single time you entered. Originally, I thought "well, so what, gambling is still pointless even if it's free" but when they explained in more depth it all became clear as to why they had been going there every single night for the last month.

The game they played was designed in such a way to provide a loophole to two cunning young travellers - if they could work it out. If there are two of you, one places their free bet on the "Banker" and the other on the "Player". Regardless of the outcome, one of them is always going to win, and the two gamblers split the money between them, every night leaving with what is essentially free money. Usually our coupon would be for 30 or 40 thousand Won which is about 30 or 40 dollars. It made perfect sense to do this! As a poor traveller, it is a great opportunity to go and pick up free money to cover one's daily budget and then basically live for free.

So, of course, I took this opportunity and went for the previous four nights prior to this particular situation at hand, every time leaving with free money. They also provided free food and drinks and we even received some gifts during the Lunar New Year in the form of beauty products and food. All in all, it was a win-win visit every time, every day. However, the number of factors all leading up to that one particular climax were so randomly assembled that it would have been impossible to try to replicate it again.

During this specific evening at the casino, I went with a Chinese guy, who I met at the guesthouse and he'd been to the casino with me every evening. I bumped into him randomly on the beach a few days prior and I dragged him into the casino to be my partner-in-crime, ensuring us both easy cash every night for the foreseeable future. On that day, we went in and grabbed our 30,000 Won and had a scrumptious free dinner after. We left and were about to pick up yet another gift on our exit, expecting it to be more dried seaweed like the day before. We were told to wait; usually I just bulldozed through and they gave gifts to us earlier than everyone else. But this night, they would not give in, and we had to wait for the bloody seaweed. Thank goodness we did wait though, because if we had just grabbed our seaweed and left, we would have never known about the raffle, let alone win it.

We were given a coupon upon entry, which we thought was just for the gifts, but it turned out to contain a five-digit code. This all made sense when they kept calling out numbers and people would go up to collect prizes. "Ah, a raffle, how great," I sarcastically thought. I checked my ticket number haphazardly and with apathy. I just wanted to grab my seaweed and sleep. I have hated raffles since childhood, like the school raffles where you merely wait for it to finish and occasionally win an awful prize of biscuits or suchlike.

A couple more numbers were called, and a couple more gambling geezers went up to collect their prizes. Another number was called "*4062*" and before I could check my number, my Chinese gambling partner let out a squeal of jubilance and zoomed excitedly over to the speaker. But, shortly after the number was read, the words "Moir, Cody" came from the speaker. What the flip, that's me! We must have gotten our vouchers mixed up, but they certainly said *my name* from the loudspeaker. I went rushing after my Chinese friend and subsequently took my prize. I showed them my I.D, my membership card, and put my signature in the box.

To my utmost elation, the prizes weren't just chocolates or toys, but my prize was actually the iPhone Xs, arguably one of the best phones in the world at the time and certainly one of the most expensive. It was just crazy how if I hadn't met the Russians, I wouldn't have been at the casino, and if my Chinese friend had met me at the previously planned time an hour before we actually arrived, we would have walked away empty handed, or if we had been allowed our seaweed early, there would have been no iPhone. It seems to me that these things are meant to happen, for some strange unknown reason. The only task at hand was to turn the phone into months of sleep and food money! Full Power luck always comes your way when you are Full Power inside and out, spreading love wherever you go, and manifesting what you need. What you give, you get. If you send the desire from a true place, into the cosmos, good things generally swoop your way sooner or later. But nonetheless, it must have been the luck of the Irish.

"Cody, cigarettes no have meat inside," proclaimed one of the Russian lads at the hostel, in a thick Ruski accent. Well, I guess, come to think of it, I've known that fact for an extremely long time, but I gave thanks for the information nonetheless. They enjoyed making statements about me not wanting to eat meat. Busanhouse Guesthouse was hilarious. I stayed there for cheap thanks to the hosting app Couchsurfing. The host was a Korean guy called Mr. Cha, who used to be a biology teacher, but he quit his job to run a guesthouse and to live a simpler life. He enjoys hosting people for the cultural exchange and to make friends from all over the world. There were also the aforementioned Russian guys staying there, a Polish cyclist whose bike snapped in Taiwan and was currently living there, and Mr. Cha's friend, Noona, who was helping him out.

It was such a funny international mix that naturally brings about unusual and amusing situations. So many times, people misheard each other in the myriad of thick native accents flying around the room, and Noona had a tendency to shout random things in broken English simply because she was bored and wanted to annoy one of the Russian boys. She just shouted Viktor's name over and over in a tone which suggested desperation, so he came to her every time in panic, and sometimes she wanted absolutely nothing, and he just walked back to where he came without a word. Mr Cha was an interesting character too, with his primary catchphrase being "just kidding" - it was probably his most commonly used words. He used it so frequently because he was relentlessly picking fun at people for a laugh, albeit totally harmlessly.

My own personal teases stemmed mostly from my newly bald head which I had shaved not long before, for sake of convenience. According to Mr Cha, however, it meant that I must have been a "Neo-Nazi", yet he also claimed that I was a Muslim. When I first told him I was a vegetarian, he said that he disliked vegetarians, and things became worse when I said that I neither drunk alcohol nor smoked. He said that I was "just as bad as Muslims", quickly adding that he was "just kidding". So, depending on his mood, I was either a Neo-Nazi or a Muslim, but to be fair he could be very amusing sometimes.

We helped him to clean the guesthouse and cook, which worked in his favour and ours also, because it meant that we were able to sleep and eat for mere pennies. It was a nice place to be all in all, and I was there for ten days in Busan before I got the boat to Osaka, Japan. South Korea had been wonderful, calm, conscientious and caring, but I was ever so excited to float over the sea to the Land of the Rising Sun.

Chapter Twenty-Three

The Land of the Rising Sun

Whilst on the boat from Busan, I was giddy with feelings of joy and glimmering hopes for the land to come. Japan was always a big checkpoint on my trip, and one of the places I had been most interested in visiting when I originally planned my route. In fact, I had endured so much pain just to get there in the first place; most cycle-tourists choose to go south into South East Asia for better weather whereas I had decided to stay north through China despite the insanely cold temperatures - just to get to Japan. It promised so much in my boundless imagination. It went beyond my expectations and delivered magic and wonder in a myriad of ways.

The boat was much nicer than the one from China to Korea, mostly because it didn't have as many old noisy Chinese people shouting and yelling at every given opportunity. But it also had some nice touches, for example, the crazy pee-game installed into the urinals whereby the strength and quantity of one's pee would either defeat or get defeated by the fighting character on the screen. This feature of the boat gave me an indication as to what country I was heading towards. The boat journey took around 24 hours overall and was a smooth crossing. I made friends with a young Scottish girl of Russian heritage, who was popping over the sea because of her fascination with Anime cartoons and the Japanese language. We watched an interesting yet slightly bizarre entertainment show on the boat with crossdressers singing karaoke and were glad to have a debrief after the show in our common language.

When leaving the boat, my new Scottish friend whizzed through customs with ease, unlike me. The lady at the desk asked: "Why haven't you filled this in?" She was pointing to the box on the immigration form saying, "hotel name". The reason I hadn't filled it in was because I was yet to book anything. With the internet nowadays you can just book a place and check-in within minutes, so I was going to do exactly that when I got to Osaka city centre. But this blank box created some suspicions about my intentions, and they brought me into a small office room to the right of the customs desks.

I had a feeling that I was going to be there a while, so I told them to tell my Scottish friend not to wait for me, and off she went. There I was, sat waiting for the immigration police to question me, thinking: "bloody great, after all this, I'm not even going to be let into the country". Well, I was lucky to have even made it over the water, because when I checked into the boat on the Korean side, she asked for my outward flight ticket from Japan. Upon telling her that I hadn't booked any flights because I was going to get a boat to Australia, she told me that I couldn't enter Japan without one. God, I can't quite remember how I managed it, but I somehow convinced her that I *was, in fact,* allowed to enter Japan without any outgoing tickets, even though I wasn't sure that was the case. I'm quite good at getting my own way when I want something enough. And I certainly did want it.

But here I was, awaiting potential eviction from a country that I'd barely even stepped foot in, let alone wheels. I'd managed to negotiate my way across the sea, and now that I'd made it over, I was pretty sure they were going to send me straight back on the next boat to Korea.

I sat there for a while waiting for one of the old and stern sensei looking fellas to storm on through the door, but to my surprise the officer that walked in was a very attractive young Japanese woman. I was careful to ensure that I didn't start flirting with this beautiful immigration officer because it would have led to my imminent deportation for sure. Instead she just asked me some very blunt and interrogating questions and I remained equipoised (despite the fact that I wanted to marry her there and then).

"What are you doing in Japan?", she asked, which already put me on the backfoot and made me feel suspicious of myself. But I knew I wasn't a terrorist just because I hadn't filled out which hotel I was staying in, so I answered with unwavering confidence "I am cycling across the world, and I am going to cycle through Japan on my way to New Zealand". Although her English was pretty good, this was slightly too complicated for her to comprehend (it is difficult for many English people to wrap their head around too).

As I tried to explain a little further, with every word I became more and more suspicious in her eyes. She went out to get one of the older guys and they both came back in together. He was clearly her senior, and he spoke better English. I explained that I wanted to marry his co-worker and asked for his consent. Just kidding, I didn't do that. Instead, I explained again that I was going to cycle from Osaka to Tokyo, and that I didn't write any hotel in Osaka because I hadn't yet booked one.

He wasn't convinced and probably thought I had a screw loose. I don't blame him because I frequently ponder upon the same thing. He continued to ask me "how much money do you have?", and "do you have a degree?" all of which I found to be highly personal and somewhat offensive. But to be fair, he did need to find out if I was to be suitable marriage material for his colleague. Well no, he was just sussing me out. I was getting slowly pushed into a corner of doom, but behold, I had an epiphany! I suddenly whipped out my phone with glee and showed them the detailed map of the route I'd taken from London to Osaka by bike and boat, and suddenly it all made sense to them both.

They were somewhat in awe and now genuinely happy to have me in their country, to the point where they were wholly apologetic for the interrogation. They stamped my passport with the three months visa free entry, and boom, I was finally in Japan! The young immigration officer asked comically if I was going to cycle up Mount Fuji and I said of course not. We had a good laugh together after the misunderstanding had surfaced, but unfortunately, she was working, so nothing could come of it, marriage-wise. Oh well, plenty more sea in the fish. I think that's the saying?

Off I skipped and off I jumped, now free to roam the country that promised so much. I got to customs where Buddha Bike was waiting patiently in his equipoised state of zen, and it sure was good to see him. I looked around and saw about 30 customs officers looking at me. It was most certainly intimidating, and once again I felt like a terrorist even though I was one hundred percent sure I wasn't. I guess that usually the 30 officers would be dealing with the 300 passengers that get off the boat all at once, but due to my hour delay, I was now the only person left to go through customs and was lucky enough to have all their attention just for myself. Woo! I usually like attention, having been a drama queen all my life, but customs officers are a tough crowd.

But knowing that I had no drugs or explosives, I waltzed on through like the confident human I am and had zero issues. They took away my dried chickpeas (I'm not sure why, but I was happy they did so, because they tasted awful and they'd been sat in one of my panniers for months. Ew), and I was all good to go. One officer bantered about rugby and said how the world cup was in Japan this year. Once again, they started off stern and ended up playful and lovely. I had a good feeling that the next three months in Japan were to be bloody delightful!

I jumped on Buddha Bike and began cycling once more, voyaging through the 16th country of the trip thus far. I started on the pavement and eagerly went onto the road, because nowadays I have a strong distaste for cyclists who cycle on the pavement endangering the poor pedestrians, bless their cotton socks. So off I went to head onto the road, but I hesitated briefly and stopped in my tracks, realising I was heading for the wrong side of the road.

Damn, what a surprise it was to find out that in Japan they actually cycle on the *left* side of the road, like back home. This was the first time since leaving England that this had been the case, which meant that I'd spent the previous year cycling and surviving the road life on the right-hand-side, everything from roundabouts to junctions. Now all of a sudden, I had to re-shift my adaptation back to how it was before.

I was puzzled as to why this was the case in Japan, but I later found out that it was the British that assisted Japan in creating their first ever trains and railway system, so that when they designed the rail system they ensured that the trains would travel left-and-left. This dates to many centuries ago back in the time of swords, when people used to walk left-and-left on the street, in order to keep their sword's handle further out of reach from potential opponents walking past them. Fascinating stuff, eh?

So here I was, cycling along from the port towards my first Japanese city - Osaka. I soon adapted to riding on the left and felt at home with it - literally. My first impressions were very potent and vivid, in the sense that it was very clear from the moment I started rolling along, that I was in a whole new land, and one that was distinctly unique from the previous Asian countries that I'd been in.

Japan is Japan, unlike any other place, and that was to be felt the whole time I was there. Everything had an air of order to it, but a smooth style. For example, when I eventually arrived into outer Osaka after 20km or so of riding, I was blown away by how very suave and tasteful the taxis looked. This sounds like an overstatement or a form of joke, but honestly, I looked at these Japanese taxis with a deep aesthetic appreciation, quite like how one would react to a catwalk model in a really lovely coat. It's challenging to describe without sounding as though I have a strange sort of taxi fetish, but they were so clean and incredibly fashionable (as far as short-term-rental-automobiles go). They had a polished deep black exterior, with a well-matched forest green text for the number plate and even the drivers were wearing smart white gloves and what looked like high-end tuxedos. Taxis in Japan are ridiculously expensive, but with that type of style in your ride, what does one expect?

The smooth stylistic situation only increased as I cycled further into central Osaka. My primary mission was to find Wi-Fi in order to book where I would stay during my time in the city. As you already know (because it nearly got me deported) I didn't have a hostel booked as of yet. So, I saw a hotel on my right and headed over to steal their Wi-Fi connection. This was generally an accepted thing to do in most countries, but as I got closer to the front façade, it looked increasingly fancy. I thought I'd give it a try anyway.

It became clear that it was a high-end five-star hotel when the doorman arrived to take my bags. I told him I wanted to speak to reception first and he showed me the way. They were ever so helpful and gave me the password for the internet; there was even a robot there if I needed help. I went to the toilet (very nice toilets) and sat down in the lobby (very nice lobby) and before I logged on, I had a little look around me. Everyone was immaculately dressed, and everything was particularly clean and tidy. In Korea there were pockets of fashionable people here and there, but for an awfully long time through Central Asia and China, fashion had been a peripheral privilege for a small middle-class minority, and I hadn't seen all too much of it. Here in the five-star lobby, everyone was dressed oh so well.

It's funny, because one may naively expect in Japan to see people still wearing kimonos and wooden clogs, but mostly people were dressed like very fashionable Londoners from a few decades ago. In fact, this could summarise my initial reaction to the style of Osaka, in that it had a retro flare to it, as if it was the height of style about 30 years ago. It's hard to explain, but I knew that I liked it. For something to be modern yet retro in the same moment is quite an achievement.

215

I booked the cheapest hostel I could find online and headed over there. Huge skyscrapers started to pop up and this was more of the type of scene I expected from Japan's third largest city. I arrived at the hostel and was warmly welcomed by a lovely young Japanese woman who was very bubbly and giggly. Her English wasn't great but she was shocked by my trip and found the whole thing very amusing and she laughed a lot about it, which I found very amusing also - amusement, being amusing in and of itself. My room was a multiple dormitory, probably about 20 individual beds, not exactly like the world-famous capsule beds of Japan but close enough. Yet once again, extremely tidy and very tasteful in design.

I only had a few days to spend in Osaka, because I was just waiting for my parents to arrive after a year and a half of not seeing them. It was like a child awaiting Christmas Day, and other than Christmas Eve, the few days prior are mere obstacles to the day itself. This is how I felt, so eagerly anticipating the moment when I could hug my parents and hold them tight. I was longing for a unique kind of embrace, a very different hug to the usual.

I would still have missed them if I'd have gone on a conventional "gap year", but considering the myriad of hurdles I'd survived in order to arrive in Japan in one piece and alive, it was to be a different type of reunion. Having survived the infamous "Tunnel of Death", the insanely dangerous Kyrgyz drivers, and the most totalitarian regime imaginable in Western China, it felt like a miracle to still be living and breathing in one unified bodily experience. This made the prospect of hugging the people who made me in the first place, all the more magical in my imagination. It took up most of my headspace, but nonetheless I was still ready to enjoy my first few days in Japan, the Land of the Rising Sun. So, off I went to explore it.

Already the stroll from my hostel to the nearest metro station brought forth views of otherworldliness. There was a huge building which created a sharp arch which looked like a building from Star Wars. I noticed that the manhole lid of the sewers contained a wonderful image of the Osaka castle, which was actually where I was headed at that very moment. It was the nicest manhole lid I've ever witnessed during these 24 years of mine. They could well have left it blank like in so many other countries, but they turned the mundane, inanimate thing into a small work of art. This was the first detail among many that made Japan shine as a place which valued the beauty of all small things.

I took the metro to the famous Osaka castle. One might ask why I took the metro instead of cycling. In huge cities on a rest day, I would generally leave Buddha Bike wherever I was sleeping and take the underground to wherever I needed or wished to go. This was mostly because a "rest day" for me *really* did mean a rest day. In order to get to the metropolis in the first place I had cycled hundreds of kilometres and my body was truly in need of a *full* day of rest. Besides this, most of the Asian metropolises I'd visited had been awfully dangerous to cycle around and the distances between places were often huge.

The castle did not quite fit my preconceptions of what a "castle" would usually look like. It looked very different to the big brick fortresses that have defended England throughout the ages, but I guess that should be the case because Japan is, after all, on the other side of the earth. It resembled somewhat more of a religious building and was truly beautiful. It had a mostly white exterior, with blue tiles on the roof (which comes to its corners with the signature East Asian flick on the end, a feature present on nearly all important Chinese and Korean architecture). It had five stories in all, all with the same flicked roof edges, and the whole castle was embellished with fine fringes of gold here and there. It was quite a sight to behold, and one I'd not seen before.

I'd seen a lot of magnificent buildings during my time cycling through China and Korea but nothing quite like this - it was unique, for it was Japanese, and it happened to be my first major historical Japanese building I'd laid my eyes upon. It was to be the first of many after I'd been to Kyoto. I learnt that it was originally built hundreds of years ago, and shortly after I learned that it had been destroyed three times and this remake was made in the 20th century. It's always slightly disappointing when you find this out, but it turned out that this happened to be the case for nearly every amazing historical building I saw in Japan. The reason for their destruction was either because of crazy pyromaniac ninjas seeking revenge, or ground shattering earthquakes, or any of the other crazily dangerous natural disasters that Japan is subject to. But regardless of when it was built, it was still stunning, and I was lucky to see it with my own eyes.

On my way out I was reading a sign about how one of the emperors of Japan had taken his own life in this castle, and then out of the blue came an old Japanese man with a young Australian traveller. The old man was explaining to the Ozzie boy about the suicide, in broken English. I smiled at them both and I was greeted in a very friendly manner by both of them, namely a low and deep bow from the old man. We soon made friends and then the old man started explaining to the both of us. It was a very random encounter, but I was happy to have a tour guide and now two new friends. From nowhere, the old man gifted me some small origami parrots that he had made himself. They were very professional and an awful lot better than what I could do, by a long way. My paper aeroplanes at school didn't even fly. He showed us the peach blossom trees that were early bloomers and then treated us to ramen for dinner.

When we first walked into the restaurant, all of the staff shouted something in Japanese simultaneously pretty bloody loudly, and it went something like: "IRRASHAIMASE!!!" Of course, I didn't have a clue as to what it meant, but from the benign reaction from the other diners I could tell it was nothing bad. I just assumed it was a welcome shout that they used for every customer. It really was quite loud though, and awfully enthusiastic, quite different to the barely audible nor passionate greeting you get in British restaurants.

Well it wasn't so much of a fancy dining affair, but had more of a fast food vibe to it. There were numerous Japanese men in suits, who I assume had just finished work, lined up on what looked like bar stools, slurping their ramen noodles very loudly, clearly enjoying them. We went upstairs and our old Japanese friend ordered us miso ramen, and it was very tasty to say the least. It was incredibly kind of him and he asked for absolutely nothing in return other than our company, of which we were happy to give because he was just so nice, and great company himself. He also gave us our very own chopsticks and even more origami gifts. It had been an amazing first day in Japan, and all the better due to this kind hospitality.

Osaka was a place of many firsts - many experiences that I'd never had before, and probably will never have again until I return to Japan. For example, the first time you walk into a Japanese "pachinko" is certainly one to remember. It's essentially a room full of flashing lights and random noises from the outside, so it's natural to want to go check it out and see what's going on inside.

But as soon as you open the door you get bombarded with a deafening sound of hundreds of machines making their own high pitch thundering arcade sounds, all coming together to accumulate into a huge electronic roar. It's almost enough to make you scream like a young child on a rollercoaster and run straight back out into the street again. But my curiosity always propels me further into these situations. It turns out that they are basically pinball machines but technically the Japanese version of gambling, because casinos are banned in Japan. It's essentially a way for middle aged men to waste their hard-earned money on useless yet incredibly stimulating games. It's still permissible to smoke inside so there's a constant cloud of smoke lingering in these places, and pretty young waitresses go around keeping the sad old men hydrated and fed, in order for them to keep wasting their lives.

It really was a whirlwind of an experience and one that's so loud and overstimulating that you kind of want it to swallow you up and spit you back out as quickly as possible. This is exactly what happened, and back on the street, it felt like the most peaceful place on earth in direct comparison. But of course, it was still central Osaka and in fact not peaceful and still rather wild, yet so much calmer than inside the pachinko room. A couple streets down from where I was, stood Dotonbori - one of the most famous streets in Osaka, so I thought I'd check that out as well.

It was also pretty nuts. All the way down the street were humongous plastic replicas of whatever the shop was selling. It was mostly food, so the calamari place for example had a huge squid on top, and the crab place had a gigantic red crab. They all seemed to have long lines of people wanting their food, so the slightly outrageous marketing must have been working pretty bloody well. Once again, this street was another type of phenomenon that I'd never encountered before. At this point, I'd been travelling non-stop for over a year and had spent four of those months in Eastern Asia, so you'd think I'd seen it all, but Japan was showing me that I most definitely had not. Most certainly not!

I spent a few days overall observing and enjoying Osaka, dipping my toe slightly into the cultural and social waters of Japan, but the next stop was seeing my parents in Kyoto and I was oh so ready to see them after so long.

I checked out of my hostel in Osaka and got back on the bike once more and started pedalling towards the people who brought me into being. The ride was a mere 50 kilometres into Japan's ancient capital - Kyoto. I thought it would be a straightforward half-day, but it turned out to be slightly more complicated (as always). My navigation app told me to just follow the river and follow the bike path.

Awesome, I'm always overjoyed to see a bike path on the route because it's always free of cars and so much more enjoyable for cycling, normally at least. I cycled pretty much the entirety of South Korea on bike paths and it was an absolute pleasure, but it turns out that Japan has planned its bike paths slightly differently. I understand the idea of putting some form of barrier in place to deter larger vehicles like motorbikes or small cars from using it. In China they didn't have any barrier at all; their so called "bike

220

paths" were full of every conceivable type of motorised two wheeled vehicles, all whizzing past you, in every possible direction. But the Japanese planners had done the opposite and have been so cautious that they decided to put the barriers so close together that I couldn't even fit Buddha Bike through at all with all his panniers on. This was so bloody irritating because they were very frequent, and there was literally no other way around, apart from lifting the 50kg set-up over the barriers which certainly wasn't a simple task. I must have gone through this arduous process about four times in total, before totally having enough.

In the end, I decided to abandon the bike path all together and jump onto the main road. In comparison to the constant stopping and starting with the barriers, it felt like I was flying along and getting ever closer to my parents in Kyoto. I was rushing too because I didn't want to arrive too much later than them, and was eager to see them. I was getting some good momentum together, before something stopped me stationary in my tracks. I got off to check out what it was, and it turned out to be a piece of my bungee cord that had somehow got tied around my disk-brakes and the wheel itself, rendering it completely unturnable. This wasn't what I needed at all. I had a quick go at dislodging it from the wheel, but it wasn't budging.

Being so close to my parents, but now unable to move any further towards them, felt very frustrating. All sorts of thoughts were going through my head, especially considering how strictly I felt towards taking vehicles for help. I had to just find the nearest bike shop, but the main problem was that I couldn't even move the bike. Luckily a Japanese road cyclist stopped and gave me a hand. It turned out that amidst my panic, I had diagnosed the problem as one which was worse than what it was in reality. I just took off the back wheel and pulled hard at the chord before it eventually gave way and came out. My wheel was good as new and I was all dandy to continue to Kyoto. Phew!

At the next convenience store I got to, I used the Wi-Fi to tell my mum and dad that I'd be late. It turned out that they also had a delay on the train and they too would be late - great! All was well and off I went, luckily with no more dramas. I came in towards Kyoto and it seemed to be much more of a "city" than I'd imagined it to be, albeit there were some amazing ancient Japanese buildings that popped up here and there, already. I'd actually arrived slightly earlier than my parents, but it was almost perfect timing.

They had booked a lovely Airbnb in a historical part of Kyoto, and it was an old-fashioned town house with a traditional wooden bath, and in fact the whole interior design was made to be as traditional as possible. I followed my map down some smaller side roads and eventually arrived at the address. I spoke to the host and she was still cleaning, so I waited outside for one of the classy looking taxis to arrive. About ten minutes later a taxi pulled up and, although I couldn't see through the windows, I knew it must have been them.

My mother hastily sprung from the vehicle towards me while my father sorted their luggage. It was a soft maternal embrace with a woman who was very happy to see me in the flesh, alive and well. We held each other for a long time fully experiencing our relationship as mother and son, in person, which we hadn't been able to do for over one year. My mum cried a lot less than I expected, and I think a lot less than she expected too. My dad had finished sorting the suitcases with the help of the tuxedo-clad taxi driver, and eventually I could share a similarly warm embrace with my dad which felt strong yet tender. I was as happy as them to still be in one piece after such a long and challenging journey. It was a sweet moment, and a big checkpoint for the trip at large. We went inside and all caught our breath. We now had ten days together, so there was no need to rush our reunion.

Our host made us feel at home, and showed us around the beautiful traditional Kyoto townhouse. Every detail of the home, from windows to cutlery was carefully picked and had a delicate air and smooth style, which I'd been impressed with since I first stepped wheels on the country. It had wooden beams and lots of charming wooden features everywhere. It had a historical feel to it despite it being a newly renovated home, that had been in her family through generations. We were lucky to be staying there, for it really was gorgeous, and much better having the whole place to ourselves rather than staying in a hotel.

Our host even took us through a map of Kyoto, going through every single possible landmark that we may wish to see. It was all useful information, but we were trying not to let it show that she was interrupting what would otherwise be a very intimate time of parents reuniting with adventuring son. We instead showed interest in her advice. Well, me and Mum did anyway, because Dad had unavoidably fell asleep during her huge monologue due to strong jet lag and simply not having slept on a noisy, uncomfortable plane. The host understood the fatigue and didn't complain of course, and eventually she'd finished and went her own way.

By this point Dad had revitalised from the nap and we were finally able to embrace fully and revel in the fact that we were actually together in person and not just on FaceTime, which, whilst being great to have, is just not quite like being in person and never will be. But here we were, all in our new temporary townhouse, enjoying each other's company. We all had a proper power nap because we were all knackered. We then unpacked, and Mum gave me all the care packages I asked her to bring, including a toothbrush and aloe vera gel, and some such things that are challenging to get whilst on the road, due to a lack of Holland and Barrett shops.

We didn't want to do any sightseeing on our first day together, because all were too tired, and we had plenty of time ahead. Instead we went to have our first Japanese dinner together. I'd been trying Japanese food during the prior few days in Osaka, and I'd been subtly adapting to the different flavours and textures of the cuisine. My parents, however, did not have this buffering period to adapt like me.

Well I'd had to adapt many times to many different countries throughout the 15 nations I'd passed through prior, so adapting and not complaining about different foods had become the norm for me. However, of course some national cuisines are easier to adapt to, like Italian and Greek for example, and others are much harder to adapt to like Tajikistan's diet of unhygienic sheep flesh and oily rice. But Japanese food, for me, was very nourishing and usually tasty vegetarian food. They do have a tendency to eat some strange things, like shark, whale and weird orange fish eggs. But then again, most cuisines have their quirks, quite like how the French eat frogs...weirdos. Anyhow, off we went to try some traditional Japanese food, and upon opening the menu, we couldn't find much at all that appealed.

My parents had recently turned vegetarian which I was incredibly happy to hear, because I think that eating less meat (especially as one gets older) is a healthy transition, because less meat generally means less fat clogging our arteries and thereby less disease within the body. This would have been fine in Japan if they were experimental with food, but it turns out that they're definitely not. I mean, I don't blame them, because half of the menu didn't make any sense even in English, and the stuff that did make sense is very rarely found in the U.K.

So, with a combination of vegetarianism and fussiness we managed to take a good half an hour, speaking very broken English using very inaccurate translations, to finally order some food. When it arrived, my mum was rather horrified to find that the cabbage she ordered was actually raw and uncooked, and her wheat noodles were completely plain with no sauce. It all must have been lost in translation and my mum wasn't too fond of the "rabbit food" but it was a good experience for everyone and we learnt from it for the next ten days together.

We spent most of our time exploring the timeless history and culture of Kyoto, which was absolutely boundless. On every street we walked down, we came across an ancient palace, temple or shrine. Kyoto used to be the imperial capital of Japan so that's why there are so many royal buildings, still standing today.

And as for the shrines, there are two main religions in Japan. The most popular faith is the Shinto tradition which is a pagan religion that worships multiple gods for multiple aspects of the world. For example, there is a God of the mountains, a God of the sea and so on and so forth, and if you are fisherman hoping for no tsunamis this year, you would go to the shrine of the Sea God to pray. Because of this, there are many shrines all dotted around. Shinto is almost inherently tied into what it means to be a Japanese person; usually if one identifies as being Japanese one will identify as following Shinto. The second main faith in Japan is Buddhism, which was originally brought over by Chinese monks. It has mostly been transformed into Zen Buddhism which is a beautiful philosophy and produces beautiful architecture and traditional zen gardens. It's not uncommon for people to identify as both Shinto and Zen at the same time, because the two faiths exist contemporaneously in society; one worships at a Shinto shrine or attends Shinto festivals but the principals of Zen are fundamental to their concept of Buddhism.

When these shrines and temples are mixed with the grand imperial buildings, the result is a huge myriad of breath-taking historical buildings everywhere. There are absolutely hundreds but we must have seen every single one during those ten days. Some of them, like the Golden Pavilion were particularly famous, so we had a packed itinerary every day in order to fit it all in and soak up all the historical goodness.

We saw so much and the result was that we'd get back every evening feeling knackered and spent. I'm renowned for planning and cramming too much in, but my parents still loved what they saw, inspired by the attention to detail and the magnificence of the design and the beauty all around us. We went to see the hundreds of deer roaming the streets of Nara, and took a stroll through the renowned bamboo forest of Arashiyama. It was fair to say that within those days my parents got a very well-rounded insight into the beauty of Japan, but most importantly we spent that time reconnecting after so long and sharing wonderful moments. It made the prior months of cycling much easier knowing that I'd see them at some point and it also made the following few months more manageable cycling alone.

The time came when they had to leave Kyoto to return back to Aldershot, our home town, and I decided to leave at the same time, not to Aldershot but instead closer to Tokyo. It wasn't easy saying goodbye but it was necessary and had to be done, so we did. I think it was harder for my mum knowing that her son would be getting back on the long arduous road to New Zealand with all the myriad dangers, yet I was fully confident in my own ability to survive and I reassured her of this. The taxi that arrived to take my parents to the airport brought an abrupt end to our emotional farewell and off they went, with a final wave - into the distance. It was once more son without parents in presence, and parents without son in presence likewise. The feeling was odd after readjusting to their constant company during those days, but I looked over at Buddha Bike leaning against our temporary Japanese family home and I knew there and then that he too is my family and my company also. Before I knew it, I was back on his back, heading towards my next stop - Shizuoka.

Chapter Twenty-Four

Hirota Sensei

The main reason I was going to visit Shizuoka was not just that it was merely on my route to Tokyo, but because a certain teacher lives there. His name is Hirota Sensei, for "Hirota" is his family name and "sensei" indicates his role as a teacher. He wasn't to teach me school subjects, instead he was to teach me Wado-Kai, a style of karate originating from Okinawa, a small sub-tropical island off the mainland of Japan. This wasn't simply some kind of tourist activity that one ought to do, but rather it happens to be the case that I've practiced this karate style since I was six years old, every Thursday in my hometown.

I'd stopped training when I was 16 mostly due to hormones and being interested in other distracting things, but I'd recently continued training after uni. I'd managed to grade to brown belt which is two grades away from black belt. My sensei back home is 8th Dan (the highest possible rank of black belt) and he put me in touch with his good Japanese friend and asked if I could train with him. Hirota Sensei agreed to this, and we arranged that I could stay at his family home, volunteer at the local primary school during after-school activities, and train karate every evening during the stay. As well as this, he happens to live on the foothills of Fuji-San, the world-famous Mount Fuji.

So, this is where I was headed as I departed from Kyoto. The prospect of top-quality martial arts tuition and a monstrous snowy volcano ahead kept me pushing pedals during this stretch. The cycling itself for this part wasn't all too dramatic but was rather comfortable in every way. It was mostly flat, with an abundance of places to get water and even a multitude of "conbini" (convenience stores) every 20km or so, where one could snack, use the toilet, and rest one's legs.

Japanese toilets are one of a kind. I mean it wholeheartedly when I say that Japan really does have the best toilets in the entire world, quite opposite to the hole-in-ground situation of Central Asia. For starters, when you sit down on the toilet seat it is already warm, and not because someone's ass has warmed it up already, but it's actually electrically warmed, so even if it's a chilly morning you won't get that uncomfortably cold seat meeting your cheeks. Alongside this, there are a myriad of buttons on the side which provide many different functions, such as playing ambient music to block the sound of your toilet business and also a function which literally showers your bum hole post-poop. It really is a delight every time you must go.

So little things like this made it such a comfortable cycle in contrast to some of the regions I'd previously endured. The car drivers were very respectful (in fact, probably the most respectful drivers from my entire trip). They gave me plenty of room when they overtook and the weather had the delicacy of early spring. My journey was pretty eventless until I got close to Shizuoka. The main road I was riding on eventually turned into a bypass, and because it was my first week of cycling in Japan, I was still somewhat unsure of the road rules. I was particularly unsure of the bypass thing, so I just risked it for a chocolate biscuit and went for it, rather than finding an alternative route. After a few beeps, and a bit more stressful cycling it became clear that bikes weren't supposed to be on a bypass: "but too late, I'm on it now so I just have to go as fast as possible until the next turn off" I said to myself.

That turn off didn't come quick enough, and alas, the sound of sirens sounded once more in this long trip of trials and tribulations. You must be reading this either shocked as to how many times I had encounters with police, or in knowing me before this trip, feeling shocked as to how there wasn't even more encounters. The flashing lights didn't particularly surprise me nor scare me considering Gunnar and I had to deal with the Chinese police nearly every day in Western China, but nonetheless it's still not what you want to see.

I pulled over and they jumped out of the car and told me in broken English that it's forbidden to cycle on a bypass in Japan. I said that I'd realised this too late and they asked me to leave at the next junction. I was kind of waiting for them to force me into the police car, but it never came and instead they were ready to escort me off the highway, allowing me to actually cycle off. I rejoiced in my head, hurrah, for this wasn't to be another sad and sodden moment of being forced into an automobile, thereby invariably accidentally cheating in my pursuit of cycling to New Zealand.

Off I cycled towards the nearby junction to depart the bypass, with the flashing lights of my police escort behind me. When we got down onto the normal roads, they used their large speaker on top of their car to shout directions to me. "Left", "go straight at roundabout" and so on and so forth.

This must have been such a strange sight for the locals, to see this obscure looking Westerner on a fully loaded bike, having directions shouted at him in a foreign tongue by the police force. It was so kind of the police to go out of their way to do this for me, and once they got me on the correct road, I waved goodbye to my new police friends and they both waved back at me with big beaming smiles, happy to have helped me on my way. But somehow that wasn't the only error of the day because later on I also managed to find myself in a tunnel that I shouldn't have been in. Don't ask me how I managed these things because I'm not too sure myself, but I will just note that navigating oneself from city to city on a push bike can be quite tricky sometimes, especially when your phone runs out of battery. I managed to exit the tunnel alive and with no flashing lights, and once again back on the normal road.

I then had some wondrous torrential rain to soak me wet through to the core. It was now fully dark, and fully rainy, but I eventually made it to the correct area. Under an umbrella by the supermarket we'd planned to meet at, was my soon to be sensei - Hirota-San.

Hirota-Sensei welcomed me into his family home and helped me to feel at ease. He showed me to my new room for the next ten days. His wonderful wife helped me to wash some clothes and we sat for our first scrumptious dinner! We went to karate training nearly every night, mostly with his personal class and his pupils, but twice we went to train with the well renowned Shimamoto-Sensei who was in his mid-eighties yet was incredibly flexible and amazingly powerful for that age. Shimamoto lived above his dojo and his whole life was devoted to mastering this particular form of martial arts. He was quite a strict and severe man, and all his pupils had utmost respect for him and the children behaved very well when training. It was inspiring to see this level of self-discipline and determination to mastering a skill.

Yet without knowing it, I think that part of the discipline I had to have for cycling had stemmed from my early years training in karate, and now this training in Japan was just reinforcing and reaffirming my ability to focus and improve myself. I felt like after ten straight days of training, my karate did improve and some of the nuances of stances and suchlike became clearer. Self-defence is a great skill to have for protecting yourself and your loved ones, but its benefits can mostly be seen in one's ability to focus and dedicate attention to one particular activity.

Hirota himself was less severe than Shimamoto and only in his fifties, yet he was equally disciplined and powerful. He was a math teacher for his day job and during the first couple days I accompanied him to his school and gave some presentations about my trip thus far, which he translated. And the week following I went into the junior school where I helped out with the after-school club, playing Japanese monopoly with the children and helping them to practice their English.

During my first day volunteering at the school, they asked if Hirota-Sensei and I could perform a small karate show for the children. We were both slightly nervous about the prospect of performing in front of lots of little energetic youths, eager to laugh at us at any given opportunity, but we both plucked up enough courage to perform.

We performed a "kata" to start with, which is essentially a combination of karate attacks and blocks which all have a set sequence akin to a very sharp and aggressive dance routine. The kids giggled a bit at the movements especially when we had to shout for emphasis, but overall, they were engaged and loved it. After this we demonstrated the pair work attacks and blocks, where we pretended to fight properly, obviously under control, but the kids fully soaked it all in and enjoyed the tame expression of mild violence.

Throughout the following week the kids treated me as if I was a karate master. I'd be surprised if a few of those children didn't go back home to their parents and ask to go to their first karate training session. The week consisted of volunteering in the day time and training in the evening. Overall it was a wonderful experience and I enjoyed my temporary Japanese family. We ate together three times a day on the living room floor, watching national T.V (which I didn't understand all too much of) and shared lots of laughter despite not speaking either party's language fluently.

The best thing about living in this area was to be able to see Mount Fuji every day. In Japan, they call it "Fuji-San" which can translate directly to Mr. Fuji, and within the Shinto religion he is deemed to be a God. It has been a place of pilgrimage for centuries. One can certainly see why, because it goes from zero to nearly 4000m above sea level sharply and suddenly; it is flat around the base and then boom, a huge volcano emerges out of nowhere. It's simply beautiful to look at, with a rim of snow constantly hemming the tip all year round. To look at Mr. Fuji every day was a real pleasure.

The time came for me to move on towards Tokyo, but in between me and the capital was a big mountain called Hakone mountain. The Hirota family were concerned about this, because old stories suggest that this mountain was very challenging to get over even since the Samurai Era. But I reassured them that I'd cycled much harder mountains in the Pamirs, and therefore not to worry.

It turned out to be really blooming hard after all. It went from zero to one thousand meters straight up, and to get up and over it in one day was a huge struggle. After my parents visited, my mum had given me lots of things like new socks, clothes and toiletries to keep me going but I didn't think too much about the additional weight until I was half way up Hakone mountain in physical agony. I know socks don't weigh much, but all the stuff together must have been pretty heavy.

I'm not sure what it was about that day, because I *had* done much worse before, as I said, but my body was aching to an incomparable degree and I had an important epiphany: "I'm really not enjoying this". It struck me like a lightning bolt, when I was forced to take a break against my will. My mind said keep on going, and my body said "no way mate, not at all, I'm stopping right now - and that's the end of this discussion". Of course, this had happened many times before, and was to happen many times again, but it was particularly poignant considering I'd recently been flirting with the idea of expanding the trip. The nature of the trip had always been a bicycle ride from England to New Zealand, the furthest you could possibly go, the other side of the world (of course with necessary boats over the water) and the return leg was always left blank in my mind.

Some of my friends said I'd definitely fly back and that I'd be sick of cycling forever. I didn't believe them, and I felt deeply in my heart that I didn't want to just fly straight back to the U.K, because that's such a boring way to end such a crazy trip, and defeats the principle of not flying. After enjoying the cycling so much overall I was toying with the idea of trying to do every continent other than Antarctica (it's so flipping expensive to get there). I was planning on getting a boat from New Zealand to Canada, and then cycling all the way down to South America, across Brazil to get a boat to North Africa and then cycling back home through Spain and France. It had some dangerous prospects, but I was keen for it, with lots of energy left in the tank and still longing for lots more adventures.

But there and then, halfway up Hakone mountain, upon being forced to stop by my stubborn pained body, the lightning strike epiphany hit me of "No way. You can't do every continent. Shorten the length of the trip - for the sake of your body" - it kind of felt like the voice wasn't my own. It was coming from somewhere outside of myself, concerned for my well-being. I felt the sincerity and the urgency of this message, and quickly stopped playing with the idea of cycling every continent. Instead, I allowed the return journey to be left as a mystery once more.

But still, I couldn't help but think about a full circumnavigation, cycling only across North America instead.
There is something very nourishing and satisfying in the idea of going east, and continuing to go east until you end up in the place you'd originally left. It's funny how heading east at the beginning of the trip gave the prospects of exotic Asia, but as I left the other side of the world, heading east would give the prospects of the known - of home. This was a delightful thought for me, going the long way around, and eventually cycling back to the home I'd cycled from all those arduous months ago.

It also went in accordance with the comments made by my good friend, Harrison, about my trip before I left. In his letter addressed to me before leaving, he wrote two particularly marked remarks. One was about appreciating "the ever-changing horizon" which will never be the same image every time I look up from the handlebars - which was unavoidably true. But the other comment relevant to the easterly pursuit was to keep up that "unstoppable momentum". This stuck with me, especially during the harder moments of cycling, as I would think about that unstoppable momentum that I'd built up since leaving home, and it was to be this same momentum that would possibly take me all the way home, all in the same direction - east.

After this epiphany, I felt like a weight had been lifted from my shoulders, and the rest of the climb up to 1000m genuinely felt easier. The prospect of a shorter trip and less mountains to climb overall helped my body to push and push, and up I went. Of course, it was still bloody hard work but I managed it and the downhill was great fun as always. With lovely views of Mount Fuji in the distance, it was particularly rewarding. I treated myself at dusk with a traditional outdoor "onsen", which is a Japanese type of spa with naturally heated spring water, bamboo all around me and a fresh evening breeze, it really was a divine way to celebrate getting up and over this renowned mountain pass. I slept well and the next day I was only one day away from the biggest city in the world - Tokyo.

The ride into Tokyo was wild. I purposefully went through Shibuya on my way in, which is home to the world's busiest pedestrian crossing, and it's mental in many senses. You'd have likely seen this crossing from an aerial perspective on a documentary or suchlike, because there's really nothing quite like this spectacle. Especially from above, seeing six streams of tiny ants all perfectly passing through one another, successfully walking to the other side somehow avoiding collision. It's quite the happening, and strangely beautiful, somewhat like seeing those huge shawls of fish swimming above the reef, or monumental numbers of birds flying in unison.

Most of these human ants stream out of Shibuya train station, which is one of the three busiest stations in the world, all three of which happen to be in Japan. Most normal people with common sense would prefer to avoid this level of chaos on a bicycle, but not me, nope - I strategically planned to pass directly through the busiest crossing. All in the name of experience and some good old-fashioned fun! It really was a bloody good laugh.

I approached the crossing with my fully loaded bicycle with the myriad of baggage mounted upon it and people looked at me as if it really wasn't a sensible idea to be embarking on this challenge. I fully knew this, and they knew that I knew this. Everyone was still queuing, waiting for the green man to finally go green, and once it did, the criss-cross exploded into a frenzy of movement and motivation of crossing, to which everyone succeeded - even me! It actually went quite smoothly, and before I knew it, I was on the other side, still in one piece. I was now free to continue towards my new Tokyo home.

When I say "home", I don't mean that I actually own a house in Tokyo, but I mean the place that was to be my temporary place of residence for one month in the mega-metropolis, once named "Edo" and now named Tokyo. I was extremely lucky to end up with this place; hostels are bloody expensive in Japan, especially for one month straight. In the end, my friend's girlfriend revealed that she grew up in Tokyo, despite being ethnically Norwegian and living in Portugal most of her life, now residing in England. She's a very international young lady, but she asked her dad to ask his Tokyo friend if they could host a young bicycle traveller. Even though she couldn't, her staff member had a spare room and I was able to live there very cheaply.

Although it was a convoluted and complicated way to arrive at such an end, it was a good situation for me and also for my housemates - because I'm a total legend. Well, that's not exactly true, but we did all get on well. I particularly bonded with Sei-San who worked for a company selling Scandinavian food and since I had studied at university in Sweden for five months, we shared a mutual interest in this part of the world. Considering I didn't have any curtains in my room, he offered to provide a lovely Swedish flag to help block out sunlight and unwanted onlookers, so I gladly accepted, and it must have looked to the neighbours that the street's new inhabitant was a Swedish nationalist making his mark.

The flag contrasted greatly with the rest of the room, which had traditional Japanese features, with six straw tatami mats on the floor and wonderful wooden trimmings offering a neat and sophisticated feeling, along with white paint on the walls. It was iconically Japanese, and this provided an interesting contrast with my new curtain. I will reiterate - I was very lucky to find this place, my new home.

Now that I had my base, I was able to simply rest my body and explore the capital city of Japan. This was an endless pursuit and when endeavouring to do this, one's absolutely spoilt for choice. For starters, my housemates took me to Akihabara, which is famously the nerd capital of Tokyo, where you find shops full to the brim with cartoon figurines from Japanese anime series, comic books, and all sorts of collectible merchandise. It really is a nerd's heaven, and to be fair, it even appealed to that small geeky part of myself, and I purchased a Pikachu Pokemon card, and a Yu-Gi-Oh card, both of which were favourites of the playground when I was a kid.

When you properly look around, it's truly staggering to see how so many companies are Japanese, especially within the entertainment industry. Nintendo, and everything that comes with it is Japanese, PlayStation also, and nearly every decent photography brand originates from Japan too.

Within the tech world, they certainly know what they are doing. Akihabara was an utter madness, with so much stimulation everywhere you looked with lights, sounds and colours lighting up every one of my senses. There was a constant electronic murmur quite like that of the pachinko machines, and the excited chit-chatter of intrigued onlookers. Neon colours refracted from every angle, which made my eyes open wide and alert.

After a full day of it, we all remarked how we were surrounded by too much information and we quickly receded to a park with less stimulation, settling in the imperial park to quieten our minds. It levelled us out, more mellow than before, and provided a more stable end to my first day in Tokyo. I was now made aware of how mad and overstimulating Tokyo could be, and this provided the foundations for my next challenge - finding zen in the biggest city in the world.

Zen, as in Zen Buddhism, blends together the core beliefs of Indian Buddhism with Chinese Taoism and Confucianism, mixed with the powerful Japanese mentality of discipline. This mix provides for a very potent practice if done properly, and gives rise to the popular saying "finding Zen". It turns out that this is actually possible in such a busy city, if you take the right measures. For starters, there are so many wonderfully peaceful parks in Tokyo which provide necessary rest from the storm of business and bustle in the inner-city. Particularly, Shinjuku-gyoen is a haven of greenery and quiet, with beautiful traditional eastern gardens and plenty of space; you can read a book there and stroll around for the day without feeling like you're in a mental metropolis.

I was very fortunate that during the time I was there it was the beginning of spring so I was lucky enough to witness the wonders of the cherry blossom (sakura) trees, in every part of their journey all the way from bud to bloom, and back to naked branch - the full cycle. This made the myriad parks all the more relaxing and gorgeous, with these light pink petals gently floating above one's head. Along with this, I'd actually managed to find a fortnightly session of Zazen (sitting Zen meditation) for ninety minutes in an authentic Zen temple where I could focus upon my breathing with correct sitting posture, thereby attempting to reach a point of stillness where the ebb and flow of unconscious thinking has less of a stronghold over your mind. Sometimes it's easy to achieve this state of calm and equipoise and other times it's harder, but regardless it was a wonderful opportunity to find peace in a city of such business and busyness. I somehow managed to balance my experience of utter madness and mayhem and nourishment and rest - both of which I needed during my month's break from cycle touring.

As if things couldn't get any better, one of my bestest buddies ever in the whole wide universe, Leyth, came to visit me in Tokyo! At that point, he was studying for one semester in Taiwan as a part of his global entrepreneurship masters and he thought he'd just pop over the ocean to see his brother whom he hadn't seen for over a year.

We had a whale of a time, exploring the temples of Tokyo, the music scene and all the little pearls of beauty here, there, and everywhere. It was so refreshing to spend time with a friend that I'd spent so many years with, and we already knew each other well, so there was no guessing or starting from scratch. We not only spoke the same language, but we share the same sense of humour, and interests in music. Sharing all of this in person rather than just over Skype was so refreshing and was exactly what I needed, because after spending so much time on the road with so many different people it can become quite tiring meeting new people all the time and leaving them straight after any bond had been made. But here, with Leyth, we were building on what was already an unbreakably strong bond and we loved every minute of seeing one another in real life once more. Unfortunately, all good things eventually come to an end, and after a solid week of exploring and partying together, he had to go back to finish his term in Taiwan before his final semester in San Francisco. But it wasn't to be the final time that I would see him during my Full Power Bike Ride, albeit the next time was in a completely different context.

It was a shame that Leyth departed merely a few days before the "Kanamara" religious festival because he would have found it blooming hilarious. I think it's hard not to find it hilarious as an outsider. It's essentially an annual celebration of a giant pink steel penis. This may sound slightly weird to you, and yes, that's because *it is* weird. It's based on an ancient story where a young princess couldn't sustain any relationships with men because every time, she made love to them, their penis would get bitten off by an evil demon that resided inside of her. To combat this, she asked for help from the local blacksmith who made her a

238

steel penis which she could use to break the teeth of the demon, which is exactly what she did, and it worked, hence the celebration of the big steel penis. I'm not too sure if this story was actually true and whether it happened or not, but it has made for a rather humorous celebration of people dressed up as dicks, licking willy shaped lollipops, whilst following around the massive pink steel knob named "Elizabeth" being carried around by the numerous drag queens of Tokyo. It was quite the celebration and Leyth would have loved it, but there's always next year.

Another celebration I was lucky to witness during my time in Japan, was the changing of the imperial era. The old emperor was getting too old and decided to step down from his position, thereby passing on the crown to his son. This is a huge deal in Japan and marked the changing of the entire era! I was lucky enough to be waved at by the old emperor by pure chance on his final public visit. He was being escorted by numerous police motorbikes and literally out of nowhere he looked in my direction and waved back at me, looking me directly in the eye. I was told by local Tokyoites that it is extremely rare to even see the emperor at all as a local, let alone to exchange a wave with him. The transition period stretched over a number of weeks with plentiful Shinto religious ceremonies marking the switch, but eventually the night came and it was to be marked at midnight, quite like the transition from New Year's Eve into New Year's Day.

Once again, I stumbled upon it, with a few of my friends. We saw loads of people crowded around the Shibuya crossing and it was suspiciously busier than usual, in the pouring rain. We decided to wait around to see what would happen, and we then found out that people were waiting to cross over on the first ever crossing of the brand-new era and for sure we wanted to be a part of it. Midnight eventually struck, and amidst the hundreds of umbrellas, the police were trying to control the crossing, asking people not to enter the middle part, but some people broke through the police line and it erupted into a full-blown party in the middle of the road celebrating the new imperial era of "Rei-Wa". It was something extraordinary to witness and I was very happy to be a part of the dancing and leaping to commemorate such a transition.

Unfortunately, the time came when I had to depart Japan and continue my cycling towards New Zealand. In some ways I was glad to be getting back on the road, for I'd become somewhat soft again living in Tokyo with all the myriad conveniences at my constant disposal, with a bed every night for one month straight, and a definite supply of water and food wherever and whenever I wanted. For sure that was lovely for a period, but after some time I could feel myself softening up and becoming a city person once more, rather than a savage bike-riding animal that feared nothing and never winced at any feeling of pain (okay, maybe I'm over exaggerating but you get the idea). Basically, I was longing for some more hardship, to get back to the arduous and tumultuous life of cycling every day, and having to hunt in order to find a place to lay my head when the darkness comes. This may sound like a horrible lifestyle to some, but I genuinely enjoyed it and the feeling of getting ever closer to the antipode of my home was always rewarding. I felt well rested, and I'd had my share of wonderful Japanese experiences, so I was definitely ready to move onto the next chapter. On the other hand, I knew that I was going to miss Japan and long for certain aspects of the culture that will forever have a resting place in my heart. I knew I would miss the politeness, the manners and the bowing, the kindness, the simplicity and the architecture, the martial arts, the food, and the overall Bushido - the soul of Japan.

Just to detour slightly into the world of bowing in Japan, it was sincerely a sacred action. In every strata and demographic in society, everyone bowed to everyone. It was such a beautiful action, of lowering your ego, and showing your respect for the other person. I absolutely loved it, and loved Japan in its totality. I soaked it all up, like a dry sponge thirsty for moisture, ready to absorb all water possible. I was recommended a book titled "Bushido - the soul of Japan" and although it will be a great read, I think I will already have a firm understanding of what it will tell

240

me. For after cycling across the country and soaking up as much as I did, I felt like I had glimpsed directly into the soul of Japan as though I were looking intently and earnestly into the eyes of a lover. This is a country with a very rich core, and a culture that stems from that core will of course be a rich and valuable one. It is one that will stick with me for the foreseeable future, not only within the Zazen sitting meditation, or the kata of my karate, but subtly in every way that I carry myself, and how I treat life and those around me.

For example, in Japan it is not uncommon to show respect to an empty space. A void piece of emptiness, no? In the West we may see it as lunatic behaviour to bow when leaving a place, directed at the empty place itself, but in Japan the space is respected for the fact that the emptiness provides the possibility for life to happen within it. Quite like the value of a frame and canvas allowing the possibility of an artistic masterpiece. For how could we have an evening bath if it wasn't for the emptiness and contents of the bathroom itself. Without knowing the meaning, I've actually been doing this since I was six years old, when I entered and left my karate dojo (essentially just a school sports hall) in my hometown. I used to feel a bit silly doing it because I didn't understand the intention behind the action, but now, having seen where this action was birthed, I perform the action with a renewed sense of meaning. Even after having left Japan, I often find myself bowing in gratitude at the home of a host, or bowing in thanks for a gorgeous woodland. This is something I took with me for the remainder of this Full Power Bike Ride, and in my life at large, regardless of whether people may think me weird. Anyhow, most people already know I'm a weirdo.

There wasn't all too much land left for me to traverse now on the final leg to my finish line, New Zealand. I was sad to leave Japan, but when it's time to go - it's time to go. Instead, one must stay rooted firmly in the present moment and look forward to the joys to come.

The next questions: "where am I going?" and "how will I get there?" The "where" part had always been known to me, even from the moment when I left my house in Aldershot on my noble steed, Rasta Bike (now known as Buddha Bike obviously, please do acknowledge him by his new name and respect his change in faith). It was always the plan to cycle through the huge and mystical continent of Australia after cycling across Asia. This was still the plan, yet I experienced some hurdles which threatened to firmly block the path between me and that plan.

Essentially, my three-month tourist visa got rejected, which not only came as a surprise but also as a real pain in the ass. For starters, the application process in and of itself was bewildering, with a multitude of tourist visas to choose from. It was all rather comical: I'd managed effortlessly to succeed in many online visa applications throughout foreign countries with strict immigration and sometimes with obscure language barriers, yet here I was, struggling with an application for an English-speaking country, which is part of our very own "Commonwealth". How did I get my Chinese visa so easily, yet struggle with my Australian one?

Well, I read an article which had a hyperlink to one of those many tourist visa options, which seemed right on the spot, so I went forth and applied for it. It turned out that it was the wrong one - great. The one I should have applied for was the three-month visa which is free and gets answered within one day. But the one that I'd accidentally chosen, required a payment of 200 dollars (£100), takes three weeks to get a response, and also asks for pages and pages of information, including financial info. It was exactly this financial information of mine which made the immigration officer deem me as being in an improper position to travel through Australia. In a way, they were kind of right, I did have insufficient funds to travel for three months in the way they expected - eating in restaurants every day and sleeping in a hotel every night. Little did they know, that by my standards I had more than enough to travel in the way that I do - mostly eating cold baked beans out of the tin and sleeping in my tent most nights.

Yet I wasn't in a position to start arguing my case, because that's not what they wanted to hear. So, I took the sensible option, and just went straight ahead to apply for the free visa that I should've done in the first place. This time around, it did only take one day for the response. It was another rejection. It turned out that my subsequent application had flagged up as someone who'd already been rejected once, and considering I didn't supply any evidence of additional funds, it simply got rejected once more. This time around, I wasn't all too calm about the verdict, for it posed the possibility that I would have to change my plan.

I was gutted, because Australia had always been that last huge leg before New Zealand where I would have earned my victory and achievement after the trials and tribulations that this huge continent would inevitably bring. But now, what was I to do? Detour to South East Asia, which is going in the wrong direction, and thereby lose that catapult momentum which had gathered during the course of the ride? Or just go straight to New Zealand but risk the feeling of an insubstantial level of challenge and adventure between my month of rest in Tokyo and arriving at the finish line.

I didn't want to give life to either of those options, so my only option was to apply once more for the Ozzie visa and make it a third time lucky, once and for all. I asked my parents to lend me some additional funds (of which I intend on paying back in due course) and I gained some professional advice about the application. This time round, I provided all the necessary evidence and also a thorough explanation of my bicycle trip and what I would be doing in Australia. It was a nail-biting couple of weeks, but luckily, just before my Japanese visa ran out, I was finally granted the thumbs up and green light to cycle through Australia!

The next question was how I was planning to get there. Well, boat of course, because after all, I was doing the whole trip by bike and boat, so I was obviously going jump on the boat from Japan to Australia and baddabing baddaboom, I'd be there in a jiffy. Yet, quite like the visa situation, this part of the process became unavoidably complicated. I'd managed to get all the way from England to Japan with merely bike and boat, hopping over the sea on passenger-ferries and I'd assumed that this would be the same situation to Australia, but it turned out that was not the case at all.

There is literally *not one* single passenger boat linking Japan and Australia, which crushed my plan into oblivion. "Okay, so which other boats can I take then?" Well, considering it was the middle of winter in Australia, there were no cruises taking this route, and not one single sailing boat looking for crew (not that I'd have been all too much help as crew anyway with zero sailing experience). So, the only option I was left with was cargo ships, and I thought that'd be fine. Once again, I was wrong. It was challenging to find contact details but, in the end, I asked for a quote from a cargo ship travel agent, a sort of middleman conduit. The quote that came back explained that there *is* a boat, but it will take a total of 28 days on the sea, and at £100 a day, costing me £3,000. Shit. I physically did not have the funds to pay for that, and even in a parallel world where I could fund that ride, spending a month on a boat with no stops sounded like a nightmare. I asked a different company and received a similar outrageously expensive quote.

I was left with no options, and ultimately, I was forced by circumstances into flying. This was by no means what I wanted - I sincerely wanted to avoid flying. It's somewhat ironic that the trip was founded in my not wanting to fly to New Zealand, and yet I now had to do so just at the last leg of the journey. However, it was somewhat liberating considering the trip had already been born, and after doing some research and finding out that cruise ships and cargo ships are just as bad for the environment as planes, if not worse in some ways. It was almost liberating to let go of my absolutism and dogmatic beliefs in regard to flying.

I think that this matter deserves some explanation, rather than just being skimmed over sharply because air travel was such a vital part of the original seedling and subsequent evolution of this trip.

The entire concept of my Full Power Bike Ride grew and evolved from one single seed - the seed of not merely flying to New Zealand, and instead finding an alternative overland method for reaching the antipode. With this in mind, I couldn't help but feel like some form of hypocrite and failure for giving in to flight travel once more. But I was cornered by a lack of choice and had to give way to that reality.

Once I relaxed and let go of my tense feelings, I actually felt a sense of freedom and liberation from my strangling anti-flying ideology. I tend to do that a lot when I take a pledge to do something for the better, in that I believe in it so wholeheartedly that I become rather dogmatic and inflexible around that belief, quite like the Jahovah's Witness, for example, who is equally as irritating in their unmovable faith in their personal conception of God and overly eager to spread that dogma. So, letting go of this strict rule of mine ended up feeling more liberating than sad or dismal.

I still believe in keeping air travel to a minimum, for it is unquestionably polluting, let alone boring when compared to overlanding, but in this case, for jumping over the ocean - it was the only feasible and reasonable option. The seed had done its job in blossoming into a beautiful flower of such a journey, and at this point it felt less important in how I crossed the water. I had the "where", and now I had the "how", so all that was left was to take the leap and turn the page onto the next chapter of my story, Australia!

PART FIVE – A TWO-WHEELED ODYSSEY THROUGH AUSTRALASIA

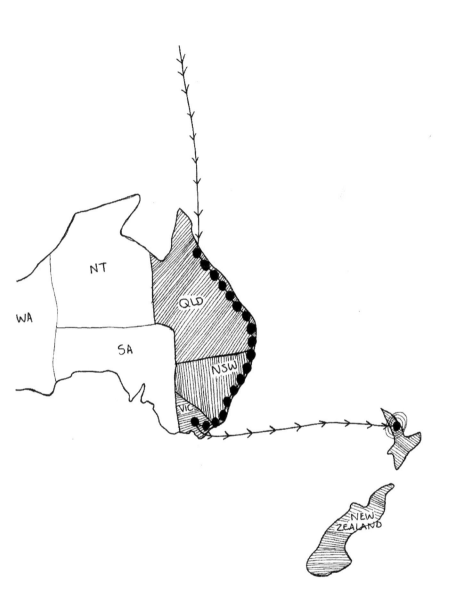

Chapter Twenty-Five

'Straya Mate - the Wild Wild Land

It's in moments like the one I'm about to describe, where it fully dawned on me how much I loved this wild, rugged, untamed landscape. I mean, I was essentially lost after having taken the "wrong" turn. And yet, as soon as I redefined my situation and reminded myself that there are *no* wrong turns in life, and that I'm exactly *where* I'm meant to be *when* I'm meant to be there, I suddenly looked around and realised that I was in paradise.

I had come off the main road and was taking the dirt road through the national park instead. It was so much quieter; you could properly hear the whistle and tooting of the songbirds rather than the roaring and gurgling of the dirty engines of the Motor Monsters. I looked over at a field full of kangaroos, smiling to myself as a couple of them hopped away on their hind legs, but they were quite far away so I couldn't see their cute little facial features. But all of a sudden, a few kilometres down the road I found myself right beside two small kangaroos grazing on the side of the road! I slowly brought myself to a standstill with my breaks and did my best not to scare them away. They stood there for a while, somewhat startled by this peculiar trippy fellow with his bike and all his bags, but after fully surveying me and concluding that I wasn't much of a threat, they went on with their business and munched some more foliage. I offered them a piece of dried apricot each and threw it in their general direction, but they kindly declined the offer by paying me absolutely no attention whatsoever. I watched them as they nibbled away and went on with their kangaroo business as the sun was settling on the horizon over yonder. It was quite a rarity to have that opportunity, so close. I had become used to seeing the dead and mutilated remains of kangaroos on the side of the main road, so to see them living and thriving was quite a sight. They are marvellous creatures, and it's no wonder that they're the national animal of Australia (along with the pretty swaggy emu on the coat of arms).

I let them be and said goodbye, knowing all too well that they wouldn't quite understand the utterances of my human language. I eventually rode out onto the part of the detour that I had been most concerned about, namely the beach. The main road was no good at all, mostly because of the risk of being crushed under the unforgiving wheels of Motor Monsters. Alternative routes, however, have their downsides too; it's like turning into a dead end with no way to keep going. It shortly became clear that this was the case for this attempted shortcut, as I came onto the beach and looked around. I soon accepted my failure and took it on the chin rather than getting frustrated with myself. But what made defeat all the more palatable was the sheer gorgeousness of my surroundings.

The light from the sunset was the perfect shade of red and at just the right potency to softly illuminate the lagoon to my right, and the bright white sand dunes to my left. Perched upon the lagoon were the rare and beautiful black swans with their red beaks of a similar hue to the setting sun. Beyond the dunes I could hear the metronomical lapping of the ebb and flow of the great ocean's waves. This, I thought, was just the right place to get lost. And as the evening got darker and darker, the possibility of pushing my bike over the sand to the nearest village became less and less likely. I surrendered myself to staying the night on that beautiful beach - oh dear, what an awful pity and agonising fate that was, resting in such a gorgeous place and having to wake up to those views again in the morning. Oh, poor me.

Speaking of agony on a serious note, however, my forearm was hurting good and proper. I'd developed a strange injury in the tendon of my forearm at this point of the cycling through Oz, probably because that region had been so hilly, and I'd been doing long distances every day (so I could get to Melbourne before my visa ran out). It was a strange and tender pain, and even hurt when I did minor tasks like brushing my teeth or picking up my water bottle, let alone cycling up and down hills all day. So before you're quick to conclude "oh great, another bit of writing about being in a beautiful place", please do understand that I was also in pain and it was actually quite chilly at the time (being mid-winter) so my situation wasn't perfect, I was just making the most out of it. When you're lost in Australia, you're still lucky to be lost because the natural world is simply oh so lovely.

And oh so tropical in the north, which was my first observation when arriving in Australia from Tokyo. Okay, let's keep it chronological and start from the top, thereby documenting some of the things that happened between arriving in Cairns, and cycling all the way down to where this majestic detour happened, in southern New South Wales (a bloody long way from Cairns).

I'd never been in the Southern Hemisphere before in my life, and I'd never been in a tropical country either, so I was arriving in uncharted territory. As soon as I walked out of the doors of the airport, I was literally hit with the foreignness of this land. The white cockatoos with their crazy yellow Mohicans sung strange songs, and some multi-coloured rainbow parakeets flew overhead boundlessly. I put my bike back into one piece and eventually got everything ready to go. I'd only been cycling for five minutes from the airport when I saw my first Australian snake. It was bloody big and bloody dark--which is never good news--but luckily for me it was off the road...and dead. Its head had been decapitated and it lay there lifeless; a menacing image and a warning sign that these types of beasts were really lurking in the surrounding wilderness.

251

After all, Cairns is situated in tropical North Queensland and it is full of rainforest, with a list of some of the world's deadliest snakes and spiders crawling and slivering along its forest floors. I know that Ozzies love to scare the English tourists about all the mythical monsters that could kill them in an instant, but to be fair, there really were many creatures that could end your life in a mere second if you were unlucky enough to cross their path. So, there was a reason for caution, and as I cycled away from the huge dead snake, I knew that I had to treat this wild, wild land with utmost respect.

Another thing that struck me almost as suddenly was something that felt like a missing jigsaw piece in this tropical jigsaw puzzle. With all the crazy flora and fauna, where were all the tropical people? Although it's a tough subject, we know essentially that the British colonial fleets came along and wiped most of them out in the late 18th century. It's much more multifaceted than that of course, but it would mostly explain why I was on the other side of the world surrounded by such foreign nature, in every sense of the word, yet most of the locals looked the same as me - British. I won't dwell on this topic all too much here, for I'm merely noting my initial observations fresh off the boat, so to speak. But I will come back to this topic, because although it's a touchy subject and people get easily offended by it, I consider it to be a vitally important discussion when understanding the incredible continent of Australia.

Queensland was pretty epic in many ways, especially tropical North Queensland. I cycled from the airport to my host's house in Cairns. I had previously met the wife of my host in Istanbul, in an elevator. Yeah, it does sound odd, but I'm telling the truth! I randomly got chatting to two middle aged Ozzie ladies who I shared an elevator with, in the old capital of Turkey, and then we ended up spontaneously having coffee together when we arrived at the cafe on the top floor. We spoke about my trip, and about Australia. I remarked that I will probably be cycling the east coast of Australia when I eventually arrive there, and they offered to

252

host me when I finally arrived, but I'm not sure if they even thought I'd get that far, having the entire Asian continent to cycle in between. But a couple of weeks before my arrival I emailed them both and they said that of course I could stay with them! However, both were actually out of town at the time, but Anna's husband offered to host me nonetheless.

They had a beautiful home at the top of a very steep hill (which was blooming hard work to cycle up) and it was walking distance from the botanical gardens. John, Anna's husband, fed me great food and let me rest up in the comfiest conceivable bed ever (I'd been pretty much sleeping on the floor in Tokyo in traditional Japanese style so I'd forgotten what it was like to sleep in a genuine hundred percent bed). It felt like I was rejuvenating on top of a memory-foam cloud. During the following couple of days, I was lucky enough to do what everybody absolutely must do when they're in this part of the world - witness the Great Barrier Reef. It really is a spectacle to behold. It turns out that the coral which comprises the reef is actually very similar to a jellyfish type animal rather than a plant, and is a genuinely living organism. Unfortunately, it is currently at risk of bleaching from human pollutants, and in fact most of the magical and rare wildlife living within the reef system is also at risk of extinction, because, after all, humans don't really give a shit about nature en masse. We were warned to be very conscientious before we went down, so that we didn't touch the coral at all and respected the nature as a whole. It was a gorgeous concoction of colours and sparkles underneath the water, with multicoloured fish all swimming around amidst the reef, like a little underwater city, city fishies going about their business in big groups or alone. We were very lucky to witness an endangered deep-sea turtle gently gliding along, and even an eagle manta ray flying through the water gracefully and effortlessly without qualms or stresses. Some people even saw mini sharks beneath us (albeit they were harmless ones and luckily there weren't any killer ones around). It was a magnificent sight and I was very lucky to have witnessed it.

I also visited some tropical rainforests near Cairns which were so diverse with flora and fauna that I'd never seen before, all so alien to me. I didn't see any, but they were the home of the prehistoric cassowary birds which are huge blue flightless birds that look like dinosaurs and are an integral part of the distribution of rainforest seeds. I probably didn't see any because they too are a massively endangered species - hooray for humankind. If the natural world could speak English, they would probably rename us as "human unkind" instead, eh? It seems that our current name isn't so fitting. Anyway, I had a good look around in the few days I was there in Cairns, but I was eager to get back on the road. After a long rest of three weeks in Tokyo, I was more than ready to get back on the bike and readapt to the cycle touring lifestyle. Also, I was well aware that I only had three months on my visa to traverse the entirety of the east coast all the way down to Melbourne. I knew it was going to be quite tight, timewise, but especially tight if I stuck around too long up north getting lost in my exploration - which could've been easily done, because it was all so fascinating and peculiar. But no, I grabbed myself by the horns and began my cycling the following day. I looked at some maps, got my stuff together, and got back on Buddha Bike!

The following day I said goodbye to John, my lovely host, and I hit the road. I jumped straight onto the Bruce Highway which was to be the road I'd be cycling on non-stop for the next few weeks. The word highway makes it sound like it was busier than what it was, in fact, it was actually quite benign and pleasant, as far as highways go at least. It was just a lane each way and the traffic wasn't all too heavy, although you would occasionally get a 4-by-4 (which the Ozzies call "yutes") that would fly past way too fast, but it was absolutely nothing when compared to the awful drivers of Turkey or Kyrgyzstan. The road would quite frequently pass over these little "creeks" which was also a relatively unknown word for me.

Creeks are basically just narrow tributaries that stem from the main river and connect with the sea- but these ones were particularly ominous and dangerous. Why, you may ask -

well...crocs of course! Tropical North Queensland is home to some of the most dangerous crocodiles in the world, and even the locals regard it as a serious concern and would warn you not to swim or camp near any given water source, for it wouldn't be long until you became a croc's snack.

And when they said, "any water", they really meant *any water* because there were both freshwater and saltwater crocodiles in this part of the world, so even on the beach you're not particularly safe from their hungry bellies. What made it worse, was the actual method in which they'd snack upon your feeble human body. Firstly, they'd creep up on you without you noticing, snap their ferocious jaws clamped shut upon your neck or leg or whichever place they so pleased, and within a blink of an eye they would have you underwater spinning you around in a whirlpool vortex quicker than you could think of the word "shit" and then they would do this until you drowned, at which point they would then stuff your lifeless body carefully and meticulously into the roots of a tree and leave you there for numerous weeks until your flesh matured, and *then...and only then*...you'd be their snack. So, I think that it goes without saying that I'd rather not be in that position myself. And when I cycled over the bridges of these creeks, I'd always look down, and although I couldn't see any crocs directly, I just knew with my deepest intuition that there were heaps and heaps of them waiting patiently under those murky dark waters simply waiting for their moment to snap.

But luckily there wasn't all too much to be concerned about as long as you weren't an idiot, but it just so happens to be the case that I am, in fact, an idiot. So, I did have to be super careful with my decision-making skills, and firmly ensure that I didn't flirt with death and get too close to any water. Well I'm still here to tell the tale some months later, so it's clear that I didn't get stuffed into any tree roots by a prehistoric reptilian monster, so that's a plot spoiler for you. I passed over many bridges that went over these creeks on my first day of cycling, and simply marvelled at the view that would be presented to me on both sides. At points it really did look like I was cycling through the Amazon rainforest, with a long winding river and endless forest for as far as the eye could see. It really was a wild land, and the adventure-level was high! I was enjoying it, and glad to be there, in the infamous land of 'Straya mate.

One aspect of North Queensland that came as quite a surprise was that it shared many similarities to the cowboy areas of Texas and suchlike in The States. It all became clear when I found out that this region of Australia is one of the largest distributors of beef in the entire world, similar to places like Texas. Beef farms seem to breed a certain type of farmer the world over, which is not necessarily good nor bad, but these cowboys can tend to be an interesting kind. In the States they call them "hillbillies" or "rednecks", but in Australia they call them "bogans" which is a term I'd never heard before. Before I arrived, I had a naive conception that all Australians were like my Ozzie friends I'd met abroad – a kind of surfer people who eat organic food and have golden wind-swept hair, with sand in between their toes. Of course, these people do exist, especially in places like Byron Bay, but in this region of North Queensland you were more likely to cross paths with Bogans than with this stereotypical surfer type.

By all means, I'm not saying they're all bad people, of course they're not, and I'm not writing this book to constantly criticise the locals because that would be ridiculous and obnoxious, but I'm merely noting my observations and this is one of them. They tended to have beliefs that one could call racist, whether that be towards the pesky Chinese "coming over to our country and taking over" or to the indigenous "black fellas, who sit around doing nothing and just taking money from the state". We have the same issues of attitude in the UK of course, but there it was particularly loudly voiced, along with the huge trucks, and a similar style of dress, I couldn't help but compare them to the infamous cowboys of Texas, and I couldn't help but write about it here.

But within any social group or subculture there are always good eggs, and one of those good eggs was my man Brendan who helped to dry my tent one morning with a leaf blower. Okay, I know that's fully weird without the context, but please allow me to explain. Well basically, I continued a particular challenge of mine that I'd been doing through Europe and had to discontinue come Georgia - namely, not paying a penny for accommodation. So now the plan was to do the same for Australia - to find somewhere to sleep every night for three months without breaking the bank. That's exactly what would have happened if I just stayed in hostels willy-nilly in Australia - I would have been very broke very fast because accommodation is so very expensive there.

I was a sincerely lucky boy, to have many friends dotted here and there down the east coast, and lucky that they too had friends of friends who were willing to help a cyclist in need. But all the nights where I didn't know anybody personally, I had to find a good place to pitch my tent without getting caught or causing any drama. That point soon came where I found myself in a small village looking for a place to camp, because I didn't know a single soul. I'd finished my dinner at this point, and it had become somewhat late and dark. The prospect of cycling an extra three kilometres to the nearby showground (basically the village sports fields where you could sometimes camp, with emphasis on "sometimes") became less and less inviting. I looked across the road and there seemed to be a pretty decent patch of grass outside the local theatre.

Of course, in a big city there would be no way you could camp outside the theatre because the security guards would be straight on your back in a matter of minutes. But here, it was only a small sleepy town - and in the literal sense too, for it seemed that everyone were *actually* sleeping anyway, so it didn't even matter where I camped because no one was on the streets to witness my camping spot regardless. It was raining slightly, and the grass outside the theatre even had some canvas canopies covering the space from the downpouring elements. Perfect, I thought, well-perfect I thought naively.

I was awoken at 3am by a peculiar sound of something mechanical jolting back and forward. It scared me to begin with, because it could've been some big mechanical spider for all I knew, in my dreamlike daze of delirium. I came to, and realised it of course wasn't this, but I was shocked further by an additional sound of water streaming from this machine. Whatever it was, it began squirting water in all possible directions at quite a force. "Oh, bloody hell!", I thought, I'd only gone and pitched my tent a matter of inches away from a sprinkler. Before I knew it, water was seeping into my tent through the innumerable holes that had slowly formed during my huge cycling voyage from England to Australia. The horrid machine didn't stop its relentless squirting and therefore it just continued to come into my tent bit by bit. I mean, it wasn't like someone was pouring a bucket of water over me at 3am, it was just more like someone had slightly left on a dripping tap, to drop on top of me inside my tent for one whole hour. There's no harm in a little bit of Chinese water torture now is there?

There was no point of getting out of my tent to try solving the issue because it really wouldn't have helped. What would I have done anyway? It's not like I could have kicked the sprinkler to death. I decided to go for the more sensible option of sleeping and pretending that it was all just happening in a dream and not in real life at all. This is certainly a positive aspect of the melting reality of dream states and waking states. The fact that the two states can blur and blend into one another makes for some useful self-deception at times of distress. I used this same tactic during the aforementioned windiest day of my life in Western China, as I convinced myself that it was only in my dream that my tent had snapped. So, I continued my sleep, outside the theatre, in a little pool of water at the bottom of my home, as the sprinkler continued to spread its noisy wrath upon me.

Eventually I woke from my awful dream to realise that, in fact, it had actually happened in real life. But it wasn't that I gradually awoke gracefully from R.E.M (rapid-eye-movement) sleep to N.R.E.M (non-rapid-eye-movement) and then into waking life, yet instead I was violently shaken out of sleep at 6am by the ferocious sound of yet another machine - a leaf blower. The loud sound came out of nowhere and henceforth just continued at the same volume. I thought about maybe trying to go back to sleep and just wait till the leaf blowing person finished, but I quickly ushered that thought out of my head considering that my camping spot could have possibly been illegal. This was a genuine concern whenever I had to find a free camping spot in Australia, or the world over. If you leave at sunrise without disturbing anyone you should generally be okay and avoid a penalty fine, but in this case it seemed that an official council worker had come to me instead, and before sunrise.

I had no choice but to get up and apologise to the person for camping in a negligent spot. If I was to receive a 200 dollar fine, it would have been the worst camping spot imaginable. I slowly managed to drag my soggy wet gear out of my tent in a tired and sulky state. I approached the leaf blowing man to apologise and explain myself, but when I arrived to him it was actually *he* who began to apologise:

"I'm really sorry mate if I woke you up" he said, in a somber and genuine tone.

"Oh, erm, no worries mate. I also apologise if I'm in your way at all" I replied, with equal sincerity.

"Don't mention it buddy! Where are you from?"

The pleasant conversation continued quite like this from that point onwards. It's funny how I was expecting a rather angry and irritated leaf-blowing-man but instead was welcomed into a new day by a lovely young fellow named Brendon. His kindness extended even further when he helped me to dry my soggy tent by using his leaf blower and then advised me as to where the sun will rise - thereby where the best spot was to dry my soggy gear. A staff member from the theatre came out, equally uncaring about my being there, and he even brought me out a morning cup of tea. The kindness warmed me to the core and along with the sun it helped to dry my gear. We all spoke together for a couple hours, and I eventually left with dry equipment and began my cycling further south towards Melbourne, blessed with the gift of kindness - prepared to take on yet another challenging day in the rough and rugged land of 'Straya.

I was heading towards Townsville (can we just take a moment to appreciate the indecisiveness of the people who named this town. It's hilarious that they didn't know whether to call it a town or a village, so they just called it both), where I was to be greeted by my first Warm Showers hosts since leaving from Cairns. I was excited for it, to cherish the comforts that are few and far between when camping. But I still had quite a way to go. I passed through a small town called Tully, which happens to be the wettest town in the whole of Australia, which isn't really too hard to be honest, considering that the vast majority of the country is as dry as a crumpled raisin. They had a huge golden boot marking the height of the record-breaking year of rainfall they had - a bit strange, but fair enough.

I stopped off at the town's backpackers just to get a bit of food and company before heading to the showground to set up my tent. I asked for some vegetarian food at the counter, to which the young lady looked quite baffled. Eventually we managed to throw together a few sides into one meal.

It must have been about half an hour of waiting time, which is fine, but I just wanted to confirm that all was well in the kitchen with my alien order. My query was met by the boss, who was a sour faced old lady who clearly didn't want to speak with me. I asked her if my order had been sent through and whether the chef definitely knew the pasta was to be without meat. For sure she had gotten out of bed on the wrong side because she erupted with negativity and rudeness from out of nowhere. I told her she was being rude and she asked me to leave, and not in a polite way whatsoever. I don't expect everyone to be civil all the time, of course not, but if you're running a service that relies on customer service then you can't shout at people who just want to confirm their order.

But it slowly sunk in, that her rudeness felt more paramount only because I'd spent three months prior in the most polite country in the world, Japan, where even the youngsters in the convenience stores bow to you when leaving and genuinely thank you for your custom. So, in comparison to that, I felt somewhat offended, because that would never ever happen in Japan, not in their wildest dreams. But I guess if I came straight from London to Tully, it would have felt normal and I wouldn't have been concerned with her rudeness.

Anyhow, I apologise if I sometimes overemphasise the troubled side of my contact with locals, it's just that it remains a lot more concrete in one's memory than the endless kind people who go out of their way to help you. Either way, I think it's important to note both the positive and negative experiences with people, because it prevents dangerous generalisations like "they're all lovely" or "they're all horrible" – which is never the case, because humans are naturally diverse. I went on with my life anyway and didn't let the situation affect my peaceful sleep.

The following morning, I continued on the Bruce Highway, which had soon become my routine: taking down camp and then jumping on the one straight road that would take me all the way to Brisbane. At some points it would get a little bit boring when the only surroundings were sugar cane fields. For some reason there was so much sugar cane, and it would stretch for miles and miles for as far as the eyes could see, so it's not the most stimulating landscape. But what made up for it was the absolute beauty of the eucalyptus trees. I'd never fully seen this tree before, as in, observed it with my heart, and for some reason it felt so sacred and powerful. They have a huge tall trunk, where the bark would chip off in naturally artistic ways, revealing numerous shades of bark, and their leaves all have a slight curve to them, possessing a deep shade of bluey green. When you split the eucalyptus leaf in half you get the gift of smelling the deep pungent smell of loveliness

261

which delightfully tickles the inside of your nasal tunnels. It's difficult to explain why, but it really is a special tree in many ways, so it was always a pleasure to watch them roll by my peripheral vision as I cycled along. Occasionally I would find myself stopping when the sunlight was just right, and simply appreciating the sheer beauty of these trees.

The highway wasn't all too bad traffic-wise, but it started to get busier the closer I got to Brisbane. Usually there was a decent hard shoulder, but that would disappear when going over the bridges over the creeks, so I had to be careful of the big farmer's yutes. I'd been cycling for a couple weeks on this road and I literally hadn't met one single cyclist. The road probably only felt safe relative to all the other countries with the most dangerous drivers imaginable. And probably after having cycled for so many months on main roads with Truck Dragons hurtling past me, I had become complacent and at ease on the road, regardless of the drivers. So relative to itself, it was still a dangerous road to the locals, and the big cars still went far too fast, and this would likely explain as to why people weren't stupid enough to risk their lives on this road - only me. I later found out that this road alone is responsible for 17% of all traffic related deaths in the entirety of Australia (it's a big country), so I think it's fair to say that I had become complacent by this point.

I'd also come to terms with the fact that I wouldn't meet any other cycle tourists, quite unlike the Pamir Highway where you would meet fellow two-wheeled mad men every other day. Comparatively, the Bruce Highway was a lonely road. Until one day, a cyclist from out of nowhere gently overtook me at a friendly pace and started a conversation:

"Hiya mate, how's it going?"

"Oh, hello...fine thanks! Where you off to?" I replied.

"I'm cycling to Townsville, what about you?"

"Me too!"

It was an unexpected moment. He was a South African man, middle aged- probably just under 50. He was a kind fellow who spoke with a very thick South African accent (which I'm awful at imitating). We didn't cycle together for all that long, because he wanted to spend the night at a beach which was a 20km detour off the main road, whereas I wanted to continue towards my Warm Showers hosts in Townsville. Albeit, we did still cycle together for half a day. His setup was quite different to mine, for he had more of a "bikepacking" setup which is much lighter and where you only bring the main equipment you need for a weeklong trip or so, which is rather different to the pannier setup where you bring everything you need to cycle across the entire world, which is what I had. Therefore, I was much heavier, bulkier and thereby much slower than him.

He whizzed off in front and I put every ounce of my energy into trying to keep up with his pace. It was really quite challenging to be honest, and somewhat stressful in some ways. It wasn't just the baggage weight difference, but also a matter of strength - his calf muscles were absolutely huge and bulging out from his legs. It's possible that trying to keep up with my new friend was one of the reasons I really hurt my knee ligaments which only properly surfaced the following day. When cycling alone you quickly adapt to your own pace of cycle touring, mine being very slow and steady, yet his was very fast and aggressive so that clash of style jarred my body notably.

I will note here also that it was bloody boiling hot in the north of Australia at that point in time. I timed it pretty well to avoid the Australian summer, knowing all too well that it would have fried me to a crisp, spitting me out as a genuine blood-red lobster. But although I arrived in the middle of winter, it was still boiling hot in North Queensland, because it's so close to the equator, and they only have two seasons - hot, and ridiculously hot. This was the closest I'd ever been to the equator and probably the closest I will be for a long while. The sun had a feeling of potent intensity. The UV rays themselves were particularly powerful, and it felt that they could really do some damage if you didn't protect yourself properly. Therefore, I smothered myself all day in 50+ sun cream, knowing full well that my white English skin wouldn't be able to take that level of UV intensity. One thing that helped me to deal with the heat was the wind.

The wind was pretty strong in the north, so it helped to cool me down. The only issue was the direction of the wind - in my face, travelling south to north. It was horrendous, for the first two weeks leaving Cairns, I had to endure the toughest head wind relentlessly all day. I'd experienced worse in the Central Asian deserts and in western China, but still, it was pretty bloody strong nonetheless. So although it cooled me down, it also happened to slow me down too, which is never fun, because I was already slow enough with all my weight and I didn't need a helping hand to cycle even slower, but alas, I had one.

I didn't realise that these winds are called the "trade winds" and have always travelled from south to north even since the days of the first European explorers, and it's these very winds that they used to navigate the east coast of Australia. It's the same all year round, for as long as records began. Every local I bumped into told me that I was cycling the wrong way and that I should've started in Melbourne, but I retorted that I was cycling to New Zealand from England, so the only direction for me was south.

So, a combination of powerful head winds, a half day of keeping up with an unusually strong middle aged South African, along with other hidden factors - contributed to a random aggressive pain in my lower knee. It first surfaced just a few kilometres outside of Townsville. I'd nearly arrived, almost there, and then boom - a seriously painful feeling throbbed in my knee. "Bloody typical" I thought, but I equally thought "radical acceptance bro, radical acceptance. You signed up for this trip- so keep going!" I was actually very lucky during this trip to avoid any serious injuries; I was even somewhat lucky to avoid death. I'd had innumerable aches and pains in every possible part of my body, especially when cycling in the mountains, and even dislocated my shoulder in the Korean sauna, but was yet to suffer from any lasting injury. But shit, this was my first serious injury and it could even have stopped my trip there and then. I did the cycling equivalent of hobbling and limping on my bike, slowly and painfully inching closer to my hosts during those final few kilometres to Townsville.

I arrived somewhat distressed and in pain, and the hosts were absolutely awesome - making me feel as comfortable as possible. Just by pure chance, the lady of the couple happened to be an English doctor, which was incredibly convenient. The gentleman of the couple was a Scottish teacher who was equally lovely. The kind doctor lady helped to look at my knee and advised me on how to rest it properly meanwhile. I mentioned the wind and the South African, but she remained curious and thought it could be something to do with my saddle height. "Hmm," I thought, this is something I hadn't considered, so the following day I went into the local cycle touring shop. The man in the shop was a cycling wizard, a two-wheeled Gandalf one could say, and after some scrutinous assessment of my saddle height, he declared that it was, in fact, far too low for my height. I felt like a proper silly billy. After landing in Cairns from Tokyo I had to re-assemble my bike from its boxed form, and I'd set the saddle height far too low- and this, in turn, lead to a repetitive strain injury in my knee. The wizard adjusted it to its correct height, and off I went to rest some more, with utmost gratitude for the Gandalf mechanic.

Townsville was a wonderful town/ville. It was full of glorious traditional "Queenslander" homes which were built on a kind of stilts, in order to allow cool air to travel underneath the home, thereby cooling the entirety of the house during their boiling summers. They are made from a lightweight wooden cladding, and painted in a myriad of light, cool colours. Although Australia as a modern nation state is a very young country, these are the most historical residential homes, with some of them looking very old and run down - but when cared for they remained lovely and still fully functional. The road where my hosts lived was full of white Queenslanders, some of them quite large and fancy – glorious when the sun reflected off of them.

Townsville has a large rock hill behind the main town, which almost resembles a kind of Uluru rock, just not in the desert and less staggering, but still quite epic with the iconic red dirt of Australia. I went for a long walk, stretching my legs and exploring, during which I had my very first experience with the famous laughing kookaburra. I didn't have a clue what it was, but I was fascinated by its neckless body. Compare it directly to the famous Australian ibis bird which urban folk prefer to call the "bin chicken" (because it spends its whole time in bins rummaging around scavenging for food). The ibis has a long neck in between its body and head, somewhat like a bird giraffe (sort of), yet the kookaburra has no neck at all, so it's a very peculiar sight. But add to this a loud and unusual birdcall and you have overall a very fascinating bird. When I was a teenager I used to take the piss out of birdwatchers and rue the day that I would ever take a notably lengthy interest in birds of any kind, but it seems that the day has come, as I'm talking for a rather long time right now, about...well, birds. But this one was pretty fricking cool! Its song sounds like a loud mocking cackle, as if it is laughing directly at you, whilst hiding amidst the canopies of glorious eucalypts. They only exist in Australia and Papua New Guinea, so it really was the first time I'd ever seen one in all my life, and it really brings out the childish feeling of freshness and novelty. Think back, if you can, to the times when you were a wee infant, effortlessly in a state of awe and wonder, whenever you first witnessed *anything* however "mundane" or "normal" it now is to the adult eye.

If it makes it easier to imagine, think of your niece, nephew or children. The first time they come into contact with a lampshade, or a bicycle bell, or for that matter - anything at all, it is the most exciting prospect in the world, for it is the very first time they've had that experience and thereby inherently bloody exciting. This is exactly how I felt during my first few weeks in Australia- like a child, experiencing these phenomena for the very first time, ever. For the locals, a kookaburra is a daily object, no more interesting than a car or a hat, but for me, the foreign English cyclist- it was a fascinating creature. Think how the very first European explorers

266

must have felt, back when the land was much wilder than it is today, experiencing the craziest of things they'd never even imagined before.

Apparently when the biologists sent back drawings of the duck-billed platypus to England, the public literally didn't believe at all that there could be such a mammal: that could lay eggs, with the bill of a duck, the tail of a beaver and all sorts of other mystical features. They thought it was a big joke and that the biologists had just chucked four different animals into one, maybe for an April fools or something. But lo! the duck billed platypus *does* exist, in this wild, wild land of 'Straya.

Anyhow, I digress once more. Kookaburras are cool. I enjoyed my walk, taking in all the new things that kept presenting themselves to me. I rested my leg, was fed glorious food by my hosts and was ready to tackle the road once more, on my way to Brisbane. Once I got back on the back of Buddha Bike, I was expecting the same pain as before, but as if magic had been sprinkled on the bike by the mechanical wizard- there was no more pain at all. Such a simple adjustment of the saddle height was enough to remove the problem altogether. I was back to normal health, and ready to continue my cycle southwards to New Zealand.

One of the most famous aspects of Australia is the sheer vastness of the landmass. Obviously everyone knows that it's a big country, simply by looking at it on a globe, but when you cycle practically every inch of its coast from north to south, you get to understand seriously how large the country really is. It's not as boring as the Kazakh and Uzbek desert where there is literally nothing for as far as the eye could see, but at least I had company during that leg. At this point, I was completely alone to tackle the vastness and mega distances that were in between me and my finish line. In some areas there was literally nothing other than sugar cane fields which were rather unstimulating with nothing to focus on other than pushing pedals. Sometimes I would go the entire day without seeing *any* humans at all (outside of their moving metal boxes). This is quite a challenging aspect of cycle touring - the loneliness.

I had been pretty good at keeping myself entertained, and all in all pretty fascinated with everything, but I did reach a psychological plateau in Australia where I did get rather bored and lonely. The famous extent of this vastness can certainly send you slightly crazy, especially when there's no one around to judge you. But for sure it did make me appreciate the Ozzie humans a lot more when I eventually did bump into them, and even a tiny building like a petrol station on the horizon would look like a human metropolis. It was always a wonderful sight to see a building after an entire day of not seeing one, because it essentially meant safety- specifically in the form of food and water, the absolute backbone of cycle touring. Without the fuel for the engine, the engine will essentially stop running, and that's not ideal when the engine is you.

However, regardless of how lonely I felt, I could always reassure myself that what I was going through was nowhere near as hard as it would have been if I'd decided to cycle from east to west of Australia, or vice versa - for that would have meant cycling through the Outback. That really wasn't a feat that I could possibly endure, considering I had already had a lifetime's worth of experience in cycling through huge, dry, and barren areas, although it would have been an interesting experience in and of itself. But the benefit of cycling down the east coast was that you could end a long hard day of cycling, usually with being rewarded by the gorgeous and calming sea. The ocean is timelessly a scene of beauty and relaxation, and even if you've seen it the previous day and will see it the next day, it doesn't stop being ever so gorgeous. Because the eastern coastline is so huge, there are innumerable sandy beaches that have barely even been looked at by tourists, let alone stepped on, because there are just so many little nooks and crannies. Ending the day with my own private beach was usually quite the treat. Noosa heads was particularly wonderful for example, with bright white sand

and crystal-clear turquoise water. It was in Noosa where I saw my very first koala, just chilling up in the tree being a lovely fluffy ball of grey, deeply involved in his ridiculously long sleep. Pretty much *every* beach was a delight to the eye and the mind alike.

Eventually, with the help of these wonderful beaches, I arrived in Brisbane, which is the third biggest city in Australia. It had been quite a while since I'd been in any settlement which one could classify as a "city", but this definitely was one. It showed me that Australia isn't merely a bunch of amazing animals and crazy nature, but it did also have significant human geography also. However, as with any city the world over, wherever you have rich people, you unfortunately must have poor people too. But, in this case, the poor and homeless had a different angle to their resentment and frustration of which they don't necessarily have in the UK for example. One reason for it being a different case for some of these people, is because they are Aboriginal.

Here, I will return to the topic that I briefly aforementioned at the beginning of this chapter - for I believe it to be deeply important. A situation occurred in Brisbane which struck me quite seriously. "Aboriginal" is a Latin word which essentially describes people who are indigenous to that land, but in Australia it has become synonymous with the word "indigenous" and all native people are called Aboriginals. For the first time in my entire trip, I was expected to distinguish between people who were essentially classified as indigenous and those who weren't. Whereas in the previous 18 countries I had cycled through, it was simply a matter of those people being from that country: Kazakh people in Kazakhstan, Japanese people in Japan, and so on and so forth, but in Australia there were two groups. It was also my first time cycling through a country that had been a part of the British Empire, and a current member of the "Commonwealth".

Before visiting, I knew very little about Australian history and just knew the absolute basics: that British colonists went exploring at some point, found this huge country and just sent all the English prisoners over there as punishment. But when you learn the nuanced details of the actual act of the colonisation, it is shocking to say the least.

Originally, Captain James Cook was sent by the British Navy to survey the Pacific Ocean and explore new lands for research, where he thereby discovered the landmass of Australia. On his return, he was asked whether there were any natives on the land, to which he responded that there were "only a few along the coastline" which would be no problem at all in colonising. From this information, they decided that there weren't enough indigenous people for it to be its own nation, thereby declaring it as a "Terra Nullius" which essentially means that it is an empty land.

Whereas, in reality, the huge country was home to a massive number of Aboriginal people with almost 500 different unique tribes with separate cultures and languages. So when the British eventually sent more fleets a few years later to actually occupy and settle on the new land, they were happy enough to wipe out any natives who tried to get in their way, because they already had the green light to classify it as no one's land, thereby making it theirs for the taking. Whether it was through simply shooting them or other supposed methods, (such as purposefully and strategically introducing Western diseases) it still remains the truth that a vast majority of the indigenous population were murdered en masse, which is nothing other than genocide.

As it stands today, Aboriginal people only make up 2.4% of the entire Australian population. Even though the world regards the nation-state of Australia as having a mere 200 years of history, we have a responsibility to acknowledge the reality that this land, in symbiosis with the Aboriginal Australians has almost 50,000 years of indigenous history which is widely ignored and pushed under the carpet. I'd like to stress sincerely that this is by no means an attack on any party, whether they are British or White Australian - for anyone alive today had no role to play in this original colonisation, but I am just stating the facts and hopefully helping spread the information which may help to bring a more inclusive future to Aboriginal people, rather than treating them as outsiders and vagrants.

Another aspect of this whole state of affairs was that the British colonists, and later the Australian government didn't even classify the Aboriginal Australians as "citizens" until the early 60's, finally allowing them to vote and ironically to be classified as 'Australians' at all. I stayed with a particular host who made some pretty striking comments about Queensland as a state - remarking that Queensland was home to the world's first apartheid, even though South Africa gets the trophy, and the home to the world's first concentration camps, even though Germany gets that trophy on an international stage. Of course, do feel free to do your own research and fact checking, but regardless, it is a pretty woeful history and one that does evoke a sense of guilt being British, in a country where the British did such malevolent things. So, with all of this in mind, it was a rather awkward moment when I was in the middle of Brisbane walking past a homeless Aboriginal woman sat on the pavement. She must have gotten fed up of people looking at her with a sense of pity, and she shouted at the top of her voice:

"Feel sorry for yourselves, you sad people!" She screamed these words with such anger and potency that it made me rethink the situation entirely. She was sitting there all day watching the stress and angst that is intrinsic to any modern city life, taking in all the pain around her. When reflecting on the simple, community life that her ancestors may have lived, potentially on this exact piece of land, the contrast must have been so stark. For 50,000 years they lived a life that worked alongside nature, inextricably linked to one another, living a natural life in every sense of the word. Along with the European settlers came the European way of life which was essentially alienation of nature and the pursuit of profit, with no regards for the totality of the whole. Her words were powerful, in that they highlighted the unhealthiness of city living, where even the homeless people pity its inhabitants.

It does beg the question of how different things would have been, if the colonists had actually adopted the tribal way of living and gone back to nature, rather than forcing their capitalist ways upon the locals. The world would be a very different place today if Captain Cook had brought back lessons of living in unity with the natural world and a life of minimalism and community, instead of simply creating another new colony for the Empire, in which there were already many - incessantly feeding the growing greed of the Crown. It was a difficult thing to hear the anger in that woman's voice and not be able to do anything positive to help directly, but at least it did make me consider the respect I should have for these people and to act more considerately than normal, considering the history involved. We can't change history, but at least we can learn from it when going into the future, and hopefully thereby live a future where we create less suffering and pain to all people of all nations.

Despite the sociological issues that come with cities, they do often give a well needed respite from the loneliness of the bush. I made the most of being surrounded by sociable people and enjoyed myself whilst being there. I stayed with a friend from Bath who had been living there for a while and we shared stories, laughter and enjoyed each other's company. I went to an art museum, and even a music event which was nourishing, for I love music and I love humans - put those both together and it's always a recipe for fun. I enjoyed myself then got ready to get back on the road. My next major city was Sydney, a huge 1000km away from Brisbane, so I had to ready myself once more for the loneliness and vast spaces ahead. Of course there are smaller settlements along the way, and I knew some people that were scattered down the coastline, but still from city to city the distances were so huge when compared to the distances between English cities on our comparably tiny island.

Once again, I had to get together the courage to return my focus to a life of incessant cycling all day every day. There's really not a lot else to do when you're in the middle of the bush. This is why at some points it's rather difficult to write about this cycling trip, considering that some days were really actually very boring. I woke up, packed down my tent, got on the bike, pedalled all day, set up my tent to sleep in and repeated that process, sometimes for a week or so without anything particularly noteworthy occurring. For me, that was generally fine because I learnt how to keep myself entertained without much stimuli, but in terms of writing about it, there's some points in the trip with not all too much to say about it. But at this point in time there was not too much need for self-motivation, because I knew that I was so close to the final destination of New Zealand, that this knowledge alone was enough to push me through those final kilometres.

Chapter Twenty-Six

A Whale's Tail in New South Wales

I stopped off in Byron Bay for a little while, which is a pretty incredible part of the world. It's where most of the Australian surfer stereotypes derive from with innumerable young guys with salty, long, blonde locks, surfboards in their arms galloping along the beach into the swell and surf of their holy waves. It's a sight to behold. It's full to the brim with organic cafes and vegan restaurants, which some people may despise but I was in my element. It is also the eastern-most point of mainland Australia and therefore the first place in the entire country to see the sun in the morning. It's stunning, but one moment struck me as being a particularly once-in-a-lifetime viewing.

I was sat on the beach around dusk, meditating and taking it all in, the yellow sun turning tiger orange, then transitioning into a deep red. At precisely the point when the sky turned a hue of pink, a gigantic whale's tail came flying out of the water, close to the bay, where it came crashing back down into the sea water, leaving a mighty *splash* behind. It was majestic in every way. Such a humongous creature, with all its sheer might, simply waving and saying hello to all the humans gaping in awe of its magnificence. It was rather fitting to be in the state of New South Wales, having front row seats to this new southern whale. It was actually perfect timing, because thousands of adult whales were making their annual migration from Antarctica, all the way up to Northern Australia where they have fun making lots of babies before heading back to Antarctica - which is a ridiculously long journey by sea. I felt remarkably lucky to see one so close.

During the ride from Byron down to Sydney, I tried my utmost to find some smaller backroads rather than sticking to the highways. I'd mostly been staying on the main road, pretty much from when I started in Cairns. It was much more efficient time-wise, but I was really starting to get sick of the big yutes going so dangerously fast past me, and I knew it was just going to get increasingly worse as I got closer to Sydney (the busiest city in Australia). I planned my route thoroughly and headed through some national park forests.

They were beautiful. The journey was much slower, and in some regards much harder when the surface wasn't always fully sealed, but all in all it was such a joy. Just having a break from a constant stream of vehicles passing you and endangering your life is a huge sigh of relief. For once, I could listen to the silence around me, merely the sound of my tyres surging through the sand, with the wild cries of birds from varying heights and from many angles. This passage revitalised my love for cycle touring, because it finally felt like an adventure again. It's too easy to just stick to the main road and constantly head south but going through the forests was wild and real.

I arrived slowly but surely into Sydney using the back roads, still in one piece. The Sydney Opera House looked better in real life, and is still to this day a rather cool and modern piece of architecture. With the Harbour Bridge standing proudly behind it, Sydney's main attractions are a sight to behold. It's a rather hectic city with so many high-rise buildings, and large quantities of vehicles, so you can imagine it was challenging to cycle through. But still, in comparison to some Chinese cities, it was a walk in the park. However, this was the first main city to be settled by British settlers 250 years ago when the main fleets first arrived in Botany Bay, not far from Sydney Harbour. A lot of the city is thus designed to function for entirely different modes of transport and ways of living. It seems that people in the olden days weren't forward thinking enough to make their city planning account for the 21st century - how very selfish of them! It's not the end of the world, it just creates some heavy traffic and angry drivers.

I celebrated my 23rd birthday in Sydney, and an old school friend, Brad, happened to be in town that same day. We went to an art museum together, a children's theme park, and then we went bowling. It was a very fun day and nice catching up with him. Unfortunately, I couldn't stick around much longer, and had to leave the following day due to my visa running out, somewhat like an hourglass.

Ultimately, it is never all too pleasant to be racing against the clock and at this point I was coming up against the hilliest part of my entire Australian cycling chapter - East Gippsland. It certainly wasn't akin to climbing up the sheer absurdity of the Pamir mountains, for example, but it was still very hilly. Up and down, somewhat relentlessly; as soon as I went down, I was going back up again. This wouldn't have been an issue if I wasn't racing against the clock, and if Melbourne wasn't actually still quite a long way away. Melbourne was essentially the finish line, not only for my Australian cycling chapter, but also for the entirety of the Full Power Bike Ride at large. It was to be the last cycling part of the entire trip, and thus the red ribbon was to be cut there.

Obviously *New Zealand* was the destination, but unfortunately you can't cycle over the sea and so Melbourne was the finish line. With this end in mind, I gritted my teeth and persisted with the same insane commitment and determination that I'd had ever since I left my house on my bike all those many months prior. To make matters even harder, it pissed with rain pretty much non-stop for a couple of weeks on end. It really didn't stop but luckily my clothes were waterproof so it didn't matter too much. You wouldn't expect that much rainfall for Australia but it was their winter and by this point I was actually quite far south and considerably far away from the equator. This did help to support some unique and amazing trees, with even little pockets of rainforest in this region. It seems that where the cycling is hardest work, it usually happens to be very beautiful.

Ironically, it's exactly this region that I'm talking about that was most seriously affected by the Australian bush fires of early 2020. It's crazy to think that there was so much rain at the time when cycling through, and a bush fire in that area would have seemed an extremely unlikely prospect. Some people have blamed the fires purely on "climate change" in all its myriad forms but I feel this is simply a blanket term that's rather unhelpful for this situation at least. The modern state of Australia has lost touch with its natural world, like nearly every other modern nation-state has also done. By contrast, during Pre-European settlement, the Aboriginals would systematically and intelligently create artificial bush fires, in order to clear the grassy undergrowth prior to the hottest part of the year. In doing so, it would rid the bushland of a perfect catalyst for uncontrollable forest fires. In creating their own, controlled, forest fires before the height of summer, they would consequently avoid the wrath of uncontrolled bush fires, of the type we've just witnessed. For 50,000 years this technique had worked for the native people there, but it seems that this traditional knowledge has seemingly been lost.

It's not surprising, considering that the European settlers notoriously disregarded the Aboriginals from being intelligent in any way, shape or form. In fact, they likened them more closely with animals than humans. And one could argue it is exactly this neglectful mentality which has helped to create these uncontrollable fires. Obviously, there are a myriad of other factors involved, and these points alone aren't enough to explain these extreme fires, but I think they are certainly contributing factors. I think that this ancient knowledge should be discussed, and brought forth back into the modern national consciousness. Maybe then, and only then, will this issue improve with time.

In the furthest south-easterly corner of the Australian mainland, I was still en route to Melbourne, and one thing that kept pushing me forward to the finish line was knowing that I was meeting my friend, Hannah, who was to cycle with me during the final leg. We met during our Erasmus term in Stockholm university. She's Australian born and bred and she mentioned at the time that I should visit her at some point but little did I know that I actually would - by bicycle. We cycled together for five days straight, still racing the clock to get there before my visa ran out. It was so much fun cycling with somebody else for a long period of time - the first time I had done so since leaving Gunnar, my American friend. Australia had been a pretty lonely state of affairs, so it was deeply appreciated to have company during this final stretch. We played loud music, chatted, snacked and lived together for those five days; it was so refreshing for cycle touring to be a shared experience once again. We took it in turns to shield one another from the ever-prevailing head wind, which provided well needed respite for this final excruciating leg. You could imagine, by now, I was so flipping knackered from all that relentless cycling, now around 3,500km in Australia alone, over the course of the prior three months. My body was simply ready to rest, forever, so getting a little bit of wind blockage was fully appreciated. We kept each other motivated through the force of friendship and laughter, and, before we even knew it, we had reached the finish line!

It was an epic feeling of achievement and gratitude. I had put in so much hard work, and received so much kindness from pretty much everyone I'd bumped into, and now I had cut the red ribbon, and finally had something to show for it. I was proud of myself. The cycling was now over, and I could finally rest my body. I stayed in an amazing community in Melbourne called "Crunchytown" where we all helped each other make food for over 30 international guests, and everyone helped to clean up after every meal. It was a proper community. There were no rules in Crunchytown apart from one sole rule – at the end of every meal, every person must lick their plate without fail. I would love to explain this in more detail, but I feel that I would need to write a whole new book just to scratch the surface of this fascinating and bizarre wonderland. I had one final party to let out some steam and to well and truly celebrate the huge achievement that I had just accomplished. Despite the need for rest, I danced literally all night, not only celebrating what had just been and gone in the gorgeous continent of 'Straya, but for what was about to come, New Zealand!

Chapter Twenty-Seven

The Full Power Destination - Aotearoa

I arrived! I arrived at the antipode, the original destination of the trip, the mystical land from my childhood imagination - New Zealand, the Land of the Long White Cloud, Aotearoa!

On one hand it felt somewhat anticlimactic arriving by plane from Melbourne, considering the trip was born on the grounds of not flying to New Zealand, but there were *no* viable alternatives. So many incredible, unforgettable moments had occurred during my trip, which would never have been possible at all if I merely flew from the UK. I was completely knackered when I touched down, royally sleep deprived from my celebratory party in Melbourne, and I was welcomed by mid-winter rain and freezing wind. At five o'clock in the morning, ridiculously tired touching down in the busiest urban area in the country, wasn't exactly the magical arrival one may have imagined. Big cities are merely big cities, so it wasn't the most stunning place to arrive, which could have been slightly depressing considering that I'd put so much pure energy and determination over the previous nineteen months leading up to this arrival, which in reality, wasn't actually that special at all. It was actually pretty bleak.

But luckily, I'm not easily saddened and remained positive at heart. I was bloody happy to be there and so relieved to have finally arrived. I felt utterly liberated, as if a huge weight had been lifted from my shoulders and dropped down a deep crater. I'd achieved what I set out to achieve, and now needed not to push myself incessantly towards that goal. Finally, this constant longing to keep going and keep going towards my destination could slowly float away into the ether of the cosmos, for I had done what I'd set out to do. I gave myself a jolly good pat on the back. I didn't expect instant gratification or to see all the beauty as soon as I'd arrive. I know that good things come to those who wait. I had only ever heard amazing things about this country and I had wanted to visit since I was about ten years old, always dreaming of this mystical land on the other side of the world. I knew that gems were waiting for me there, they just didn't appear straight away. Besides, this part of the trip had a different aim to my previous aim of making distance and continuing moving forward and further, further and forward. Now that I'd arrived, it was more about laying down some roots and staying in one place long enough to feel the merits of stationary life, like long term friendships, a sense of community, and a properly well-rested body. I was even looking forward to getting a job, living a little bit of a "normal life" for a while, and to have a little money to my name. Of course, I planned to eventually travel this wild and gorgeous land but when I first arrived this was not the focus. Before, I would have to earn some money and get grounded in my temporary home, enjoy resting after having cycled there from England.

Counterintuitively, with so much angst and anticipation leading up to the arrival, the actuality of my life in New Zealand was rather normal and comparatively dull. I stayed for a totality of two months, but during that time I achieved exactly what I was looking for - a slow and steady life. My focus wasn't on crazy adventures and insane stories of madness, because I'd had plenty of those en route. I just wanted to live a normal life, and my bank balance didn't allow me much scope for frivolous activities.

Back down to earth - this was my priority and focus. I had to do all the preliminary steps to even get a job in the first place, like open a bank account, get a New Zealand phone number, and wait for my IRD number. I then applied for a few different jobs, and in the end, I got two - one working in a bike shop (which was a rather fitting role, if I do say so myself) and the other in a camping shop (also quite fitting). In fact, I basically had three jobs because I was also volunteering at the hostel I was living in – "Fat Cat".

Fat Cat was a very special place, because not only was it a hostel but it was also a community; we lived together and did everything together. There were so many wonderful people from all over the world, and there was always an opportunity to dance and have fun, regardless of the time of day, be it in the kitchen, the living room, outside or wherever. It was a constant party, and that made coming home from work all the easier. We actually had three fat cats, as a part of the community and also loads of chickens that we would feed every morning. There was a small vegetable patch that would gift food to us, and heaps of wild mint all around which we would use for our morning tea. Once a week we took it in turns to cook for everyone, sometimes for up to forty people, which is quite a huge feat if you've never done that before. Then after dinner everyone would pick a card out of the hat which would be a personal chore, and before you knew it, all the work was done and we could go back to playing guitar and games and laughing.

Once I started working, most of my life was either at Fat Cat, or at work. I was starting to make a little bit of money, saving it, and settling into quite a nice routine. I did go on a few small trips to the surrounding areas of Auckland, but really not many places overall. However, the places I did see were absolutely stunning. Auckland itself isn't that nice at all, especially the city centre. But we were located out in the western suburbs and not all too far from the western beaches on the Tasman Sea. All in all, when you consider the surrounding beaches and sub-tropical islands around Auckland, it actually ends up being a pretty gorgeous neck of the woods, so I was very lucky to live there for two months.

But of the entirety of New Zealand, I barely witnessed a fraction before something huge happened. I was planning to continue working until the new year, and then at the start of 2020, I would start cycling down to the southern part of the South Island, before eventually crossing the Atlantic and cycling across North America, back home.

But alas, life did what life is best at doing - throwing a spanner in the works and toppling one's plans. Something dramatic came out of the blue, changing not only my plans but my entire future.

PART SIX – AN UNEXPECTED ENDING

Chapter Twenty-Eight

Fragility

All of a sudden, in the blink of an eye, my trip sharply changed direction. Before one could even say "Go!" I had already packed up my entire life in New Zealand, quit three jobs and found myself back on the other side of the world, in the opposite hemisphere in a location I'd never thought I'd find myself again - Budapest, Hungary.

So now, not only was I still away from my family home in London, but I was also a long way removed from my new home in Auckland. Even if I tried, I couldn't have felt any more ungrounded, and confused as to where I was. It takes a while to settle into a place and ground oneself, and I'd only just managed to do so in Auckland, yet here I was, having ripped myself away from a location that I'd only just glued myself to. Now, of all places, I find myself in Hungary?

Well, life is bloody unpredictable, is it not? We spend our whole time trying to understand it all, organising everything, putting things into a routine - then *kapow*, life throws a bulldozer into your path and smashes your feeble order into oblivion. My bike trip was over - the Full Power Bike Ride had officially ended. One of my closest friends in the whole wide world, Leyth, had nearly died.

He had a subarachnoid haemorrhage, which essentially means the bursting of an artery in the brain leading to

287

excess internal bleeding. It was caused by an aneurysm, which is a weakened bulge of an artery wall which subsequently ruptured. This whole internal catastrophe in his brain lead to Leyth having a stroke and a seizure, there and then on the spot - collapsing. He was just about to play a game of football in Budapest but had been there in the first place to do a speech for the European Union Climate Committee. Before he had a chance to play football or make the speech, this all happened inside his brain, and he collapsed instantaneously.

There were literally no prior signs of severe medical concern, other than a few minor headaches; those around him were therefore frightened, to say the least, by his abrupt collapsing and subsequent fitting for the following fifteen minutes. Luckily--and it couldn't possibly have been timed any better--he was standing next to a trained medical doctor and was immediately rushed to hospital and placed on the operating table.

I've known Leyth since we were sixteen years old, and we've been having fun and causing mischief for the past seven years non-stop. We met at college and clicked immediately, bonding over a shared music taste and philosophical stance. The late teens are tender years; you're learning intensely about yourself and the world around you, whether you like it or not. Sharing this whole learning process together formed an unbreakable bond. Together we delved deep into the rabbit hole of spirituality and political philosophy. Some of the things we discovered blew our minds, leaving us forever touched and nurtured by such findings, and this formed an incomparable friendship between Leythy boy and I. We even made some music together, in which we spoke of the things we'd learnt, in the form of rap and poetry. Anyone who has embarked on an artistic endeavour with a loved one will know how that can solidify a friendship even further.

We both went to university in the west of England, and travelled extensively together all over Europe via train, going to numerous epic music festivals, and essentially having the time of our lives. When I remark that he's one of my closest friends, I

288

don't say that half-heartedly. He makes me cry with laughter, dance even more euphorically than I already do, and smile with even more potency. He's a wizard, a warrior, and an angel. The last time I saw him was when I was in Tokyo, Japan, during this Full Power Bike Ride. We had an absolute blast, living life to the fullest in the busiest city in the world. He is an absolute legend.

So, one can only start to imagine the sheer agony it caused me to learn that Leyth was lying on his ridiculously premature deathbed. I was staying overnight at a friend's house in Auckland. That day, I'd received two random messages from his sister and friend from university, both of whom I'd not spoken to for months. I knew something wasn't right, but come on, what could go terribly wrong with a healthy twenty-three-year old? I waited to reply until later, refusing to believe that it was urgent. But just before I went to bed that night, a random jolt of concern for Leyth's wellbeing shot through me, causing me to check my phone one last time. Alas, there was another message from his sister, Noor, this time in the form of a voice note. I listened. I played it out loud, and both me and my friend were utterly shocked by the content of her message. She explained to me what I explained to you at the start of this chapter, but the difference was the sound of devastation which permeated the core of every word she shared.

I was twelve hours ahead of her at the time, literally about to turn the light off and fall into a deep slumber before I checked my phone. I felt numb and speechless - my friend and I just sat there in silence for quite a while, dumbfounded. I really didn't know what to do, because I felt an overwhelming sense of shock and emotional numbness. It was far too drastic of a situation, far too late at night, and I simply could not respond. I felt like a computer system glitching and malfunctioning, physically inept at processing the information at hand. I decided to simply sleep and call Noor in the morning. I thought about him all night and sent him as much love and healing energy as I possibly could.

Upon awakening, I knew that there was only one thing left for me to do - fly to Budapest on the next available flight. His sister had made it clear to me that it was still a life or death situation for him and that the next few days of surgery were vital for his survival. Regardless of what direction he would take, I knew that I only had only one option and that was to be by his side, not on the other side of the world. As it stood, I felt so horrifically removed from the situation, literally so far away. It pained me and put everything into perspective suddenly and violently. I realised there and then that my trip had already finished, because my mission was already completed. The Full Power Bike Ride was simply a cycle ride from England to New Zealand, and I had made it! I'd cycled 24,000 kilometres across twenty countries and the red ribbon marking the finish line had already been snipped.

Anything more than that was just added arbitrary extras, not necessary at all. I didn't *have* to save loads of money in Auckland, and I didn't *have* to cycle back across the States. This whole situation showed me clearly that I was wasting my time in Auckland, being so far away from my loved ones, when anything like this could happen. I wasn't enjoying it that much anyway - it rained an awful lot, and the working days really weren't all too much fun.

When the friend I was staying with woke up the following morning, I made it clear that my ride was over and that I was getting the next possible flight to Budapest. I packed up my entire life, quit my three jobs, and that evening jumped on the twenty-seven-hour flight to Budapest, leaving my newly formed life in New Zealand behind for good. Life certainly is a peculiar thing.

It was a rather challenging flight, not only due to the huge duration, but also the circumstances. It felt slightly strange going back in the direction I'd come, spending all those arduous months on a bicycle to get to the other side of the world, only now to be coming all the way back by air. But I didn't question my decision for one millisecond, because I knew deep in my heart that it was the right thing to be doing. I couldn't stop thinking about Leyth and his condition, but I never thought of the worst-case scenario, and remained positive.

After leaving Dubai, we flew over Iraq for an hour or so. It is a beautiful country from the air with a surprising amount of water and mountains. It's not just the war-stricken Middle Eastern desert that our media leads us to believe. Leyth's dad is from Iraq, and lives there currently, so seeing the wonderful landscape of Leyth's ancestral roots gave me hope. And the name "Leyth" means "lion" in Arabic. From above, it looked like a land of resilience and strength, and this is exactly what Leyth has in abundance, so seeing this aspect of his roots reassured me. We then passed over Turkey, into Europe, and before I knew it, we were touching down in Budapest.

I'd been to Budapest twice before and I didn't expect to be back ever again, let alone in those circumstances. I got a taxi from the airport straight to the hospital and we passed through some dodgy and dirty neighbourhoods. This didn't do great things for my confidence and I started imagining the awful deteriorating hospital that Leyth had been chucked in. But with every turn we made, the buildings became slightly more promising, until we eventually arrived on the road of the hospital where all the buildings were particularly splendid. The taxi came to a stop next to a big mansion with a resplendent facade. The driver told me that this was the hospital, and at that point I knew that Leyth was in the right place.

As it turned out, this couldn't have been any truer; the neurosurgeon who operated on Leyth's brain was essentially the best neurosurgeon in the entirety of Europe when it comes to haemorrhages. I was reunited with Leyth's family where we exchanged huge lengthy hugs, and they told me that I could go straight in to see him which I hadn't been expecting so soon. I put on the medical robes and shoe covers and went into the intensive care unit to be finally reunited with Leythy.

He looked different to how he looked when we last said goodbye to each other in Tokyo. There must have been about seven different tubes all going into different parts of his body serving a multitude of different functions. He was still in a medically induced coma, being given a concoction of morphine and codeine, sending him into a different dimension. Bless him, also bald and nude, with only the white bed sheets covering his private parts. It was tough seeing him like this, especially considering his usual demeanour and glowing excitement of life. On the one hand, it was quite difficult seeing him in this state, yet on the other hand, it was amazing to see him still alive.

There was a tube attached to a machine that was essentially helping him to breath and to continue fighting. In the midst of all the inner neurological turmoil, he had developed a severe chest infection, pneumonia, which his body had to fight on top of everything else. We were told that he had to stay on this breathing machine until his chest got better, and thereby had to stay in the coma with his hands tied down just in case he tried to pull all his tubes out; apparently this is what he did every time he came into consciousness. We knew deep down that this was for the best, although the selfish part within wanted to see him talk and move, but we just put these thoughts aside and allowed the professionals to do their job.

We spoke to him softly, every day for almost a week. Occasionally, when the sedation wore off, he would momentarily open his eyes and squeeze one's hand if you were holding his, which always gave us a huge surge of happiness to see these functions still intact. But when he became too aware and started wiggling around, trying to rip the tubes out of his body, the nurses would rush back over and sedate him once more. We were told that it would probably be another two weeks with the breathing machine, and therefore the same level of sedation and lack of response.

When we came in the next day during visiting hours, we were absolutely shocked to see Leyth awake and sat upright! The breathing machine had been removed, and we were profoundly surprised! They said that his tests the night before had been very positive, showing that he no longer had pneumonia and his body could now support him to breath on his own. This meant less sedation and gave him back the ability to speak. This was always our main concern: would his mental faculties be in the same position they had been before the haemorrhage or would they be significantly impaired?

Thank goodness they were good as gold, and he was exactly the same Leythy as before, just slightly more drugged up. It was a day of utmost elation, for we were celebrating his life and the gift he had been given of renewal. He was obviously very tired and confused, but we were able to actually talk to him:

"I haven't seen you for a while mate," were the first words he said to me, with his understandably croaky and dry voice, and he looked rather shocked to see me at all, knowing that I should have been in New Zealand.

"I've come back for good now bro to help you on your path to recovery. The Full Power Bike Ride has been completed." I told him.

His eyes lit up, albeit rather surprised but happy that I was now by his side. This moment made all the pain from the previous week absolutely dissolve and it was a day for celebration. I felt 100 times more elated seeing him alive and well, than when I arrived in Auckland a couple months prior. This was the true arrival: the arrival of life and the continuation of a strong unbreakable friendship. He did come out with some rather comical things in his state of semi-delirium; something about him being called a Christmas tree by the nurses, and the Welsh rugby team being in the same room as him, and all sorts of other hilarious nonsensical remarks, but he was cracking loads of jokes and being his same old self.

There were merely a few more days of this, before we were surprised once more by him being moved out of the intensive care ward. He was completely off the sedation by this point, with a different tube being removed every day and slowly working his way back towards full health! Physiologically, he was exactly the same as before, but the only thing that was significantly different was his right leg, which had barely any movement in it at all. During the seizure, he had a stroke which impaired the movement in his right side. Luckily the right arm became fully functional, but the right leg was still slightly lacking movement. Yet, as we know – there's nothing that an infinitely focused and powerful mind can't achieve, and his path of recovery is a true display of exactly that determination and relentless passion for health. He spent an extra week in the sub-intensive ward, where we were able to play card games, listen to music, and even take him outside into the courtyard.

The first time he went outside in two weeks was a moment to behold, as he looked at the autumnal leaves with delicate awe and the attention to detail that a toddler has for the world around them. That was exactly it, a new life, seeing things for the first time since his new life had begun. It was amazing to witness and it filled our hearts with phenomenal joy. Luckily, his insurance company sorted his private air-ambulance back to London, and after a couple days at a neurological hospital in London, he was discharged and safe to return to his family home where he is now.

It was an absolute miracle that he recovered so quickly, coming out the other side as wonderful as before. Anything could have happened, but things have turned out as good as we could have ever imagined. And maybe that's exactly it – imagining. He put every ounce of his strength into imagining a positive and healthy future for his body and his right side, and ultimately he didn't waver in the slightest with that focus, and thus we see the epic results of recovery and rejuvenation. If you are lacking inspiration in your life, and feel that you are struggling to get a grip of yourself and can't achieve what you want – please do yourself a favour and take a wee green leaf out of Leyth's book, and show yourself, like he did, that *anything is possible* if you well-and-truly put your mind to it. For at the end of the day, reality is in our mind, it is processed in the head, and if we see our goal in our mind's eye and only ever give light to that reality – it will thereby come into actuality, and boundless fruition. Believe in yourself.

Chapter Twenty-Nine

A Full Power Conclusion

The Full Power Bike Ride was exactly the sort of trip I needed at this point in my life. I achieved absolutely everything that I wanted to - and more. I proved to myself that really anything is possible if you truly put your mind to it and give every ounce of your enthusiasm, even if it is an arbitrary and crazy challenge. It was an incredibly healing experience, having spent an awful lot of time alone, processing things that I otherwise wouldn't have been able to do surrounded by other humans. I was able to make some exciting plans for the future, experiencing a myriad of thoughts in my little cranium on the open road, plotting what to do with this gift we call life.

Ultimately, I feel that I have transitioned from a boy to a man throughout this entire experience. During the trip, I had to grow up fast with no one else to call on but myself in times of distress and hardship; I looked adversity straight in the eye and laughed at its feebleness. I now know pain like it's my closest ally, having spent so much time in each other's company. I know his weaknesses and he knows mine. I've proved to myself that you don't have to simply give up when times get hard and painful, for you can simply beat him at his own game and keep on going with a smile on one's face and a passionate heart still beating strong. Leyth had learnt this lesson well and truly. Struggle and anguish are absolutely integral to living, so what is the point in running away from them if they will still be

296

there the next day? Cycling up mountain after mountain, across desert after desert, has taught me to face these facts and to just keep on keeping on, for this is all we can do in life, without sending ourselves insane by resisting the inevitable and the intrinsic. A positive attitude is the absolute key in everything we do, and I have proved to myself the unboundedness of this asset. Once you train your mind to be unwaveringly positive, it's an attitude that just keeps on giving.

I have made innumerable international friendships and connections that will remain forevermore, and I have completed my true university Degree of Life, having learnt so much about so much. But most importantly, having peeled away different layers of personality and brought myself to a more minimalistic way of life, I feel as though I have reached somewhat closer to my *true* destination of liberation. Mental freedom and clarity are the best place to arrive at, for if you can truly understand that paradise is merely a state of consciousness, it means that you can reside in paradise regardless of wherever you are physically or geographically.

If you keep the sun shining brightly inside of yourself, it makes the whole world a lot brighter outside too.

Realistically, there is no way at all that I would have been able to benefit in the myriad ways I did, if it wasn't for the sheer unconditional kindness from people who were, at the time, total strangers. It is absolutely inspirational, to receive relentlessly waves after waves of love and compassion from people you barely even know. It's funny, that before I had even left for my trip, I received some stern words of advice from people around me, that one could call negative. For example, one piece of advice was: "do not trust anyone." That was it. As clear as daylight, with no beating around the bush, the advisor made it of paramount importance to alert me that people are inherently bad within, and therefore you can't trust anybody you meet. In fact, the vast, vast majority of experiences I had were exactly the opposite and proved that sentiment to be irrelevant and redundant.

Time and time again, I was provided with supreme kindness and it was that and that alone which made the whole trip possible. The kind smile from the old lady on the street, the warm welcome of a family allowing me (a dirty cycling stranger) into their home to feed me and help me rest, the sincere advice of a local showing me the best route to go. Honestly, I can't overstate it enough – people are beautiful. People are intrinsically kind deep down, and it is merely one's environment and socialisation which turns people "bad" or untrustworthy.

People are amazing and I love everyone to bits. The support I received was unbelievable, and I shall be eternally indebted, forever wishing to help others in return. Ultimately, it's not a matter of "giving it back" to those individuals themselves, but to "give it forward" to someone else who is in need. I must remind myself throughout my life (and please do remind me if I forget at times) that it is now my duty to care and support people in need, because I had exactly that, for two years straight, so paying it forward is the only just way to respond.

Leyth's situation taught me the sheer importance of friendship and community, and how that reigns far superior to one's own personal goals and journeys. Life is a shared experience after all, so if we can all support each other in times of need, it will make the whole trip an awful lot easier. I believe that I'm exactly where I need to be, when I need to be there, and in that sense, there are no wrong turns.

It feels great to be back in London, U.K, with all my family and beautiful friends. Leyth is getting better every day and returning to his Full Power health. Who knows, maybe I will return another time in my life to cycle the other half of the world, but at least for now I can relax fully, knowing that after cycling 25,000 kilometres across 20 countries - I finally completed what I set out to do: to cycle the length of the planet from England to New Zealand in the most Full Power way I possibly could!

FULL POWER! I LOVE YOU ALL!

The Full Power Bike Ride

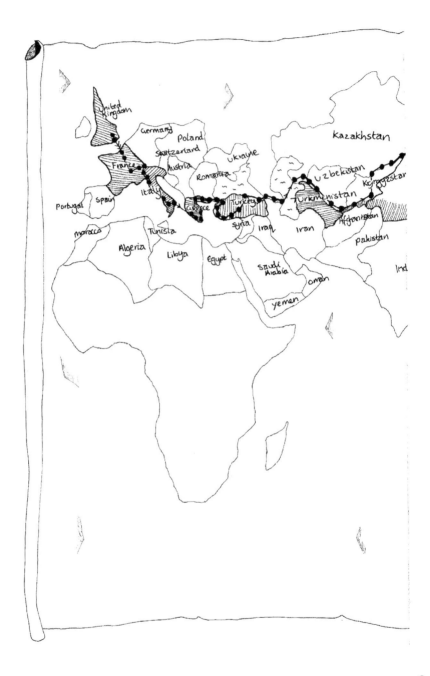

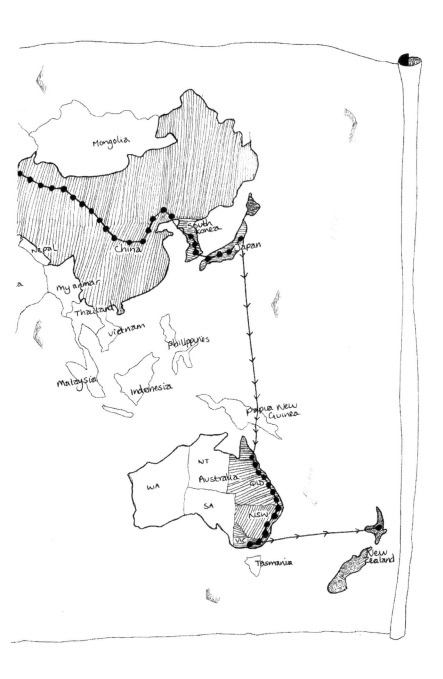

Afterword

Some final thoughts:

A Little Dash

On your gravestone
There will be a little dash,
No more than an inch wide
Inbetween your day of birth
And your day of death,
Signifying the space
inbetween your first and last breath.

This little dash
Marks the entirety of our existence
The totality of our human experience,
Our. Entire. Life.

A lifetime is not one that one should waste,
Treated with hate and distaste,
It's an utter miracle
that we are even here on Earth in the first place.
We have a choice every day when we wake,
In how we choose to live this day.
Do we choose to move
In a mundane way?

Or do we choose to live,

truly live
The adventure
Through the eyes of a child
A creative imaginative mind
Seeking
Novelty and newness
in every petal of a flower
and every droplet from a raincloud
For when you look closely at the details of this world,
You can see concealed the divine beauty
of the Universe manifest in oh so many forms
All equally as bountifully beautiful as eachother

We can choose beauty, to be seen through our eyes
We can choose wonder and awe
when we watch the bumble bee fly by
or when we smell spring blossoming
This is our choice,
who else's?

Equally, we have freedom to choose the opposite
To choose boredom
The grotesque and grotty version of everything
We can label every situation as "the worst thing ever"
If we so please.
Do you please?
Do you really wish to be unhappy?
I'm not sure anybody truly does.
This is our choice.
Who else's?

But the monkey mind leaps from branch to branch
Fiending, lusting for pleasure
And fearing, frightened of pain
Therefore we choose security,
the mundane,

the routine way of living
To avoid going insane

But in doing so,
we miss out on the wild unboundedness
of adventure and exploration
We miss the boat
We stop seeing the playfullness
that we once did when we made incredible sandcastles
And watched the multitude of colours sparkle
within the bubbles

It's our choice whether we wish to be happy
or whether we wish to be sad
To perceive things as good
or to see them as bad
Whether we want to be sane
or we want to be mad.
So why taint your brush with the colours of doom?

We have one dash
Only one little dash
No more than an inch wide
Which will mark the entirety of our lives
Let's make it represent the best possible life
we could ever ever live.
Let's all leave a living legacy of love
For love is the only meaningful thing we can give
It's the only thing that will keep this human race alive
the only thing that will make this species thrive.

So let's smash the dash! Full power!

Thank you so very much for reading this book. I sincerely wish
you the very best in your life ahead.

My warmest regards,
Cody Moir

If you'd like to see some photographs from this trip, please head to www.codysfullpowerbikeride.com! There are plenty on the website.

Printed in Great Britain
by Amazon